SOCIAL PROBLEM SOLVING

SOCIAL PROBLEM SOLVING

Theory, Research, and Training

Edited by

Edward C. Chang
Thomas J. D'Zurilla
Lawrence J. Sanna

American Psychological Association
Washington, DC

Published by
American Psychological Association
750 First Street, NE
Washington, DC 20002
www.apa.org

To order
APA Order Department
P.O. Box 92984
Washington, DC 20090-2984
Tel: (800) 374-2721
Direct: (202) 336-5510
Fax: (202) 336-5502
TDD/TTY: (202) 336-6123
Online: www.apa.org/books/
E-mail: order@apa.org

In the U.K., Europe, Africa, and the Middle
East, copies may be ordered from
American Psychological Association
3 Henrietta Street
Covent Garden, London
WC2E 8LU England

Typeset in Goudy by World Composition Services, Inc., Sterling, VA

Printer: United Book Press, Inc., Baltimore, MD
Cover Designer: Naylor Design, Washington, DC
Project Manager: Debbie Hardin, Carlsbad, CA

The opinions and statements published are the responsibility of the authors, and such
opinions and statements do not necessarily represent the policies of the American
Psychological Association.

Library of Congress Cataloging-in-Publication Data

Social problem solving : theory, research, and training / edited by Edward C. Chang,
Thomas J. D'Zurilla, and Lawrence J. Sanna.
    p. cm.
  Includes bibliographical references and index.
  ISBN 1-59147-147-8
  1. Problem solving. 2. Life skills. I. D'Zurilla, Thomas J. II. Chang, Edward C.
(Edward Chin-Ho) III. Sanna, Lawrence J. IV. Title.
BF449.S67   2004
153.4'3'—dc22   2004000024

British Library Cataloguing-in-Publication Data
A CIP record is available from the British Library.

Printed in the United States of America
First Edition

To Tae Myung-Sook and Chang Suk-Choon who, as educated and concerned immigrant parents, together solved problems in their strange new world with love, dedication, and great sacrifice for their children. I will always remember, cherish, and share the lessons they have taught me. To my older sister Helen, for helping me to solve my problems by reaching out to others. To my wife, for being a model problem solver no matter what the circumstances and challenges. To my little Olivia, for testing and training my abilities to be a better and more effective problem-solving dad each and every day. To Tom D'Zurilla, my mentor, for teaching me the skills to be a thoughtful and effective teacher and researcher. And finally, to the Varneys and the Chapmans, in loving memory of Mickey.
—Edward C. Chang

To my wife Lola, for her love, caring, and companionship.
—Thomas J. D'Zurilla

To my mentors and students of the past, present, and future.
—Lawrence J. Sanna

CONTENTS

CONTRIBUTORS

Alan S. Bellack, Veterans Administration Capitol Health Care Network Mental Illness Research Education and Clinical Center and University of Maryland School of Medicine, Baltimore

David R. Black, Purdue University, West Lafayette, IN

Ronald L. Bonner, Federal Correctional Institution—Allenwood, Allenwood, PA

Edward C. Chang, University of Michigan, Ann Arbor

George A. Clum, Virginia Polytechnic Institute and State University, Blacksburg, VA

Lynnette M. Cook, University of North Carolina at Chapel Hill

James V. Cordova, Clark University, Worcester, MA

Christina A. Downey, University of Michigan, Ann Arbor

Thomas J. D'Zurilla, Stony Brook University, Stony Brook, NY

Timothy R. Elliott, University of Alabama at Birmingham

Greg A. R. Febbraro, Drake University, Des Moines, IA

Marianne Frauenknecht, Western Michigan University, Kalamazoo

Joan S. Grant, University of Alabama at Birmingham

Albert Maydeu-Olivares, University of Barcelona, Barcelona, Spain

Sarah E. Morris, Veterans Administration Capitol Health Care Network Mental Illness Research Education and Clinical Center and University of Maryland School of Medicine, Baltimore

Doreen M. Miller, Southern University, Baton Rouge, LA

Shilagh A. Mirgain, University of Wisconsin Medical School, Madison

Arthur M. Nezu, Drexel University, Philadelphia, PA

Christine Maguth Nezu, Drexel University, Philadelphia, PA

Andrew D. Palmatier, Drexel University, Philadelphia, PA

Alexander R. Rich, University of South Florida, Tampa

Jenni L. Salata, University of Michigan, Ann Arbor

Lawrence J. Sanna, University of North Carolina at Chapel Hill

Eulena M. Small, University of North Carolina at Chapel Hill

Wendy N. Tenhula, Veterans Administration Capitol Health Care Network Mental Illness Research Education and Clinical Center and University of Maryland School of Medicine, Baltimore

Sam Vuchinich, Oregon State University, Corvallis

Victoria M. Wilkins, Drexel University, Philadelphia, PA

Marni L. Zwick, Drexel University, Philadelphia, PA

FOREWORD

Being asked by Edward C. Chang, Thomas J. D'Zurilla, and Lawrence J. Sanna to write a foreword to this volume provided me with the opportunity to reflect on when my involvement in social problem solving first began. An event that stands out in my memory goes back to the late 1960s. I can vividly recall Tom D'Zurilla and I sitting in my backyard, talking about the possible development of a problem-solving intervention that could be added to the array of available behavioral techniques already in use. At that point in time, the introduction of cognitive interventions into behavioral therapy was in its early stages; the label *cognitive–behavioral therapy* was not yet in existence. Still, those of us at Stony Brook (i.e., D'Zurilla, Jerry Davison, Stu Valins, and myself) and several of our behavioral colleagues at other institutions (e.g., Albert Bandura, Peter Lang, Arnold Lazarus, Michael Mahoney, Don Meichenbaum, and Donald Peterson) firmly believed that although methods based on classical and operant conditioning had made important contributions, more work was needed. Tom and I were particularly interested in developing an intervention that not only would help clients cope with specific life problems but also would afford them a skill that they could use in dealing with a variety of problematic situations.

In addition to the beginning cognitive movement within behavioral therapy, another important context that set the stage for us working on the development of the social problem-solving model was a criticism that had been made of behavioral therapy—or behavior modification, as it was sometimes called. This criticism came from our psychodynamic colleagues, who maintained that the directive nature of our interventions undermined the client's autonomy and independence. At the time, the terms *control* and *manipulation* appeared in the behavior therapy literature, which were associated with the methods and findings that were extrapolated from research in the laboratory setting. These methodologically based terms, together with the relatively more structured and directive nature of the interventions, led to our psychodynamic colleagues accusing us of functioning much like puppeteers in our clients' lives. To counter this accusation, many of us began to frame behavioral interventions as methods for helping clients develop self-control or self-regulation in their lives. This focus eventually evolved into the notion of therapy as coping-skills training, whereby clients were being taught to become their own therapists. Training in social problem solving provided a most natural way of making this happen.

Still another context for our development of the problem-solving model was our work with college students. The original clinic set up by the psychology department at Stony Brook—Psychological Services—was established both to provide therapy to undergraduate students and to serve as a training facility for our newly developed clinical psychology training program. On the basis of much of our clinical work with undergraduates, it became clear that many of our clients were having difficulty making the transition to the college setting. They were continually confronted with a variety of problematic situations associated with having become a college student, which was exacerbated by the growing pains that came with a newly formed university (e.g., crowded dorms and inadequate library facilities). What became apparent was that the failure to effectively deal with these situational challenges often resulted in their experiencing anxiety, depression, and other psychological problems. As a result, Tom and I focused our research efforts on the facilitation of competence in college freshman. We defined competence in a functional way—namely the ability to deal effectively with those issues inherent in the problematic situations that one typically encounters, while minimizing any possible negative consequences.

Our involvement in studying competence in college freshman quickly led us to recognize that they clearly were not the only population that was confronted with problematic situations. Indeed, we noted in our 1971 *Journal of Abnormal Psychology* article that for all of us, "Our daily lives are replete with situational problems which we must solve in order to maintain an adequate level of effective functioning" (p. 107).[1] As suggested by Harry Stack Sullivan several years earlier, problems in living are part of the human condition. We all experience them, need to accept them as a fact of life, and need to learn how to cope with them.

As we sat there in my backyard discussing problem-solving training, Tom and I had a sense that we might be on to something—not a clear realization but more of an intuitive sense. It was a feeling that a problem-

---

[1] D'Zurilla, T. J., & Goldfried, M. R. (1971). Problem solving and behavior modification. *Journal of Abnormal Psychology, 78,* 107–126.

solving intervention might contribute to behavioral therapy—and perhaps therapy in general. We never anticipated that it would gain as much recognition or utility as it has.

As the result of the efforts of Chang, D'Zurilla, Arthur M. Nezu, Albert Maydeu-Olivares, Sanna, and countless other workers in the field—including many of those who have contributed to this important volume—there are applications of social problem solving for a wide variety of problems in living. Just to mention a few, problem-solving training has been used for stress management and for dealing with life transitions, substance abuse, couple relationships, family conflict, adolescent conduct disorders, suicide risk, schizophrenia, anger management, stress of caregivers, and a variety health-related problems.

In every area of applicability, social problem solving has allowed individuals to gain a better sense of control over their lives. Not only does it help to resolve the distress of encountering difficult life situations and their possible negative consequences, but with the experience of successful coping and increased competence also comes an enhanced sense of self-efficacy—an important key to psychological well-being. As so comprehensively illustrated in this volume, the implications of effective problem solving can indeed be far reaching.

—Marvin R. Goldfried, PhD
Stony Brook University

PREFACE

Life is complex and dynamic, filled with many enriching experiences. These experiences are what make life meaningful. When some experiences become bothersome and troubling, a person may feel uncertain about how to deal with them, or a person may try to cope but nothing seems to work. That is when experiences become problems. But experiencing problems and finding ways to deal with them effectively also serve to make life meaningful and promote growth and development. Even in extreme cases involving clinical dysfunction, some have argued that such individuals are experiencing "problems in living" with which they are unable to cope effectively. In that regard, social problem solving represents a broad and complex theory of how we go about solving problems in our day-to-day lives, from problems that are simple and benign to those that are complex and involve multiple causes and consequences. Social problem solving also represents a key form of intervention within contemporary psychotherapy and education, a way to better manage the demands of everyday living in a world that is often complex and unpredictable and sometimes irrational. It was thus for both mundane and compelling reasons that we decided to embark on this volume.

Before this book, no single volume existed in which leading researchers, practitioners, and educators came together to share their expert and experienced thoughts on the power of social problem solving. We put together a book that would offer readers multiple perspectives, insights, and directions in understanding social problem solving as an important theory that has driven wide-ranging scientific research and as an important means of training to empower and elevate the lives of individuals. We believe that social problem solving can help individuals free themselves from the problems they face or the distress that these problems cause. We recognize that some problems may be difficult or impossible to solve, but we believe that considerable value remains in understanding and promoting effective social problem solving to foster the novel insights and methods in which problems that seem insurmountable ultimately may be conquered in incremental steps, across time and across individuals. Moreover, we believe that problems can be solved in different ways. When problematic situations or circumstances are manageable or controllable, a good problem solver tries to find ways to change them for the better. However, when such situations or circumstances are unchangeable or uncontrollable, one can still use problem solving to find ways to accept and tolerate with less distress that which cannot be changed or controlled.

In putting together this volume, we emphasized a balance between theory, research, and training. Thus, one will find that most of the chapters on social problem-solving research also address the issue of training. Likewise, one will find that the chapters on problem-solving training also focus on research. We tried to be comprehensive in our coverage of social problem solving. Because social problem solving occurs in a social context, it was important for us to include an appreciation of how social problem solving may operate effectively (or ineffectively) within individuals, couples, caregivers, and families. However, we simply could not include everything. There is much that we do not know and much work that remains to be done. Despite this, we believe that this book will inspire in the reader much excitement about the future of social problem solving and its value in helping individuals and groups. Solving problems in life is meaning making, and thus we hope that this volume contributes to helping individuals seek and find greater meaning in their lives.

We acknowledge the support, guidance, and insights proffered by the contributors to this volume. Without their expertise and enthusiasm, this book simply would not have been possible. We thank Susan Reynolds at the American Psychological Association for giving us the opportunity to edit this volume and for her encouragement and support. We also thank the production and development editors at the American Psychological Association, especially Kristine Enderle, who helped ensure that the book was complete and ready for publication every step of the way. Finally, we thank the many individuals, including the contributors of this book, who continue to help shape and guide our excitement about the future of social problem-solving theory, research, and training.

SOCIAL
PROBLEM
SOLVING

INTRODUCTION:

SOCIAL PROBLEM SOLVING FOR THE REAL WORLD

EDWARD C. CHANG, THOMAS J. D'ZURILLA,
AND LAWRENCE J. SANNA

According to ancient Greek philosophers such as Aristotle (1908/350 B.C.), practical wisdom, prudence in judgment (*logos*), and action in the real world (*praxis*) were considered to be among the highest virtues attainable by an individual. In later years, numerous educators and psychologists have echoed these sentiments. Despite these early views, the role of problem solving in adjustment did not receive serious scientific study until the second half of the 20th century. In their seminal article on problem solving and behavior modification, D'Zurilla and Goldfried (1971) called for a major research effort to study the role of social problem solving in adjustment, as well as the efficacy of problem-solving training as a clinical intervention and prevention approach. They argued that such training would lead to more positive, generalized, and durable behavior changes because individuals would learn general skills that would enable them to enhance their functioning in a positive direction and deal more effectively with future problems.

Since the publication of this classic article, there has been an explosion of studies on the topic of social problem solving and problem-solving training and therapy in the clinical and counseling psychology literature. Within the past decade, research interest in this subject has also grown rapidly in other areas of psychology as well, including cognitive, social, developmental, organizational, and health psychology. Reviews of this research literature have appeared in a number of chapters and books during the past two decades (D'Zurilla, 1986; D'Zurilla & Nezu, 1982, 1999; Nezu & D'Zurilla, 1989; Nezu, Nezu, & Perri, 1989). However, before this volume, no edited book has been published that addresses so many issues and ideas related to an understanding of social problem solving as both a wide-ranging theory of adjustment and as an effective form of therapy. This volume brings together leading experts in the area of social problem solving to share their thoughts on social problem-solving theory, research, and training. Indeed, the interconnectedness of social problem-solving theory, research, and training are explicit across all of the chapters in this volume.

OVERVIEW

This volume is separated into four sections. The first section focuses on providing a broad overview of social problem-solving theory. In chapter 1, Thomas J. D'Zurilla, Arthur M. Nezu, and Albert Maydeu-Olivares introduce fundamental concepts involved in the study of social problem solving. These authors go on to provide a critical review of major social problem-solving models and measures, with specific attention to the popular social problem-solving theory of D'Zurilla, Goldfried, Nezu, and Maydeu-Olivares. In addition, these authors present a problem-solving model of stress that forms the foundation of problem-solving therapy. Following this broad conceptual and methodological overview, Alexander R. Rich and Ronald L. Bonner, in chapter 2, provide critical discussions of possible determinants (mediators) of social problem solving for answering *how* social problem solving may develop and of possible interaction factors (moderators) of social problem solving for answering *why* social problem solving may be effective for some and not for others. These authors make a convincing case for considering social causes and contexts within problem-solving theory.

The second section of this volume focuses on research linking problem solving with adjustment. Beginning this section, Arthur M. Nezu, Victoria M. Wilkins, and Christine Maguth Nezu, in chapter 3, provide an up-to-date review of the extant literature examining support for the involvement of social problem solving in negative affective conditions (e.g., depression, worry, anxiety) and for the involvement of social problem solving as a moderator of the association between stressful life events and psychological distress. Based on their analysis of findings reported in more than 50 different studies conducted on social problem solving, these authors find positive support for the involvement of social problem solving in both situations. Extending the examination of social problem solving, stress, and negative affective conditions further, George A. Clum and Greg A. R. Febbraro, in chapter 4, focus on how social problem solving and stress contribute to suicide risk. These authors provide a careful review of the extant literature supporting a link between stress and suicide risk and supporting a link between social problem solving and suicide risk. This leads to a practical discussion by these authors on the effectiveness of social problem-solving treatments to help individuals better manage stress and reduce their level of suicide risk. In chapter 5, Sarah E. Morris, Alan S. Bellack, and Wendy N. Tenhula provide evidence for the usefulness of applying social problem-solving theory to the study of extreme psychotic behavior—specifically, schizophrenia. In reviewing the complex literature on schizophrenia, these authors not only identify significant problem-solving deficits among individuals with schizophrenia, but they also identify some promising evidence supporting the idea that social problem-solving abilities can be bolstered to improve social functioning in this population. Going against the traditional focus on negative conditions, Edward C. Chang, Christina A. Downey, and Jenni L. Salata, in chapter 6, focus on a much-needed examination of social problem solving and positive psychological functioning. Based on a review of the limited available literature and on analyzing recently collected data on psychological well-being, these authors conclude that social problem solving is not only important for understanding negative functioning, but it is also important for understanding, and perhaps promoting, positive functioning. In chapter 7, Timothy R. Elliott, Joan S. Grant, and Doreen M. Miller go beyond a discussion of psychological conditions to also consider physical conditions. These authors provide an important discussion of the multiple roles of social problem solving found in understanding behavioral health, ranging from the role of social problem solving in pain behaviors to the role of social problem solving in promoting positive functioning among individuals with health-related problems. An implicit theme running through the previous chapters of this section is that the exercise of greater social problem-solving abilities is adaptive, whereas the exercise of poor social problem-solving abilities is maladaptive. Extending important research and theory on mental simulations, Lawrence J. Sanna, Eulena M. Small, and Lynnette M. Cook, in chapter 8, provide a thought-provoking discussion of how timing, among other critical factors, and the exercise of certain problem-solving abilities can interact to determine positive and negative outcomes.

The third section focuses on problem-solving training and therapy for different populations. Beginning in this section, Marianne Frauenknecht and David R. Black, in chapter 9, discuss the importance of problem-solving training to meet the multiple health and educational needs of children and adolescents. These authors provide an integrative review of the many different problem-solving training programs that have been developed and used in this population and highlight common elements across the different programs that have been found to be the most effective in promoting the needs of children and adolescents. In chapter 10, Arthur M. Nezu, Thomas J. D'Zurilla, Marni L. Zwick, and Christine Maguth Nezu offer a comprehensive review of problem-solving therapy guidelines for working with adults, and evaluate findings obtained from 48 outcome studies using problem-solving therapy to treat adults for various conditions and problems. From their review, the authors highlight the greater efficacy of problem-solving therapy over no or alternative interventions and discuss novel and innovative ways in which such therapy may be used in working with adults. Extending the focus of the previous chapter, James V. Cordova and Shilagh A. Mirgain, in chapter 11, look at problem-solving training for working with adult couples experiencing distress. These authors provide a useful and comprehensive review of major therapeutic interventions predicated on social problem-solving theory used to promote positive functioning and constructive motivation between partners and identify positive support for the effectiveness of incorporating problem-solving training elements in working with distressed couples. Within family systems perspective, Sam Vuchinich, in chapter 12, provides a valuable discussion on the application and usefulness of problem-solving training in working with distressed families. The author notes four basic ways in which problem-solving training may be used to work with distressed family members, and he provides practical guidelines for using such theory in families. In chapter 13, Christine Maguth Nezu, Andrew D. Palmatier, and Arthur M. Nezu provide a valuable look at problem-solving therapy as an effective or promising intervention for helping caregivers of individuals dealing with a variety of illnesses, from cancer to stroke.

In the fourth section, Thomas J. D'Zurilla, Edward C. Chang, and Lawrence J. Sanna, in chapter 14, conclude the volume by reflecting on some of the main concerns raised in the previous chapters and with thoughts on future directions for social problem-solving research and training.

SOCIAL PROBLEM SOLVING AS BOTH A USEFUL THEORY AND A USEFUL THERAPY

We attempted to promote a balance of theory, research, and therapy in developing a comprehensive volume on social problem solving. It is our hope that in doing so, this volume will have a strong appeal to researchers and to mental health professionals alike. To reiterate an earlier point, social problem solving is neither a theory of adjustment nor an effective therapy to promote adjustment; rather, social problem solving refers to both a theory *and* a form of therapy. The wide-ranging impact of social problem-solving theory and therapy is identified and documented throughout the pages of this volume. Accordingly, we believe the relevance of this volume also extends to everyday people who find themselves dealing with real and complex problems in living.

REFERENCES

Aristotle. (1908). *Nicomachean ethics* (W. D. Ross, Trans.). Oxford, England: Clarendon Press. (Original work written in 350 B.C.)

D'Zurilla, T. J. (1986). *Problem-solving therapy: A social competence approach to clinical intervention.* New York: Springer.

D'Zurilla, T. J., & Goldfried, M. R. (1971). Problem solving and behavior modification. *Journal of Abnormal Psychology, 78,* 107–126.

D'Zurilla, T. J. & Nezu, A. (1982). Social problem solving in adults. In P. C. Kendall (Ed.), *Advances in cognitive–behavioral research and therapy* (Vol. 1, pp. 201–274). New York: Academic Press.

D'Zurilla, T. J., & Nezu, A. M. (1999). *Problem-solving therapy: A social competence approach to clinical intervention* (2nd ed.). New York: Springer.

Nezu, A. M., & D'Zurilla, T. J. (1989). Social problem solving and negative affective conditions. In P. C. Kendall & D. Watson (Eds.), *Anxiety and depression: Distinctive and overlapping features* (pp. 285–315). New York: Academic Press.

Nezu, A. M., Nezu, C. M., & Perri, M. G. (1989). *Problem-solving therapy for depression: Therapy, research, and clinical guidelines.* New York: Wiley.

I

WHAT IS SOCIAL PROBLEM SOLVING?

1

SOCIAL PROBLEM SOLVING: THEORY AND ASSESSMENT

THOMAS J. D'ZURILLA, ARTHUR M. NEZU,
AND ALBERT MAYDEU-OLIVARES

In this chapter we describe the social problem-solving model that has generated most of the research and training programs presented in the remaining chapters of this volume. We also describe the major assessment methods and instruments that have been used to measure social problem-solving ability and performance in research as well as clinical practice.

The term *social problem solving* refers to the process of problem solving as it occurs in the natural environment or "real world" (D'Zurilla & Nezu, 1982). The adjective *social* is not meant to limit the study of problem solving to any particular type of problem. It is used in this context only to highlight the fact that we are interested in problem solving that influences one's adaptive functioning in the real-life social environment. Hence, the study of social problem solving deals with all types of problems that might affect a person's functioning, including *impersonal problems* (e.g., insufficient finances, stolen property), *personal or intrapersonal problems* (emotional, behavioral, cognitive, or health problems), *interpersonal problems* (e.g., marital conflicts, family disputes), as well as broader *community and societal problems* (e.g., crime, racial discrimination). The model of social problem solving presented in this chapter was originally introduced by D'Zurilla and Goldfried (1971)

11

and later expanded and revised by D'Zurilla, Nezu, and Maydeu-Olivares (2002; D'Zurilla, 1986; D'Zurilla & Nezu, 1982, 1990, 1999; Maydeu-Olivares & D'Zurilla, 1995, 1996; Nezu & D'Zurilla, 1989).[1]

MAJOR CONCEPTS

The three major concepts in the D'Zurilla et al. model are (a) problem solving, (b) problem, and (c) solution. It is also important for theory, research, and practice to distinguish between the concepts of problem solving and *solution implementation*. The definitions presented are based on concepts previously discussed by Davis (1966), D'Zurilla and Goldfried (1971), D'Zurilla and Nezu (1982, 1999), and Skinner (1953).

Problem Solving

As it occurs in the natural environment, *problem solving* is defined as the self-directed cognitive–behavioral process by which an individual, couple, or group attempts to identify or discover effective solutions for specific problems encountered in everyday living. More specifically, this cognitive–behavioral process (a) makes available a variety of potentially effective solutions for a particular problem and (b) increases the probability of selecting the most effective solution from among the various alternatives (D'Zurilla & Goldfried, 1971). As this definition implies, social problem solving is conceived as a conscious, rational, effortful, and purposeful activity. Depending on the problem-solving goals, this process may be aimed at changing the problematic situation for the better, reducing the emotional distress that it produces, or both.

Problem

A *problem* (or problematic situation) is defined as any life situation or task (present or anticipated) that demands a response for adaptive functioning but no effective response is immediately apparent or available to the person or people confronted with the situation because of the presence of one or more obstacles. The demands in a problematic situation may originate in the environment (e.g., objective task demands) or within the person

---

[1]Several variations and modifications of this social problem-solving model have appeared in the clinical, counseling, educational, and health psychology literature (see Black & Frauenknecht, 1990; Crick & Dodge, 1994; Elias & Clabby, 1992; Frauenknecht & Black, 2003; Spivack et al., 1976; Tisdelle & St. Lawrence, 1986). In addition, similar models and perspectives have also been described in the literature on geropsychology and organizational psychology (see Poon, Rubin, & Wilson, 1989; Sinnott, 1989; Sternberg & Wagner, 1986).

(e.g., a personal goal, need, or commitment). The obstacles might include novelty, ambiguity, unpredictability, conflicting stimulus demands, performance skill deficits, or lack of resources. A particular problem might be a single time-limited event (e.g., missing a train to work, an acute illness), a series of similar or related events (e.g., repeated unreasonable demands from a boss, repeated violations of curfew by an adolescent), or a chronic, ongoing situation (e.g., continuous pain, boredom, or feelings of loneliness).

An *interpersonal* problem is a special kind of real-life problem in which the obstacle is a conflict in the behavioral demands or expectations of two or more people in a relationship (Jacobson & Margolin, 1979). In this context, interpersonal problem solving may be described as a cognitive–interpersonal process aimed at identifying or discovering a resolution to the conflict that is acceptable or satisfactory to all parties involved. Hence, according to this view, interpersonal problem solving is a "win–win" approach to resolving conflicts or disputes rather than a "win–lose" approach.

Solution

A *solution* is a situation-specific coping response or response pattern (cognitive or behavioral) that is the product or outcome of the problem-solving process when it is applied to a specific problematic situation. An *effective* solution is one that achieves the problem-solving goal (i.e., changing the situation for the better or reducing the emotional distress that it produces), while at the same time maximizing other positive consequences and minimizing negative consequences. The relevant consequences include both personal and social outcomes, long-term as well as short-term. With specific reference to an interpersonal problem, an *effective* solution is one that resolves the conflict or dispute by providing an outcome that is acceptable or satisfactory to all parties involved. This outcome may involve a consensus, compromise, or negotiated agreement that accommodates the interests and well-being of all concerned parties.

Problem Solving Versus Solution Implementation

Our theory of social problem solving distinguishes between the concepts of problem solving and solution implementation. These two processes are conceptually different and require different sets of skills. Problem solving refers to the process of *finding* solutions to specific problems, whereas solution implementation refers to the process of *carrying out* those solutions in the actual problematic situations. Problem-solving skills are assumed to be general, whereas solution-implementation skills are expected to vary across situations depending on the type of problem and solution. Because they are different, problem-solving skills and solution-implementation skills are not always correlated. Hence, some individuals might possess poor problem-solving skills but good solution-implementation skills or vice versa. Because both sets of skills are required for effective functioning or social competence, it is often necessary in problem-solving therapy to combine training in problem-solving skills with training in other social and behavioral performance skills to maximize positive outcomes (McFall, 1982).

DIMENSIONS OF SOCIAL PROBLEM-SOLVING ABILITY

One of the major assumptions of this theory is that social problem-solving ability is not a unity construct but, rather, a multidimensional construct consisting of several different, albeit related, components. In the original model described by D'Zurilla and Goldfried (1971) and later expanded and refined by D'Zurilla and Nezu (1982, 1990), it was assumed that social problem-solving ability consisted of two general, partially independent components: (a) problem orientation and (b) problem-solving skills (later referred to as "problem-solving proper," D'Zurilla & Nezu, 1999, and then "problem-solving style," D'Zurilla et al., 2002). *Problem orientation* was described as a metacognitive process involving the operation of a set of relatively stable cognitive–emotional schemas that reflect a person's general beliefs, appraisals, and feelings about problems in living, as well as his or her own problem-solving ability. This process was believed to serve an important motivational function in social problem solving. *Problem-solving skills*, on the other hand, referred to the cognitive and behavioral activities by which a person attempts to understand problems and find effective "solutions" or ways of coping with them. The model identified four major skills: (a) problem definition and formulation, (b) generation of alternative solutions, (c) decision making, and (d) solution implementation and verification (D'Zurilla & Goldfried, 1971). These skills will be described in more depth.

Based on this theoretical model, D'Zurilla and Nezu (1990) developed the Social Problem-Solving Inventory (SPSI), which consisted of two major scales: the Problem Orientation Scale (POS) and the Problem-Solving Skills Scale (PSSS). The items in each scale were designed to reflect both positive (constructive or facilitative) and negative (dysfunctional) characteristics. The assumption that problem orientation and problem-solving skills are different, albeit related, components of social problem-solving ability was supported by findings that showed that the POS items correlated relatively high with the total POS score and relatively low with the total PSSS score, whereas the reverse was true for the PSSS items (D'Zurilla & Nezu, 1990).

In later studies, Maydeu-Olivares and D'Zurilla (1995, 1996) conducted exploratory and confirmatory factor analyses on the SPSI. Although the results showed moderate support for the original two-factor model (viz., problem orientation and problem-solving skills), a better fitting model was found to be a five-factor model consisting of two different, albeit related, problem-orientation dimensions and three different problem-solving styles. The two problem-orientation dimensions are positive problem orientation and negative problem orientation, whereas the three problem-solving styles are rational problem solving (i.e., effective problem-solving skills), impulsivity–carelessness style, and avoidance style. These five dimensions of social problem-solving ability are measured by the Social Problem-Solving Inventory—Revised (SPSI–R; D'Zurilla et al., 2002), which will be described later. Positive problem orientation and rational problem solving are constructive dimensions that have been found to be related to adaptive functioning and positive psychological well-being, whereas negative problem orientation, impulsivity–carelessness style, and avoidance style are dysfunctional dimensions that have been found to be associated with maladaptive functioning and psychological distress (see reviews by D'Zurilla & Nezu, 1999; D'Zurilla et al., 2002). As would be expected, the constructive dimensions are positively correlated with each other and negatively correlated with the dysfunctional dimensions and vice versa (D'Zurilla et al., 2002). Each dimension is described later in the chapter.

Problem-Orientation Dimensions

Positive problem orientation is a constructive problem-solving cognitive set that involves the general disposition to (a) appraise a problem as a "challenge" (i.e., opportunity for benefit or gain), (b) believe that problems are solvable ("optimism"), (c) believe in one's personal ability to solve problems successfully ("problem-solving self-efficacy"), (d) believe that successful problem solving takes time and effort, and (e) commit oneself to solving problems with dispatch rather than avoiding them. In contrast, *negative problem orientation* is a dysfunctional or inhibitive cognitive–emotional set that involves the general tendency to (a) view a problem as a significant threat to well-being (psychological, social, economic), (b) doubt one's own personal ability to solve problems successfully ("low problem-solving self-efficacy"), and (c) easily become frustrated and upset when confronted with problems ("low frustration tolerance").

Problem-Solving Styles

Rational problem solving is a constructive problem-solving style that is defined as the rational, deliberate, and systematic application of effective problem-solving skills. As noted earlier, this model identifies four major problem-solving skills: (a) problem definition and formulation, (b) generation of alternative solutions, (c) decision making, and (d) solution implementation and verification. In *problem definition and formulation*, the problem solver tries to clarify and understand the problem by gathering as many specific and concrete facts about the problem as possible, identifying demands and obstacles, and setting realistic problem-solving goals (e.g., changing the situation for the better, accepting the situation, and minimizing emotional distress). In the *generation of alternative solutions*, the person focuses on the problem-solving goals and tries to identify as many potential solutions as possible, including both conventional and original solutions. In *decision making*, the problem solver anticipates the consequences of the different solutions, judges and compares them, and then chooses the "best" or potentially most effective solution. In the final step, *solution implementation and verification*, the person carefully monitors and evaluates the outcome of the chosen solution after attempting to implement it in the real-life problematic situation (for a more detailed description of these skills, the reader is referred to D'Zurilla & Goldfried, 1971; D'Zurilla & Nezu, 1999; D'Zurilla et al., 2002).

Impulsivity–carelessness style is a dysfunctional problem-solving pattern characterized by active attempts to apply problem-solving strategies and techniques, but these attempts are narrow, impulsive, careless, hurried, and incomplete. A person with this problem-solving style typically considers only a few solution alternatives, often impulsively going with the first idea that comes to mind. In addition, he or she scans alternative solutions and consequences quickly, carelessly, and unsystematically, and monitors solution outcomes carelessly and inadequately.

Avoidance style is another dysfunctional problem-solving pattern characterized by procrastination, passivity or inaction, and dependency. The avoidant problem solver prefers to avoid problems rather than confronting them head on, puts off problem solving for as long as possible, waits for problems to resolve themselves, and attempts to shift the responsibility for solving his or her problems to other people.

THE SOCIAL PROBLEM-SOLVING PROCESS

Based on the social problem-solving model described earlier, the hypothesized social problem-solving process is depicted in Figure 1.1. As the figure shows, problem-solving outcomes in the real world are assumed to be largely determined by two general, partially independent processes: (a) *problem orientation* and (b) *problem-solving style*. The two problem orientation dimensions and the three problem-solving styles that make up the present model are also shown in the figure. Constructive or effective problem solving is depicted as a process in which positive problem orientation facilitates rational problem solving (i.e., the deliberate, systematic application of effec-

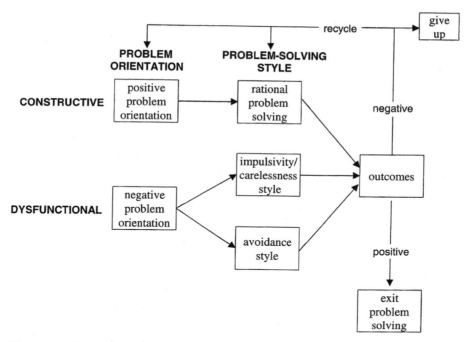

Figure 1.1. Schematic representation of the social problem-solving process based on the five-dimensional model of D'Zurilla et al. (2002).

tive problem-solving skills), which in turn is likely to produce positive outcomes. Dysfunctional or ineffective problem solving is shown as a process in which negative problem orientation contributes to impulsivity–carelessness style or avoidance style, which are both likely to produce negative outcomes. Hence, our model predicts that the most favorable problem-solving outcomes are likely to be produced by individuals who score relatively high on measures of positive problem orientation and rational problem solving while scoring relatively low on measures of negative problem orientation, impulsivity–carelessness style, and avoidance style. Moreover, when initial outcomes are negative or unsatisfactory, these "good" problem solvers are more likely to persist and recycle, or return to the problem-solving process, to find a better solution or to redefine the problem with more realistic goals. For example, after finding that a certain medical problem is incurable, the person may change the problem-solving goal to one that focuses on minimizing pain and discomfort and maximizing quality of life. In contrast, poor problem solvers, who have high scores on the dysfunctional dimensions and low scores on the construction dimensions, might be more likely to give up when initial outcomes are negative and either do nothing or try desperately to get someone else to help them solve the problem.

Empirical evidence that supports different aspects of this hypothesized social problem-solving process is reviewed in D'Zurilla et al. (2002).

ASSESSMENT OF SOCIAL PROBLEM SOLVING

In research on social problem solving, as well as research and clinical practice in problem-solving therapy, it is important to assess not only the person's general level of social problem-solving ability but also his or her strengths and weaknesses across the different components of problem-solving ability (e.g., positive problem orientation, negative problem orientation, rational problem solving, etc.). Hence, it is useful to distinguish between two general types of social problem-solving measures: (a) process measures and (b) outcome measures (D'Zurilla & Maydeu-Olivares, 1995).

Process measures directly assess the general cognitive and behavioral activities (e.g., attitudes, skills) that facilitate or inhibit the discovery of effective or adaptive solutions for everyday problems, whereas *outcome measures* assess the quality of specific solutions to specific problems. Hence, process measures are used to assess specific strengths and deficits in social problem-solving ability, and outcome measures are used to evaluate problem-solving performance or the ability of a person to apply his or her skills effectively to specific problems. An outcome measure can be viewed as a global indicator of social problem-solving ability but, unlike a process measure, it does not provide any information about the specific components of social problem-solving ability.

Problem-solving process measures include self-report inventories as well as performance tests. The self-report inventory provides a broad survey of a person's problem-solving attitudes, strategies, and techniques, both positive (facilitative) and negative (inhibitive). Some inventories also estimate the extent to which the person actually uses the problem-solving skills that he or she possesses, as well as the manner in which these techniques are typically applied (e.g., efficiently, systematically, impulsively, carelessly, etc.). The performance test format presents the person with a specific problem-solving task that requires him or her to apply a specific skill or set of skills (e.g., problem recognition, problem definition, generation of solutions, decision making). The individual's task performance is then judged or evaluated and this measure is viewed as an indicator of his or her level of ability in that particular skill area (see D'Zurilla & Nezu, 1980; Nezu & D'Zurilla, 1979, 1981a, 1981b; Spivack, Platt, & Shure, 1976).

All problem-solving outcome measures are performance tests. However, instead of testing one particular component skill or ability, these measures assess overall problem-solving performance, or general social problem-solving ability, by presenting the person with a specific problem and asking him or her to solve it, after which the solution is judged or rated on some quantitative or qualitative dimension. An example of a quantitative score is the number of relevant means, or discrete steps, that enable the problem solver to move closer to a goal (Platt & Spivack, 1975; Spivack, Shure, & Platt, 1985). Examples of qualitative scoring are ratings or judgments of "effectiveness," "appropriateness," "active vs. passive coping," and "approach vs. avoidance" (Fischler & Kendall, 1988; Freedman, Rosenthal, Donahoe, Schlundt, & McFall, 1978; Getter & Nowinski, 1981; Linehan, Camper, Chiles, Strosahl, & Shearin, 1987; Marx, Williams, & Claridge, 1992). Although most outcome tests have used hypothetical test problems, some studies have assessed participants' solutions for their current, real-life problems (e.g., Marx et al., 1992; Schotte & Clum, 1987). Compared to an interview or questionnaire format, *problem-solving self-monitoring* (e.g., D'Zurilla & Nezu, 1999) is a particularly useful and efficient assessment method for this purpose.

Rather than assessing solutions only, some outcome measures have been designed to assess one or more process variables as well, thus providing more information about the person's problem-solving ability (Donahoe et al., 1990; Getter & Nowinski, 1981; Goddard & McFall, 1992; Nezu, Nezu, & Area, 1991; Sayers & Bellack, 1995; Schotte & Clum, 1987). One example of this approach is the Problem-Solving Task developed by Nezu et al. (1991) to measure the process and outcome of interpersonal problem solving in adults with mental retardation. Using an interview format, research participants are presented with interpersonal problematic situations that include a stated goal (e.g., to make a new friend). They are then asked a series of questions that attempt to assess different process variables (e.g., the ability to generate alternative solutions, the ability to anticipate consequences) in addition to outcome (i.e., ratings of solution quality). Interrater agreement has been found to be high ($r = .83$) and estimates of test–retest reliability indicate that responses are relatively stable over time ($r = .79$). In addition, the Problem-Solving Task has been found to be sensitive to the effects of problem-solving training.

Although many different process and outcome measures have been used in social problem-solving research and training, the most popular instruments have been (a) the Social Problem-Solving Inventory—Revised (SPSI–R; D'Zurilla et al., 2002), (b) the Problem-Solving Inventory (PSI; Heppner & Petersen, 1982), and (c) the Means–Ends Problem-Solving Procedure (MEPS; Platt & Spivack, 1975; Spivack et al., 1985).

Social Problem-Solving Inventory—Revised

The Social Problem-Solving Inventory—Revised (SPSI–R; D'Zurilla et al., 2002) is a 52-item, Likert-type inventory consisting of five major scales that measure the five different dimensions in the D'Zurilla et al. social problem-solving model. These scales are the Positive Problem Orientation (PPO) scale (5 items), the Negative Problem Orientation (NPO) scale (10 items), the Rational Problem Solving (RPS) scale (20 items), the Impulsivity/ Carelessness Style (ICS) scale (10 items), and the Avoidance Style (AS) scale (7 items). Using this instrument, "good" social problem-solving ability is indicated by high scores on PPO and RPS and low scores on NPO, ICS, and AS, whereas "poor" social problem-solving ability is indicated by low scores on PPO and RPS and high scores on NPO, ICS, and AS. In addition to the five major scales, the RPS scale is broken down into four subscales (each with five items) that measure the four major problem-solving skills in the D'Zurilla et al. social problem-solving model: (a) the Problem Definition and Formulation (PDF) subscale, (b) the Generation of Alternative Solutions (GAS) subscale, (c) the Decision Making (DM) subscale, and (d) the Solution Implementation and Verification (SIVS) subscale. A 25-item short form of the SPSI–R is also available that measures the five major problem-solving dimensions but does not provide subscales that measure the four specific skills within the rational problem-solving construct. Empirical evidence supporting the reliability and validity of the SPSI–R and its short form can be found in D'Zurilla et al. (2002).

Problem-Solving Inventory

The Problem-Solving Inventory (PSI; Heppner & Petersen, 1982) is a 35-item Likert-type inventory that is described by the authors as a measure of "problem-solving appraisal," or an individual's perceptions of his or her problem-solving behavior and attitudes (Heppner, 1988). The PSI is derived from an initial pool of 50 items that are based on D'Zurilla and Goldfried's (1971) original social problem-solving model, which consists of a general orientation component (later renamed "problem orientation") and four specific problem-solving skills (problem definition and formulation, generation of alternatives, decision making, and verification). Contrary to expectations, a principal components factor analysis identified a three-factor structure rather than a five-factor structure, corresponding to the five components in the D'Zurilla and Goldfried model. The three factors and the scales that were designed to measure them were named Problem-Solving Confidence (PSC; 11 items), Personal Control (PC; 5 items), and Approach–Avoidance Style (AAS; 16 items). Unfortunately, none of these constructs is based on any particular theory of social problem solving. The most popular measure has been the total PSI score, which is used as an index of overall problem-solving ability. Empirical findings supporting the reliability and validity of the PSI are reported in Heppner and Petersen (1982) and Heppner (1988).

In an attempt to relate empirical findings using the PSI to social problem-solving theory, two different groups of investigators (Elliott, Sherwin, Harkins, & Marmarosh, 1995; Nezu & Perri, 1989) reinterpreted the three factors measured by this instrument, using the social problem-solving model described by D'Zurilla and associates (D'Zurilla & Goldfried, 1971; D'Zurilla & Nezu, 1990). These investigators have independently concluded that the PSC and PC scales are measuring problem orientation variables, whereas the AAS scale can be viewed as a measure of problem-solving skills.

Using the same social problem-solving model, Maydeu-Olivares and D'Zurilla (1997) recently conducted a content analysis of the PSI and concluded that two meaningful theoretical constructs can be extracted from this item pool. One construct is *problem-solving self-efficacy* (i.e., the belief that one is capable of solving problems effectively), which is an important subcomponent of positive problem orientation; the second construct is *problem-solving skills*. Selecting the items that most closely approximated these two constructs, Maydeu-Olivares and D'Zurilla (1997) constructed a 7-item Problem-Solving Self-Efficacy (PSSE) scale and a 9-item Problem-Solving Skills (PSS) scale. A confirmatory factor analysis supported a two-factor structure corresponding to these two scales. The PSSE and PSS scales were found to have good reliability and high correlations with the original PSC and AAS scales ($rs = -.93$ and $-.92$, respectively; higher scores on the PSI scales indicate *lower* problem-solving ability). The advantages of the new scales are that they have fewer items without sacrificing reliability and they are more clearly linked to existing social problem-solving theory. Additional empirical data on the PSSE and PSS scales can be found in Maydeu-Olivares and D'Zurilla (1997).

The Means–Ends Problem-Solving Procedure

The Means–Ends Problem-Solving Procedure (MEPS; Platt & Spivack, 1975; Spivack et al., 1985) is described by its authors as a measure of *means–ends thinking*, which has three major components: (a) the ability to conceptualize the sequential steps or "means" that are necessary to satisfy a need or achieve a particular goal, (b) the ability to anticipate obstacles to goal attainment, and (c) the ability to appreciate that successful problem solving takes time or that appropriate timing is important for successful solution implementation. Research participants are presented with a series of 10 hypothetical interpersonal problems consisting of incomplete stories that have only a beginning and an ending. In the beginning, the need or goal of the protagonist is stated and at the end, the protagonist successfully satisfies the need or achieves the goal. The instructions present the instrument as a test of imagination. Participants are asked to make up the middle part of the story that connects the beginning with the ending. The MEPS uses a quantitative scoring system that computes separate frequency scores for relevant means, obstacles, and time. The number of relevant means has been the most common MEPS score used in research. Because means–ends thinking represents a problem solution rather than the process that leads to a solution, the MEPS is viewed as an outcome measure rather than a process measure. Data on the reliability and validity of the MEPS can be found in Butler and Meichenbaum (1981); D'Zurilla and Maydeu-Olivares (1995), Marx et al. (1992), Platt and Spivack (1975), Schotte and Clum (1982, 1987), and Spivack, et al. (1976).

In a study focusing on hospitalized psychiatric patients, Schotte and Clum (1987) developed a modified MEPS that measures two process variables in addition to outcome: (a) the ability to generate alternative solutions and (b) the ability to anticipate solution consequences. Instead of the usual MEPS problems, the participants were asked to list and respond to real problems from their personal lives that contributed to their hospitalization. The results of the study demonstrated that suicidal patients generated significantly fewer alternative solutions and reported a greater number of potential negative consequences than nonsuicidal patients.

OTHER SOCIAL PROBLEM-SOLVING MEASURES

A number of other process and outcome measures have been used in studies on social problem solving. Unfortunately, many of these measures have been presented with little or no information about test construction or their psychometic properties. Some of the better process measures include the Social Problem-Solving Inventory for Adolescents (SPSI–A; Frauenknecht & Black, 1995, 2003), the Problem-Focused Style of Coping (PF–SOC; Heppner, Cook, Wright, & Johnson, 1995), and the Perceived Modes of Processing Inventory–Rational Processing (RP) scale (Burns & D'Zurilla, 1999).

Other outcome measures that have been used in social problem-solving research (including some that also measure process variables) include the Interpersonal Problem-Solving Assessment Technique (IPSAT; Getter & Nowinski, 1981), the Adolescent Problems Inventory (API; Freedman et al., 1978), the Social Problem Solving Assessment Battery (SPSAB; Sayers & Bellack, 1995), the Assessment of Interpersonal Problem-Solving Skills (AIPSS; Donahoe et al., 1990), the Inventory of Decisions, Evaluations, and Actions (IDEA; Goddard & McFall, 1992), the Everyday Problem Solving Inventory (EPSI; Cornelius & Caspi, 1987), the Practical Problems

(PP) test (Denney & Pearce, 1989), and the Everyday Problems Test (EPT; Willis & Marsiske, 1993).

Unfortunately, a major difficulty with most current problem-solving outcome tests is the lack of empirical support for their construct validity. For example, Marsiske and Willis (1995) conducted a confirmatory factor analysis on three of these outcome tests (the EPSI, EPT, and a modified version of the PP test) and found little consistency across the three tests. Specifically, the results showed that the tests were virtually unrelated to each other, typically sharing less than 5% of their variance. The conclusion was that these three tests are measuring quite different coping constructs.

These findings are not surprising considering the fact that none of these tests is based on any particular theory or model of social problem solving. At the very least, the construction and selection of test items (real or hypothetical problems) must be based on clear and specific definitions of the terms *problem, problem solving,* and *solution.* For example, in the social problem-solving model presented, a problem is defined as a life situation in which there is a discrepancy between demands and the availability of an effective coping response. Defined in this way, a test problem is likely to set the occasion for problem solving, which is the process by which a person attempts to *find* an effective solution. Because the participant's test response is the product of this process, it can be viewed as a valid indicator of problem-solving ability. On the other hand, if this definition is *not* used to construct or select test items, then one cannot assume that the test is measuring problem-solving ability. Instead, some or all test responses could simply be products of "automatic processing," or the direct, single-step retrieval of previously learned coping responses from memory (see Burns & D'Zurilla, 1999; Logan, 1988). Although the test may be viewed as a measure of coping, its validity as a measure of problem-solving ability could be seriously questioned. For a discussion of test construction guidelines that may help to maximize the construct validity of social problem-solving measures, the reader is referred to D'Zurilla and Maydeu-Olivares (1995).

Because problems in living are idiosyncratic (a problem for one person may not be a problem for another person), the most valid problem-solving performance measure may be a problem-solving self-monitoring (PSSM) method in which individuals are given definitions of the terms *problem, problem solving,* and *solution,* and then are asked to identify real problems as they occur in everyday living, attempt to solve them, and record their solutions (D'Zurilla & Nezu, 1999). After a period of time, the person's solutions are rated for "effectiveness" and the mean of these ratings is used as a global index of that individual's social problem-solving ability. If desired, this PSSM method can also be used to assess specific process variables, such as problem definition, the ability to generate alternative solutions, and decision making.

CONCLUSION

In this chapter, we describe a social problem-solving model that is based on an integration of theory and empirical data. This model consists of five partially independent dimensions of social problem-solving ability: (a) positive problem orientation, (b) negative problem orientation, (c) rational problem solving (i.e., effective problem-solving skills), (d) impulsivity–carelessness style, and (e) avoidance style. These five dimensions are measured by the Social Problem-Solving Inventory—Revised (SPRI–R; D'Zurilla et al., 2002). Good problem-solving ability is reflected by higher scores on positive problem orientation and rational problem solving and lower scores on negative problem orientation, impulsivity–carelessness style, and avoidance style. Two general types of social problem-solving measures are *process* measures and *outcome* measures. Process measures assess strengths and weaknesses in the cognitive–behavioral activities that constitute the problem-solving process (i.e., the process of *finding* a solution to a problem), whereas outcome measures assess the quality of specific solutions to specific problems. The SPSI–R is an example of a process measure. Outcome measures are useful for assessing problem-solving performance, or the ability of a person to apply his or her problem-solving skills to specific problems. Unfortunately, at this time there are no theory-based problem-solving performance measures that have adequate data supporting their construct validity. The best method of measuring problem-solving performance may be problem-solving self-monitoring (D'Zurilla & Nezu, 1999).

REFERENCES

Black, D. R., & Frauenknecht, M. (1990). A primary prevention problem-solving program for adolescent stress management. In J. H. Humphrey (Ed.), *Human stress: Current and selected research* (Vol. 4, pp. 89–110). New York: AMS.

Burns, L. R., & D'Zurilla, T. J. (1999). Individual differences in perceived information processing in stress and coping situations: Development and validation of the Perceived Modes of Processing Inventory. *Cognitive Therapy and Research, 23*, 345–371.

Butler, L., & Meichenbaum, D. (1981). The assessment of interpersonal problem-solving skills. In P. C. Kendall & S. D. Hollon (Eds.), *Assessment strategies for cognitive–behavioral interventions* (pp. 197–225). New York: Academic Press.

Cornelius, S. W., & Caspi, A. (1987). Everyday problem solving in adulthood and old age. *Psychology and Aging, 2*, 144–153.

Crick, N. R., & Dodge, K. A. (1994). A review and reformulation of social information-processing mechanisms in children's social adjustment. *Psychological Bulletin, 115*, 74–101.

Davis, G. A. (1966). Current status of research and theory in human problem solving. *Psychological Bulletin, 66*, 36–54.

Denney, N. W., & Pearce, K. A. (1989). A developmental study of practical problem solving in adults. *Psychology and Aging, 4*, 438–442.

Donahoe, C. P., Carter, M. J., Bloem, W. D., Hirsch, G. L., Laasi, N., & Wallace, C. J. (1990). Assessment of interpersonal problem-solving skills, *Psychiatry, 53*, 329–339.

D'Zurilla, T. J. (1986). *Problem-solving therapy: A social competence approach to clinical intervention.* New York: Springer.

D'Zurilla, T. J., & Goldfried, M. R. (1971). Problem solving and behavior modification. *Journal of Abnormal Psychology, 78*, 107–126.

D'Zurilla, T. J., & Maydeu-Olivares, A. (1995). Conceptual and methodological issues in social problem-solving assessment. *Behavior Therapy, 26*, 409–432.

D'Zurilla, T. J., & Nezu, A. (1980). A study of the generation-of-alternatives process in social problem solving. *Cognitive Therapy and Research, 4*, 67–72.

D'Zurilla, T. J., & Nezu, A. M. (1982). Social problem solving in adults. In P. C. Kendall (Ed.), *Advances in cognitive–behavioral research and therapy* (Vol. 1, pp. 201–274). New York: Academic Press.

D'Zurilla, T. J., & Nezu, A. M. (1990). Development and preliminary evaluation of the Social Problem-Solving Inventory (SPSI). *Psychological Assessment: A Journal of Consulting and Clinical Psychology, 2*, 156–163.

D'Zurilla, T. J., & Nezu, A. M. (1999). *Problem-solving therapy: A social competence approach to clinical intervention* (2nd ed.). New York: Springer.

D'Zurilla, T. J., Nezu, A. M., & Maydeu-Olivares, A. (2002). *Social Problem-Solving Inventory—Revised (SPSI–R): Technical manual.* North Tonawanda, NY: Multi-Health Systems.

Elias, M., & Clabby, J. (1992). *Building social problem-solving skills: Guidelines for a school-based program.* San Francisco: Jossey-Bass.

Elliott, T. R., Sherwin, E., Harkins, S., & Marmarosh, C. (1995). Self-appraised problem-solving ability, affective states, and psychological distress. *Journal of Counseling Psychology, 42*, 105–115.

Fischler, G. L., & Kendall, P. C. (1988). Social cognitive problem solving and childhood adjustment: Qualitative and topological analyses. *Cognitive Therapy and Research, 12*, 133–153.

Frauenknecht, M., & Black, D. R. (1995). Social Problem-Solving Inventory for Adolescents (SPSI–A): Development and psychometric evaluation. *Journal of Personality Assessment, 64*, 522–539.

Frauenknecht, M., & Black, D. R. (2003). *The Social Problem-Solving Inventory for Adolescents (SPSI–A): A manual for application, interpretation, and psychometric evaluation.* Morgantown, WV: PNG Press.

Freedman, B. I., Rosenthal, L., Donahoe, C. P., Schlundt, D. G., & McFall, R. M. (1978). A social–behavioral analysis of skill deficits in delinquent and non-delinquent adolescent boys. *Journal of Consulting and Clinical Psychology, 46,* 1448–1462.

Getter, H., & Nowinski, J. K. (1981). A free response test of interpersonal effectiveness. *Journal of Personality Assessment, 45,* 301–308.

Goddard, P., & McFall, R. M. (1992). Decision-making skills and heterosexual competence in college women: An information-processing analysis. *Journal of Social and Clinical Psychology, 11,* 401–425.

Heppner, P. P. (1988). *The Problem-Solving Inventory.* Palo Alto, CA: Consulting Psychologist Press.

Heppner, P. P., Cook, S. W., Wright, D. M., & Johnson, W. C., Jr. (1995). Progress in resolving problems: A problem-focused style of coping. *Journal of Counseling Psychology, 42,* 279–293.

Heppner, P. P., & Petersen, C. H. (1982). The development and implications of a personal problem solving inventory. *Journal of Counseling Psychology, 29,* 66–75.

Jacobson, N. S., & Margolin, G. (1979). *Marital therapy: Strategies based on social learning and behavior exchange principles.* New York: Brunner/Mazel.

Linehan, M. M., Camper, P., Chiles, J. A., Strosahl, K., & Shearin, E. (1987). Interpersonal problem solving and parasuicide. *Cognitive Therapy and Research, 11,* 1–12.

Logan, G. D. (1988). Toward an instance theory of automatization. *Psychological Review, 95,* 492–527.

Marsiske, M., & Willis, S. L. (1995). Dimensionality of everyday problem solving in older adults. *Psychology and Aging, 10,* 269–283.

Marx, E. M., Williams, J. M. G., & Claridge, G.C. (1992). Depression and social problem solving. *Journal of Abnormal Psychology, 101,* 78–86.

Maydeu-Olivares, A., & D'Zurilla, T. J. (1995). A factor analysis of the Social Problem-Solving Inventory using polychoric correlations. *European Journal of Psychological Assessment, 11,* 98–107.

Maydeu-Olivares, A., & D'Zurilla, T. J. (1996). A factor-analytic study of the Social Problem-Solving Inventory: An integration of theory and data. *Cognitive Therapy and Research, 20,* 115–133.

Maydeu-Olivares, A., & D'Zurilla, T. J. (1997). The factor structure of the Problem-Solving Inventory. *European Journal of Psychological Assessment, 13,* 206–215.

McFall, R. M. (1982). A review and reformulation of the concept of social skills. *Behavioral Assessment, 4,* 1–33.

Nezu, A., & D'Zurilla, T. J. (1979). An experimental evaluation of the decision-making process in social problem solving. *Cognitive Therapy and Research, 3,* 269–277.

Nezu, A., & D'Zurilla, T. J. (1981a). Effects of problem definition and formulation on decision making in the social problem-solving process. *Behavior Therapy, 12,* 100–106.

Nezu, A., & D'Zurilla, T. J. (1981b). Effects of problem definition and formulation on the generation of alternatives in the social problem-solving process. *Cognitive Therapy and Research, 6,* 265–271.

Nezu, A. M., & D'Zurilla, T. J. (1989). Social problem solving and negative affective conditions. In P. C. Kendall & D. Watson (Eds.), *Anxiety and depression: Distinctive and overlapping features* (pp. 285–315). New York: Academic Press.

Nezu, A. M., & Perri, M. G. (1989). Social problem solving therapy for unipolar depression: An initial dismantling investigation. *Journal of Consulting and Clinical Psychology, 57,* 408–413.

Nezu, C. M., Nezu, A. M., & Area, P. (1991). Assertiveness and problem-solving training for mildly mentally retarded persons with dual diagnoses. *Research in Developmental Disabilities, 12,* 371–386.

Platt, J. J., & Spivack, G. (1975). *Manual for the Means–Ends Problem-Solving procedure (MEPS): A measure of interpersonal cognitive problem-solving skills.* Philadelphia: Hahnemann Community Mental Health/Mental Retardation Center.

Poon, L. W., Rubin, D. C., & Wilson, B. A. (Eds.). (1989). *Everyday cognition in adulthood and late life.* New York: Cambridge University Press.

Sayers, M. D., & Bellack, A. S. (1995). An empirical method for assessing social problem solving in schizophrenia. *Behavior Modification, 19,* 267–289.

Schotte, D. E., & Clum, G. A. (1982). Suicide ideation in a college population: A test of a model. *Journal of Consulting and Clinical Psychology, 50,* 690–696.

Schotte, D. E., & Clum, G. A. (1987). Problem-solving skills in suicidal psychiatric patients. *Journal of Consulting and Clinical Psychology, 55,* 49–54.

Sinnott, J. D. (Ed.). (1989). *Everyday problem solving: Theory and applications.* New York: Praeger.

Skinner, B. F. (1953). *Science and human behavior.* New York: Macmillan.

Spivack, G., Platt, J. J., & Shure, M. B. (1976). *The problem-solving approach to adjustment.* San Francisco: Jossey-Bass.

Spivack, G., Shure, M. B., & Platt, J. J. (1985). *Means–Ends Problem Solving (MEPS). Stimuli and scoring procedures supplement.* Unpublished document, Hahnemann University, Preventive Intervention Research Center, Philadelphia, PA.

Sternberg, R. J., & Wagner, R. K. (Eds.). (1986). *Practical intelligence: Nature and origins of competence in the everyday world.* New York: Cambridge University Press.

Tisdelle, D., & St. Lawrence, J. (1986). Interpersonal problem-solving competency: Review and critique of the literature. *Clinical Psychology Review, 6,* 337–356.

Willis, S. L., & Marsiske, M. (1993). *Manual for the Everyday Problems Test.* Unpublished manuscript, University Park, Pennsylvania State University.

2

MEDIATORS AND MODERATORS OF SOCIAL PROBLEM SOLVING

ALEXANDER R. RICH AND RONALD L. BONNER

In chapter 1 of this volume, D'Zurilla, Nezu, and Maydeu-Olivares define social problem solving in terms of its components and processes. The following chapters richly outline the important role of social problem solving in psychological adjustment and well-being and its prevention of maladaptive coping, disease, and psychopathology. This chapter considers the complexity of this dynamic and multivariate process by examining important mediators and moderators of social problem solving. In other words, we seek to discover the biopsychosocial factors that transact to determine or influence social problem-solving capabilities, competencies, and performances. *Moderators* are variables that interact with problem situations to modify how problems are experienced and dealt with, and they provide some insight into *why* one individual is generally effective in solving social problems and another person generally is not. *Mediators* are intervening variables that "come between" the problem-solving situation and the social problem-solving process to explain *how* differences in social problem solving come about.

Social problem solving is embedded within transactionalism and the stress and coping paradigm. At any given point in time a variable can serve as an antecedent, a mediator, a moderator, or a consequence in the social problem-solving process (Lazarus, 1981). For example, at one point in time dispositional optimism may moderate the effects of social problem solving on adjustment, and at another point in time social problem solving mediates the effects of optimism on adjustment. In addition, mediational and moderational processes may not be mutually exclusive. Individual differences in trait affectivity may moderate social problem solving, whereas the effectiveness of situational problem solving is mediated by current affective states.

The research on moderators and mediators of social problem solving is in its infancy, and only a few studies have used the methodologies recommended by Baron and Kenny (1986) for testing for moderating and mediating effects. In addition, comparison across studies is difficult because of differing operational definitions of social problem solving and the use of different problem-solving measures. With this caveat in mind, we start by examining theory and research on potential genetic and early environmental influences on the development of social problem solving. Person factors are considered next, followed by a review of studies on the role of various contextual variables in influencing social problem solving. Our major focus is on theory and research pertaining to D'Zurilla and colleagues' social problem-solving model (D'Zurilla, 1988; D'Zurilla & Goldfried, 1971; D'Zurilla & Maydeu-Olivares, 1995; D'Zurilla & Nezu, 1982, 1999), but relevant research generated from other models is included.

GENETIC AND EARLY CHILDHOOD INFLUENCES ON SOCIAL PROBLEM SOLVING

No research to date has directly investigated the contributions of genetic factors in social problem solving, though twin studies on related constructs suggest that it may have genetic contributions. For example, in research reviewed by Taylor and Aspinwall (1996), optimism–pessimism was found to have an estimated heritability of .31, suggesting that more than learning and experience are involved in developing generalized outcome expectancies. In addition, Kendler, Kessler, Heath, Neale, and Eaves (1991) found that the coping styles of active coping, turning to others, and the perceived availability of social support have significant genetic contributions.

The early interpersonal environment interacts with genetic predispositions to lay the framework for social problem-solving capabilities. Social competence, including social problem-solving skills, results from complex interactions between the child and his or her environment. Parental role models, child-rearing practices, and day-to-day interactions between parents and children teach both a general orientation to everyday problems and the skills necessary for solving them (Gauvain, 2001).

As well, research suggests that the structure and support of secure attachments to proficient role models provides a context that enables young children to perform competently and to achieve socially expected goals (Masten & Coatsworth, 1998). According to attachment theory, parents provide children with working models for coping with stress and for solving everyday problems (Bowlby, 1973). As the child develops, these working models become internalized as attachment cognitions that guide and influence future experiences. Children who experience secure attachment relationships are also provided with assurances that they are worthy of being loved and cared for. Feelings of worth and value become internalized as part of the child's attachment cognitions, which lead to positive feelings about themselves and the world. Insecure attachment relationships have the opposite effect.

Secure attachment cognitions are related to social competence and emotional adjustment, whereas insecure attachment cognitions are related to poor social skills, relational incompetence, and psychopathology (Engels, Finkenaurer, Dekovic, & Meeus, 2001). Burge, Hammen, Davila, and Daley (1997) found that attachment cognitions assessed in high school predicted college and work-related stress and performance two years later.

Attachment cognitions were found to affect social problem-solving abilities among college women (Davila, Hammen, Burge, Daley, & Paley, 1996). Women with secure attachment cognitions showed better social problem-solving ability relative to women with insecure attachment beliefs as measured by the number of effective strategies for solving hypothetical interpersonal problems. Additional analysis revealed that global self-worth mediated the effect of attachment cognitions on social problem solving; women with secure attachment cognitions had higher global self-worth and better social problem-solving skills.

CONTRIBUTIONS OF PERSONALITY TO SOCIAL PROBLEM SOLVING

Stable individual differences in personality appear to affect social problem solving. The potential moderating roles of the "supertraits" of the five-factor model, positive and negative affectivity, optimism–pessimism, hope, and perfectionism have been investigated within the context of social problem solving.

Neuroticism and the Big Five

Neuroticism, also defined as negative emotionality, has been defined by stable tendencies to experience negative affects such as fear, anger, and shame (Watson, David, & Suls, 1999). However, consistent patterns of thoughts and behaviors are also associated with neuroticism. People high in neuroticism are more likely to evaluate or appraise everyday situations as threatening compared to those low in neuroticism, and as a consequence experience more perceived stress (Watson & Hubbard, 1996). In addition, high scorers on neuroticism do actually experience more stressful life events than low scorers, which suggests that negative emotionality generates negative consequences (Suls, Green, & Hillis, 1998). Neuroticism is also associated with passive and ineffective forms of coping, such as behavioral and mental disengagement, denial, avoidance coping, wishful thinking, and the venting of emotions (Carver, Scheier, & Weintraub, 1989; Scheier, Carver, & Bridges, 1994; Watson & Hubbard, 1996). High neuroticism scorers also appraise their problem-solving capabilities, as measured by the Problem-Solving Inventory (PSI; Heppner & Peterson, 1982), as more deficient than low scorers (Watson & Hubbard, 1996).

Because those high in neuroticism tend to perceive events as a threat, doubt their capabilities to cope effectively, and use more avoidant ways of coping, it seems reasonable to predict that they have deficient social problem-solving abilities. McMurran, Egan, Blair, and Richardson (2001) found support for this hypothesis in a sample of mentally ill, inpatient offenders. As predicted, those high in neuroticism scored high in negative problem orientation, impulsive and careless coping style and avoidance coping style, and low on positive problem orientation and rational problem-solving style as measured by the Social Problem-Solving Inventory—Revised (SPSI–R; D'Zurilla, Nezu, & Maydeu-Olivares, 2002).

Other members of the five-factor model may also influence social problem-solving ability. Extroversion or positive emotionality is related to stable differences in positive affectivity and the use of active, rational problem-focused coping, positive reappraisal, and the seeking of social support as coping strategies (Watson & Hubbard, 1996). However, the research linking extroversion to social problem-solving ability is mixed. Watson and Hubbard (1996) found extroversion to be only weakly related to perceived problem-solving ability as measured by the PSI, and McMurran et al. (2001) reported a low positive correlation between extroversion and a positive problem orientation as measured by the SPSI–R. The hypothesized relationship between extroversion and coping style was not confirmed in either study.

Openness was found to correlate moderately with perceived problem-solving ability in two studies as measured by the PSI (Watson & Hubbard, 1996; Watson et al., 1999). In addition, McMurran et al. (2001), using the SPSI–R, found openness to be positively related to the use of rational problem solving and negatively related to impulsive and careless coping style, avoidance coping style, and a negative problem orientation among mentally ill offenders. Open individuals report that they are able to generate diverse and creative solutions to social problems and are able to adapt if initial coping efforts are ineffective (Watson & Hubbard, 1996).

The research relating conscientiousness to social problem solving is mixed. Watson and Hubbard (1996) found conscientiousness to be moderately related to perceived problem-solving ability and use of active problem-focused coping in their nonpatient samples, and Burns and D'Zurilla (1999) found a significant correlation between Conscientiousness and the Rational Processing scale of their Perceived Modes of Processing Inventory (PMPI), which is a measure of rational problem-solving skills that is highly correlated with the Rational Problem Solving scale of the SPSI–R. On the other hand, McMurran et al. (2001) did not find conscientiousness to be significantly related to any of the SPSI–R social problem-solving dimensions among mentally ill offenders. At present, agreeableness has not been linked to any coping or social problem-solving dimension.

Affectivity

Research suggests that two distinguishable dimensions characterize mood: positive affectivity and negative affectivity. Positive affectivity refers to the propensity for people to feel active, alert, and enthusiastic and to experience positive emotions such as joy, interest, pride, and contentment. Negative affectivity refers to the propensity for people to experience pervasive negative mood and stress (Watson & Kendall, 1989).

The role of affectivity in social problem solving has been investigated. Chang and D'Zurilla (1996) found that although positive and negative problem orientation as measured by the SPSI–R shared a large amount of variance with positive and negative affectivity respectively, the two constructs were related but independent. In that study, conducted with college students, a positive problem orientation contributed independent variance to the prediction of adaptive coping beyond that of both positive affectivity and optimism; similarly, a negative problem orientation contributed independent variance to the prediction of psychological distress beyond negative affectivity and pessimism.

As traits, positive and negative affectivity may moderate social problem solving, whereas positive and negative affective states may mediate particular instances of social problem solving and facilitate long-term changes in social problem-solving ability. Momentary positive affects such as joy, interest, love, and contentment appear to broaden cognition as reflected in more creative, flexible, and open thinking (Isen, 2000), and they also appear to facilitate effective self-regulation (Aspinwall, 1998). A number of information-processing advantages appear to be associated with positive affect, including more efficient decision making and problem solving in complex situations. Positive affect appears to facilitate a greater elaboration of negative information, to engender a more detailed and flexible view of the problem, and to facilitate the integration of diverse information (Aspinwall, 1998).

There is also evidence that positive affect builds coping resources. According to Fredrickson's (2001) "broaden and build" model, momentary positive affects such as joy, interest, contentment, pride, and curiosity broaden a person's thought–action repertoire, and over the long term enhance durable personal resources for managing future threats.

Positive affect may undo the effects of negative affect (Fredrickson, 2001). For example, cultivating positive emotions during chronic stress appears to help people cope with uncontrollable stress such as that experienced by caregivers of people with AIDS (Folkman, 1997; Folkman & Moskowitz, 2000). Caregivers who were able to cultivate positive affect during their difficulties by means of positive reappraisal, goal-directed problem-focused coping, and positive meaning-making in the context of ordinary events reported lower distress and were less likely to experience clinical depression over time than caregivers who infrequently experienced positive affect (Folkman & Moskowitz, 2000).

Positive affect may also undo ego depletion (Baumeister, Faber, & Wallace, 1999). Coping with chronically stressful situations, even when that coping is successful, appears to deplete personal resources over time, as exemplified, for example, in burnout among health professionals. According to Baumeister et al. (1999), positive affect is one of the mechanisms for replenishing the self or ego (see also Lazarus & Folkman, 1984).

Positive and negative affect appears to have opposite effects on cognition and behavior. Under negative affect, cognition is constricted, fewer and less effective alternatives are generated, negative feedback is avoided, and views of the problem become more rigid (Fredrickson, 2001). One type of negative affect, dysphoria with associated rumination, appears to mediate the effects of stress on social problem solving. In a series of studies by Lyubomirsky and Nolen-Hoeksema (1995), dysphoric ruminators were found to have a more pessimistic problem orientation than nondysphoric participants and to generate less effective solutions to interpersonal problems.

In conclusion, preliminary research evidence suggests that affectivity, both as a moderator and as a mediator, affects social problem solving in many complex ways. Future research will no doubt unravel this interesting relationship.

Optimism–Pessimism

Optimism–pessimism is typically defined as generalized positive and negative outcome expectancies (Scheier et al., 1994). There is ample research evidence that optimism and pessimism affects physical and psychological health (Peterson & Bossio, 2001; Scheier, Carver, & Bridges, 2001). One pathway for these effects appears to be a result of their relationship to affect. Optimists generally report positive affective states, and pessimists typically report negative affective states (Affleck, Tennen, & Apter, 2001). Moreover, there is some research evidence to suggest that the effects of optimism and pessimism on psychological health are partially mediated by affectivity (Chang & Sanna, 2001).

A second pathway for the effects of optimism–pessimism on adjustment is through coping. Scheier and Carver (1985) suggested that optimists use more active coping to change problematic situations compared with pessimists. More specifically, relative to pessimists, optimists use more engaged coping strategies, problem-focused coping, and cognitive reframing and less denial and distancing coping (Scheier, Weintraub, & Carver, 1986).

Research indicates that optimism–pessimism moderates social problem solving independent of affectivity. Chang and D'Zurilla (1996) found that, independent of affectivity, optimistic college students had a more positive problem orientation and pessimistic students had a greater negative problem orientation as measured by the SPSI–R. In addition, optimistic college students with a positive problem orientation reported more frequent use of rational problem-solving strategies of active coping and cognitive restructuring compared with more pessimistic students. On the other hand, pessimistic students with a negative problem orientation reported using more avoidance coping, specifically wishful thinking, compared to their optimistic counterparts.

There is evidence that optimists compared to pessimists are better able to moderate their beliefs and behavior depending on the situation (Scheier et al., 2001). In unchangeable situations, optimists are better able to recognize and accept the situation and to disengage from active problem-solving efforts (Aspinwall, Richter, & Hoffman, 2001). Because of their tendency to meet problems head on and to engage in active, problem-solving coping as opposed to avoidance coping, optimists may acquire greater knowledge of problem situations and which problem-solving strategies are likely to be successful in those situations regardless of whether their active coping efforts are successful or not (Aspinwall et al., 2001).

The research findings for optimism and positive affectivity are to a large extent parallel. The difference appears to be that optimism gives rise to specific coping propensities, whereas positive affectivity has no action tendencies associated with it (Aspinwall et al., 2001; Fredrickson, 2001).

Hope

Recent research has examined the positive effects of hope in promoting psychological and physical well-being. Two interrelated and reciprocal dimensions, pathway and agency, define the hope construct. *Agency* refers to one's goal-directed determination or self-efficacy, and *pathway* refers to the perceived ability to generate successful routes or pathways for goal attainment (Snyder, Simpson, Michael, & Cheavans, 2001). Stable dispositional differences in hope have been found using the Hope Scale (Snyder, Harris, Anderson, & Holleran, 1991). Hope and optimism are similar with regard to their focus on the role of positive expectancies in affecting psychological and physical health. However, they differ in that hope includes an additional component, pathways, which is outside of the range of convenience of optimism. Snyder (1995) suggested that the positive benefits of hope are mediated by social problem solving, but research indicates that hope, in turn, moderates social problem solving. Chang (1998b) found that high-hope college students had a more positive problem orientation and a less negative problem orientation compared to low-hope students, and they reported preferring more rational problem solving and less avoidant coping.

More research is needed for us to fully understand how hope affects social problem solving. It will be interesting to determine if hope has the same cognitive and behavioral processing advantages as optimism in solving social problems.

Perfectionism

Perfectionism is defined as a multidimensional construct that involves excessive high personal standards and concerns about meeting social expectations, doubts about one's capabilities to meet those standards and expectancies, and excessive self-criticism (Frost, Marten, Lahart, & Rosenblate, 1990). Chang (1998a) found evidence that perfectionism moderates social problem solving in a sample of college students. More specifically, a doubt about one's actions was related to a negative problem orientation and the overuse of impulsive–careless coping and avoidance coping. A positive problem orientation and the use of rational problem solving were predicted by the social expectancy component of perfectionism; the greater the concerns about meeting social expectations, the lower the students' positive problem orientation and the lower the self-reported tendency to use rational problem-solving strategies.

CONTRIBUTIONS OF CONTEXTUAL VARIABLES TO SOCIAL PROBLEM SOLVING

Research suggests that one's biosocial context also influences social problem solving. Research and theory on the influence of the contextual factors of life span development, ethnicity, gender, and social relationships on social problem solving are considered in this section.

Life Span Developmental Context

D'Zurilla, Maydeu-Olivares, and Kant (1998) studied age and gender differences in social problem solving in a sample of young adults, middle-aged adults, and elderly individuals. They concluded that social problem-solving ability increases from young adulthood through middle-age and then decreases thereafter. More specifically, compared to younger adults, middle-aged adults scored higher on the dimensions of positive problem orientation and rational problem solving and they scored lower on the dimensions of negative problem orientation, impulsivity–carelessness coping, and avoidance copying style. Middle-aged adults also scored higher than elderly adults on the positive problem orientation and rational problem-solving dimensions, but the two groups did not differ on the other social problem-solving dimensions. Elderly adults differed from younger adults by scoring lower on the negative problem orientation dimension. Other research also suggests that older individuals use less problem-focused coping than younger and middle-aged adults (Folkman, Lazarus, Pimley, & Novacek, 1987).

On the other hand, Berg, Klaczynski, Calderone, and Strough (1994) found that although older adults differ from younger adults in the frequency of use of problem-focused coping, there was no difference between the groups in terms of the perceived effectiveness of the strategies chosen. Older adults also appear better able to recognize when a problem situation is uncontrollable and to cope accordingly compared with younger adults. In controllable problem situations, both older and younger adults endorse the use of problem-focused coping strategies. However, in uncontrollable situations, older adults endorsed more emotion-focused and fewer problem-focused coping strategies than younger adults (Blanchard-Fields, 1996).

Developmental differences in social problem solving appear to be moderated by the nature and emotional salience of the problematic situation. As people grow older, problem-solving goals become more concerned with other people, intimacy, and generativity (Sansone & Berg, 1993). Older adults do not differ from middle-aged and young adults in solving impersonal and low and medium emotionally salient problems. However, in interpersonal and high emotionally salient situations, older adults use more passive–dependent, emotion–focused, and avoidant strategies (Blanchard-Fields, 1998).

Lazarus (1996) theorized, with some corroborating evidence, that elderly individuals differ from middle-aged and younger adults not because of developmental differences but because of the type of stressors that they experience and the more limited coping options available to them. That is, elderly individuals do experience more uncontrollable stressors for which emotion-focused coping strategies may be the best option.

In summary, social problem-solving ability appears to improve with age, although some changes in problem solving may occur after middle-age. However, it is unclear whether these changes are related to developmental processes, contextual factors, or the moderating role of individual goals and values on the social problem-solving process.

Gender

D'Zurilla et al. (1998) conducted a fairly large-scale study on gender differences in problem solving on the SPSI–R, across samples of college students, middle-aged community residents, and elderly individuals. These investigators did not find a main effect for the role of gender as a moderator of social problem solving, but they did find that gender moderated the effects of age on social problem solving. First, high rational problem solving among middle-aged adults as compared to younger adults was found only for males. Second, the more positive problem orientation and lower avoidance tendencies in this same comparison was found only for women. The lower negative problem orientation in elderly individuals as compared to younger adults was found in males but not in females. Across age groups, men were found to have greater positive problem orientation and less negative problem orientation than women. Within age groups, these differences were only significant in young adults. Young women were also found to have lower impulsivity than young men.

Males and females differ in terms of their approach to social problems. Although males generally prefer problem-focused coping, females prefer to seek social support and to use emotion-focused responses (Ptacek, Smith, & Dodge, 1994; Ptacek, Smith, & Zanas, 1992). Female responses to stress have been characterized as "tend and befriend" rather than "fight or flight" (Taylor et al., 2000). Tending involves nurturing activities to promote safety and reduce distress, and befriending involves the creation and use of social networks to aid in the coping process. Typical measures of social problem solving may not get at the tending and befriending strategies more typical of females. Therefore, definitive conclusions about gender differences in social problem solving must wait on the development of new methodologies for assessing strategies that are used more often by females.

Ethnicity

Although research on ethnicity and social problem solving per se is most limited, promising work has been done in establishing the important role and differences between Western and Eastern cultures on optimism and pessimism (Chang, 2001). The traditional focus in Eastern culture has been on group identity and self only as it relates to the connectedness to others, whereas Western culture has focused on self, independence, and individual determination at meeting goals and one's needs, often apart from others. In the first study in this area, Heine and Lehman (1995) investigated unrealistic optimism in Japanese and Canadian college students. Canadians were found to believe more often that positive events would happen to them and negative events would happen to others. In contrast, Japanese students believed positive events were more likely to happen to others, whereas negative events were more likely to happen to them. Lee and Seligman (1997) studied attributions for positive and negative events for mainland Chinese, Chinese Americans, and White Americans. Mainland Chinese students were found to have a significantly lower optimistic explanatory style than did Chinese Americans and White Americans. The pessimistic explanatory styles of mainland Chinese and Chinese Americans were found to be significantly greater than White American students. Taking these findings, Chang (2001) concluded that Chinese American students appear to be just as pessimistic as mainland Chinese students, whereas White Americans appear to be less pessimistic than both groups.

Chang (1996) extended this research by looking at cultural differences between Asian Americans and White Americans across time on optimism, pessimism, coping, and adjustment. In this study, Asian Americans were not found to be lower in optimism but were significantly more pessimistic than White Americans. In addition, Asian Americans used more problem avoidance and social withdrawal strategies than White Americans in dealing with stressful situations.

Finally, Chang (1998a) investigated differences in social problem solving between Asian American college students and White American college students using the SPSI–R. Asian American students scored higher on the negative problem orientation and impulsive and careless coping style subscales of the SPSI–R than White American students. Additional analysis suggested that when White American students scored high in negative problem orientation, it was because of doubts about their personal effectiveness; when Asian American students scored high on the same subscale, however, it was because of previous experience with ineffective coping influenced by impulsive and careless problem solving.

These studies, of course, need to be replicated and extended to a wide variety of other ethnic and cultural groups before the relationship between ethnicity and social problem solving can be fully understood.

Social Context

To date, the research on social problem solving has taken an intrapersonal approach, neglecting the larger, interactive social context (Snyder, 1999). Within the traditional stress and coping model, the coper is conceptualized as a person who appraises and copes with stressors "individually." This model neglects the fact that people often cope with stressors in a collaborative fashion with other individuals. The social context can affect the primary and secondary appraisal of stress as well as the choice and implementation of coping strategies; therefore, the social context may influence social problem solving beyond the effects of social support (Berg, Meegan, & Deviney, 1998).

Berg et al. (1998) articulated a social–contextual model of stress and coping that has important implications for social problem solving. In this model a variety of social context–appraisal configurations exist. One is the solitary individual who appraises a situation based on his or her sole activated space. But another is the shared relational appraisal, which is a configuration in which one or both persons appraise a situation as stressful and problematic and both view it as a problem to be solved jointly. The result is collaborative social problem solving.

With the shared relational appraisal several unique coping strategies are thought to develop beyond the individual strategies as traditionally defined. For example, collaborative coping strategies entail much greater involvement with others in the actual appraisal and coping and include such unique coping strategies as negotiation, joint problem solving, division of labor, influence and control, compensation for others' deficits, and transactional dialogue with others to advance coping and move the process forward (Berg et al., 1998). Within the context of the shared relational appraisal, stressor reappraisal can occur that is active and not benign. For example, if getting a child to and from day care is considered a joint problem, the primary appraisal of stress is different than if it were an individual problem. Moreover, with both partners contributing to the solution, the secondary appraisal of coping is influenced as well.

Examining social problem solving within the social context represents a new and necessary direction for problem-solving research. The social context appears likely to moderate both problem orientation and problem-solving style.

CONCLUSION

We reviewed theory and research on a few select factors that have been examined as mediators or moderators of social problem solving, including genetics and early childhood experiences and a variety of personal and contextual factors. Although the research to date offers a promising beginning, much more research in each of these areas still needs to be done for us to understand the unique contributions of these variables to social problem solving. Moreover, real and significant advances in understanding social problem solving will only occur with improvements in research methods and procedures. Many problems in living are recurrent and are only partially or temporally solved at any given point in time. The ipsative, normative research method recommended by Lazarus and Folkman (1984), supplemented by narrative methodologies, are needed to assess problem solving as it unfolds over time for us to obtain a clear understanding of the social problem-solving process and the moderating and mediating role played by various personal and social resources (Lazarus, 1999).

REFERENCES

Affleck G., Tennen, H., & Apter, A. (2001). Optimism, pessimism, and daily life with chronic illness. In E. C. Chang (Ed.), *Optimism and pessimism: Implications for theory, research, and practice* (pp. 147–168). Washington, DC: American Psychological Association.

Aspinwall, L. G. (1998). Rethinking the role of positive affect in self regulation. *Motivation and Emotion, 22*(1), 31–32.

Aspinwall, L. G., Richter, L., & Hoffman, R. R. (2001). In E. C. Chang (Ed.), *Optimism and pessimism: Implications for theory, research, and practice* (pp. 217–239). Washington, DC: American Psychological Association.

Baron, R. M., & Kenny, D. A. (1986). The moderator–mediator variable distinction in social psychological research: Conceptual, strategic, and statistical considerations. *Journal of Personality and Social Psychology, 51,* 1173–1182.

Baumeister, R. F., Faber, J. E., & Wallace, H. M. (1999). Coping and ego depletion: Recovery after the coping process. In C. R. Snyder (Ed.), *Coping: The psychology of what works* (pp. 50–69). New York: Oxford University Press.

Berg, C., Klaczynski, P., Calderone, K., & Strough, J. (1994). Adult age differences in cognitive strategies: Adaptive or deficient? In J. Sinnott (Ed.), *Handbook of adult lifespan learning* (pp. 371–388). Westport, CT: Greenwood.

Berg, C. A., Meegan, S. P., & Deviney, F. P. (1998). A social–contextual model of coping with everyday problems across the lifespan. *International Journal of Behavioral Development, 22,* 239–261.

Blanchard-Fields, F. (1996). Emotion and everyday problem solving in adult development. In C. Magai & S. H. McFadden (Eds.), *Handbook of emotion, adult development, and aging* (pp. 149–165). San Diego, CA: Academic Press.

Blanchard-Fields, F. (1998). The role of emotion in social cognition across the adult life span. In K. W. Schaie & M. P. Lawton (Eds.), *Annual review of gerontology and geriatrics: Focus on emotion and adult development* (pp. 238–265). New York: Springer.

Bowlby, J. (1973). *Attachment and loss: Vol. 2. Separation, anxiety, and anger.* New York: Basic Books.

Burge, D., Hammen, C., Davila, J., & Daley, S. E. (1997). Attachment cognitions and college and work functioning two years later in late adolescent women. *Journal of Youth and Adolescence, 26,* 285–301.

Burns, L. R., & D'Zurilla, T. J. (1999). Individual differences in perceived information processing styles in stress and coping situations: Development and validation of the Perceived Modes of Processing Inventory. *Cognitive Therapy and Research, 23,* 345–371.

Carver, C. S., Scheier, M. F., & Weintraub, J. K. (1989). Assessing coping strategies: A theoretically based approach. *Journal of Personality and Social Psychology, 56,* 267–283.

Chang, E. C. (1996). Cultural differences in optimism, pessimism, and coping: Predictors of subsequent adjustment in Asian American and Caucasian American college students. *Journal of Counseling Psychology, 43,* 113–123.

Chang, E. C. (1998a). Cultural differences, perfectionism, and suicidal risk in a college population; Does social problem solving still matter? *Cognitive Therapy and Research, 22,* 237–254.

Chang, E. C. (1998b). Hope, problem-solving ability, and coping in a college student population: Some implications for theory and practice. *Journal of Clinical Psychology, 54,* 953–962.

Chang, E. C. (2001). Cultural influences on optimism and pessimism; Differences in Western and Eastern construals of the self. In E. C. Chang (Ed.), *Optimism and pessimism: Implications for theory, research, and practice* (pp. 257–280). Washington, DC: American Psychological Association.

Chang, E. C., & D'Zurilla, T. J. (1996). Relations between problem orientation and optimism, pessimism, and trait affectivity. *Behaviour Research and Therapy, 34,* 185–194.

Chang, E. C., & Sanna, L. J. (2001). Optimism, pessimism, and positive and negative affectivity in middle-aged adults: A test of a cognitive–affective model of psychological adjustment. *Psychology and Aging, 16,* 524–531.

Davila, J., Hammen, C., Burge, D., Daley, S. E., & Paley, B. (1996). Cognitive/ interpersonal correlates of adult interpersonal problem-solving strategies. *Cognitive Therapy and Research, 20*(5), 465–480.

D'Zurilla, T. J. (1988). Problem solving therapies. In K. S. Dobson (Ed.), *Handbook of cognitive–behavioral therapies* (pp. 85–135). New York: Guilford Press.

D'Zurilla, T. J., & Goldfried, M. R. (1971). Problem solving and behavior modification. *Journal of Abnormal Psychology, 78,* 107–126.

D'Zurilla, T. J., & Maydeu-Olivares, A. (1995). Conceptual and methodological issues in social problem-solving assessment. *Behavior Therapy, 26*, 409–432.

D'Zurilla, T. J., Maydeu-Olivares, A., & Kant, G. L. (1998). Age and gender differences in social problem solving ability. *Personality and Individual Differences, 25*(2), 241–252.

D'Zurilla, T. J., & Nezu, A. (1982). Social problem solving in adults. In P. C. Kendall (Ed.), *Advances in cognitive–behavioral research and therapy* (Vol. 1, pp. 201–274). New York: Academic Press.

D'Zurilla, T. J., & Nezu, A. M. (1999). *Problem-solving therapy: A social competence approach to clinical intervention* (2nd ed.). New York: Springer.

D'Zurilla, T. J., Nezu, A. M., & Maydeu-Olivares, A. (2002). *Social Problem-Solving Inventory—Revised (SPSI–R): Technical manual.* North Tonawanda, NY: Multi-Health Systems.

Engels, R. C. M. E., Finkenauer, C., Dekovic, M., & Meeus, W. (2001). Parental attachment and adolescents emotional adjustment: The associations with social skills and relational competence. *Journal of Counseling Psychology, 48*, 428–439.

Folkman, S. (1997). Positive psychological states and coping with severe stress. *Social Science and Medicine, 45*, 1207–1221.

Folkman, S., Lazarus, R. S., Pimley, S., & Novacek, J. (1987). Age differences in stress and coping processes. *Psychology and Aging, 2*, 171–184.

Folkman, S., & Moskowitz, J. T. (2000). Positive affect and the other side of coping. *American Psychologist, 55*, 647–654.

Fredrickson, B. L. (2001). The role of positive emotions in positive psychology: The broaden-and-build theory of positive emotions. *American Psychologist, 56*, 218–226.

Frost, R O., Marten, P., Lahart, C., & Rosenblate, R. (1990). The dimensions of perfectionism. *Cognitive Therapy and Research, 14*, 449–468.

Gauvain, M. (2001). *The social context of cognitive development.* New York: Guilford Press.

Heine, S. J., & Lehman, D. R. (1995). Cultural variation in unrealistic optimism: Does the West feel more vulnerable than the East? *Journal of Personality and Social Psychology, 68*, 595–607.

Heppner, P. P., & Peterson, C. H. (1982). The development and implications of a personal problem-solving inventory. *Journal of Counseling Psychology, 29*, 166–175.

Isen, A. M. (2000). Positive affect and decision making. In M. Lewis & J. M. Haviland-Jones (Eds.), *Handbook of emotions* (2nd ed., pp. 417–435). New York: Guilford Press.

Kendler, K. S., Kessler, R. C., Heath, A. C., Neale, M. C., & Eaves, L. J. (1991). Coping: A genetic epidemiological investigation. *Psychological Medicine, 21*, 337–346.

Lazarus, R. S. (1981). The stress and coping paradigm. In C. Eisdorfer & J. E. Adams (Eds.), *Models for clinical psychopathology* (pp. 177–214). New York: Spectrum.

Lazarus, R. S. (1996). The role of coping in the emotions and how coping changes over the life course. In C. Magai & S. H. McFadden (Eds.), *Handbook of emotion, adult development, and aging* (pp. 289–306). San Diego, CA: Academic Press.

Lazarus, R. S. (1999). *Stress and emotion: A new synthesis.* New York: Springer.

Lazarus, R. S., & Folkman, S. (1984). *Stress, appraisal, and coping.* New York: Springer.

Lee, Y. T., & Seligman, M. E. P. (1997). Are Americans more optimistic than the Chinese? *Personality and Social Psychology Bulletin, 23,* 32–40.

Lyubomirsky, S., & Nolen-Hoeksema, S. (1995). Effects of self-focused rumination on negative thinking and interpersonal problem solving. *Journal of Personality and Social Psychology, 69,* 176–190.

Masten, A. S., & Coatsworth, J. D. (1998). The development of competence in favorable and unfavorable environments. *American Psychologist, 53,* 205–220.

McMurran, M., Egan, V., Blair, M., & Richardson, C. (2001). The relationship between social problem solving and personality in mentally disordered offenders. *Personality and Individual Differences, 30,* 517–524.

Peterson, C., & Bossio, L. M. (2001). Optimism and physical well being. In E. C. Chang (Ed.), *Optimism and pessimism: Implications for theory, research, and practice* (pp. 127–146). Washington, DC: American Psychological Association.

Ptacek, J. T., Smith, R. E., & Dodge, K. L. (1994). Gender differences in coping with stress: When stressors and appraisals do not differ. *Personality and Social Psychology Bulletin, 20,* 421–430.

Ptacek, J. T., Smith, R. E., & Zanas, J. (1992). Gender, appraisal, and coping: A longitudinal analysis. *Journal of Personality, 60,* 747–770.

Sansone, C., & Berg, C. A. (1993). Adapting to the environment across the life span. *International Journal of Behavioral Development, 16,* 215–241.

Scheier, M. F., & Carver, C. S. (1985). Optimism, coping, and health: Assessment and implications of generalized outcome expectancies. *Health Psychology, 4,* 219–247.

Scheier, M. F., Carver, C. S., & Bridges, M. W. (1994). Distinguishing optimism from neuroticism (and trait anxiety, self-mastery, and self-esteem): A reevaluation of the Life Orientation Test. *Journal of Personality and Social Psychology, 67,* 1063–1078.

Scheier, M. F., Carver, C. S., & Bridges, M. W. (2001). Optimism, pessimism, and psychological well-being. In E. C. Chang (Ed.), *Optimism and pessimism: Implications for theory, research, and practice* (pp. 189–216). Washington, DC: American Psychological Association.

Scheier, M. F., Weintraub, J. K., & Carver, C. S. (1986). Coping with stress: Divergent strategies of optimists and pessimists. *Journal of Personality and Social Psychology, 51,* 1257–1264.

Snyder, C. R. (1995). Conceptualizing, measuring, and nurturing hope. *Journal of Counseling and Development, 73,* 355–360.

Snyder, C. R. (1999). Coping: Where are you going? In C. R. Snyder (Ed.), *Coping: The psychology of what works* (pp. 324–333). New York: Oxford University Press.

Snyder, C. R., Harris, C., Anderson, J. R., & Holleran, S. A. (1991). The will and the ways: Development and validation of an individual differences measure of hope. *Journal of Personality and Social Psychology, 60,* 570–585.

Snyder, C. R., Simpson, S. C., Michael, S. T., & Cheavans, J. (2001). Optimism and hope constructs: variants on a positive expectancy theme. In E. C. Chang (Ed.), *Optimism and pessimism: Implications for theory, research, and practice* (pp. 101–126). Washington, DC: American Psychological Association.

Suls, J., Green, P., & Hillis, S. (1998). Emotional reactivity to everyday problems, affective inertia, and neuroticism. *Personality and Social Psychology Bulletin, 24,* 127–136.

Taylor, S. E., & Aspinwall, L. G. (1996). Mediating and moderating processes in psychological stress. In H. B. Kaplan (Ed.), *Psychosocial stress: Perspectives on structure, theory, life course, and methods* (pp. 71–110). San Diego, CA: Academic Press.

Taylor, S. E., Klein, L. C., Lewis, B. P., Gruenwald, T. L., Gurung, R. A. R., & Updegraff, J. A. (2000). Biobehavioral responses to stress in females: Tend-and-befriend, not fight-or-flight. *Psychological Review, 107,* 411–429.

Watson, D., David, J. P., & Suls, J. (1999). Personality, affectivity, and coping. In C. R. Snyder (Ed.), *Coping: The psychology of what works* (pp. 119–140). New York: Oxford University Press.

Watson, D., & Hubbard, B. (1996). Adaptational style and dispositional structure: Coping in the context of the five-factor model. *Journal of Personality, 64,* 737–774.

Watson, D., & Kendall, P. C. (1989). Understanding anxiety and depression: Their relation to negative and positive affective states. In P. C. Kendall & D. Watson (Eds.), *Anxiety and depression: Distinctive and overlapping features* (pp. 3–26). San Diego, CA: Academic Press.

II

SOCIAL PROBLEM SOLVING
AND ADJUSTMENT

3

SOCIAL PROBLEM SOLVING, STRESS, AND NEGATIVE AFFECT

ARTHUR M. NEZU, VICTORIA M. WILKINS, AND CHRISTINE MAGUTH NEZU

According to D'Zurilla and Nezu (1999), social problem solving represents an important general coping process that, when effective, serves to increase situational coping and behavioral competence. This in turn can reduce and prevent the deleterious effects of stressful life events regarding a variety of psychological and physical health variables, especially emotional distress. If this tenet of the model is valid, then (a) social problem solving should be significantly associated with various negative affective conditions, such as depression and anxiety; and (b) effective problem-solving ability should serve to moderate the relationship between stressful life events and psychological distress (Nezu & D'Zurilla, 1989). In this chapter, we provide a selective overview of the relevant literature in support of these assumptions.

SOCIAL PROBLEM SOLVING AND DEPRESSION

Over the past several decades, many studies have been conducted investigating the relationship between social problem solving and depression. For convenience, we group our discussion of this body of research according

49

to the method of assessing social problem solving that was used, because the majority of investigations used one of the following three problem-solving measures: Means–Ends Problem-Solving Procedure (Platt & Spivack, 1975), Problem-Solving Inventory (Heppner, 1988), or the Social Problem-Solving Inventory—Revised (D'Zurilla, Nezu, & Maydeu-Olivares, 2002).

Means–Ends Problem-Solving Procedure

The Means–Ends Problem-Solving Procedure (MEPS; Platt & Spivack, 1975) comprises 10 hypothetical interpersonal problems involving incomplete stories that have only a beginning, where the protagonist's goal is specified, and an end, where he or she successfully achieves this goal. Respondents are asked to "make up the middle part of the story" that connects the beginning with the ending.

Studies that used the MEPS have generally identified a significant relationship between problem solving and depression. For example, Marx and Schulze (1991) found depressed college students to produce fewer effective solutions than their nondepressed counterparts. Similar findings were found regarding adult patients with major depressive disorder (Marx, Williams, & Claridge, 1992) and among elementary school children (Sacco & Graves, 1984). MEPS scores were also found to be significantly correlated with depressive symptom severity among a sample of college students (Nezu & Ronan, 1988). However, Blankstein, Flett, and Johnston (1992) found no differences between depressed and nondepressed college undergraduates on a college student version of the MEPS. However, they did find that depressed students had more negative expectations and appraisals of their problem-solving abilities compared with their nondepressed student counterparts.

Problem-Solving Inventory

The Problem-Solving Inventory (PSI; Heppner, 1988) is a self-report inventory that in addition to a total score includes three scales: (a) *problem-solving confidence* (self-assurance while engaging in problem-solving), (b) *approach-avoidance style* (the general tendency to approach or avoid problem-solving activities), and (c) *personal control* (the extent to which a person is in control of his or her emotions and behavior while solving problems).

Studies using this measure provide substantial evidence of a significant relationship between PSI scores and depression or negative affectivity. These cut across various populations, including college undergraduates (e.g., Elliott, Sherwin, Harkins, & Marmarosh, 1995; Nezu, 1985; Nezu & Nezu, 1987), Chinese college students (Cheng, 2001), French adolescents (Gosselin & Marcotte, 1997), patients with spinal cord injuries (Elliott, Godshall, Herrick, Witty, & Spruell, 1991), graduate students (Miner & Dowd, 1996), clinically depressed adults (Nezu, 1986a), and South African undergraduates (Pretorius & Diedricks, 1994). In addition, the PSI was found to predict recovery from a depressive episode (Dixon, 2000), as well as demonstrate that problem-solving deficits are both an antecedent and a consequence of depression (Dixon, Heppner, Burnett, Anderson, & Wood, 1993). In other words, poor problem-solving serves as a vulnerability factor for depression but can also be a consequence of depression (negative affect leads to impaired problem solving).

Social Problem-Solving Inventory—Revised

The Social Problem-Solving Inventory—Revised (SPSI–R; D'Zurilla et al., 2002) is a 52-item revision of the original D'Zurilla and Nezu (1990) 70-item, self-report inventory that was directly linked to the social problem-solving model introduced by D'Zurilla and Goldfried (1971) and later expanded and refined by D'Zurilla and Nezu (see chap. 1). Based on a factor analysis of the SPSI by Maydeu-Olivares and D'Zurilla (1996), the SPSI–R currently contains five scales, including (a) *Positive Problem Orientation* (PPO; the constructive orientation to problems in living, including, for example, a strong sense of self-efficacy and positive outcome expectancies); (b) *Negative Problem Orientation* (NPO; a negative orientation involving poor self-efficacy, negative outcome expectancies, low frustration tolerance); (c) *Rational Problem Solving* (RPS; the rational, deliberate, and systematic application of effective problem-solving skills); (d) *Impulsivity/Carelessness Style* (ICS; the application of problem-solving techniques in a narrow, impulsive, careless, hurried, and incomplete manner), and (e) *Avoidance Style* (AS; the frequent procrastination, passivity, inaction, and dependency on others regarding problem-solving attempts).

Similar to the PSI, a large number of studies using the SPSI or SPSI–R have found a significant relationship between various problem-solving dimensions and depressive severity or negative affectivity. This set of findings also cuts across a variety of sample populations, including college undergraduates (Chang & D'Zurilla, 1996), adult (D'Zurilla, Chang, Nottingham, & Faccini, 1998) and adolescent (Reinecke, DuBois, & Schultz, 2001) psychiatric inpatients, caregivers of patients with spinal cord injuries (Elliott, Shewchuk, & Richards, 2001), adolescent girls (Frye & Goodman, 2000), adult community residents (Kant, D'Zurilla, & Maydeu-Olivares, 1997), adult cancer patients (C. M. Nezu et al., 1999), and high school students (Sadowski, Moore, & Kelley, 1994). However, among these studies, there appears to be an inconsistency with regard to *which* SPSI–R scales are related to depression scores. For example, among two different samples (college undergraduates and psychiatric inpatients), D'Zurilla et al. (1998) found all

SPSI–R scales to be highly correlated with the Beck Depression Inventory (BDI; Beck, Ward, Mendelson, Mock, & Erbaugh, 1961), with the exception of RPS. A similar pattern of results was evident across four assessment points within a year regarding a sample of family caregivers of patients with spinal cord injuries (Elliott et al., 2001). Among a sample of adolescent girls, only the NPO, AS, and ICS scales were significantly correlated with BDI scores (Frye & Goodman, 2000). Haaga, Fine, Terrill, Stewart, and Beck (1995), focusing on a college student sample, also found depression scores to be related to only problem orientation and not problem-solving skills per se. Further, McCabe, Blankstein, and Mills (1999) and Reineke et al. (2001) found depression scores to be significantly related to all SPSI–R scales *except* RPS. On the other hand, in a sample of middle-aged community residents, Kant et al. (1997) found all SPSI–R scales, including RPS, to be correlated with depressive severity, which was similar to the results of two separate studies by C. M. Nezu et al. (1999) conducted with adult cancer patients.

Additional Problem-Solving Measures

Three studies that included other measures have also found a significant relationship between problem solving and depression. Because they were not focusing on real-life problem-solving, Dobson and Dobson (1981) incorporated an impersonal problem-solving task to assess problem-solving style. Their results suggested that depressed, versus nondepressed, college students evidenced various problem-solving deficits and an overall conservative problem-solving style. Goodman, Gravitt, and Kaslow (1995) used a measure that requests individuals to generate effective solutions in response to three hypothetical peer conflict situations and found that children providing less effective alternative solutions also reported higher levels of depressive symptoms.

To evaluate depression-related differences in social problem solving, Nezu and Ronan (1987) conducted two investigations—one using a measure of the effectiveness of solution ideas generated to a series of hypothetical problems and one using a measure of decision making in which participants were asked to choose the most effective solution among a group regarding a series of hypothetical problems. Results of this investigation found that depressed college students performed significantly worse on both problems-solving tasks compared with their nondepressed counterparts.

SOCIAL PROBLEM SOLVING AND SUICIDE

Investigators have also been interested in assessing the relationship between social problem solving and suicidal ideation and behavior (for a more detailed discussion, see chap. 4, this volume). For example, using the MEPS, Schotte and Clum (1982) found that the combination of high stress and poor problem-solving ability predicted hopelessness and suicidal intent in a sample of college students with suicidal ideation. In a subsequent study by these same authors, Schotte and Clum (1987) compared suicidal psychiatric patients with nonsuicidal patients on a modified version of the MEPS. They found that the suicidal patients generated less alternative solutions to problems and reported more potential negative consequences than did the nonsuicidal group. In another study with suicidal psychiatric inpatients, Linehan, Camper, Chiles, Strosahl, and Shearin (1987) scored the MEPS for active versus passive relevant solutions. They found that psychiatric inpatients admitted following a parasuicide (deliberate, self-inflicted injury) generated less active relevant solutions than those admitted for suicidal ideation without parasuicide. Problem-solving deficits, as measured by the MEPS, was also found to be related to suicide and parasuicide by several additional investigators (Biggam & Power, 1998, 1999; Evans, Williams, O'Loughlin, & Howells, 1992; Hawton, Kingsbury, Steinhardt, James, & Fagg, 1999; Pollock & Williams, 2001; Sidley, Whitaker, Calam, & Wells, 1997).

Using the total score of the PSI, Bonner and Rich (1988) found that problem-solving ability was related to hopelessness in college students even after controlling for depression. They also found that problem-solving ability moderated the impact of major negative life events on hopelessness. Dixon, Heppner, and Anderson (1991) found that positive problem orientation, measured by the Problem-Solving Confidence scale of the PSI, was negatively related to both hopelessness and suicidal ideation in college students. In another study using the PSI in a sample of young adults in an outpatient program targeting suicidal behavior and ideation, Dixon, Heppner, and Rudd (1994) found support for a mediational model in which problem-solving deficits increased hopelessness, which, in turn, increased suicidal ideation.

Using the SPSI–R, D'Zurilla et al. (1998) reported that positive and negative problem orientation were most strongly related to hopelessness and suicidal ideation in college students and general psychiatric inpatients, whereas all five problem-solving dimensions were highly correlated with both of these variables in suicidal inpatients. In another study using the SPSI–R, Chang (1998) found that social problem-solving ability predicted suicidal probability in college students even after controlling for ethnic status (White versus Asian American) and maladaptive perfectionism.

In a study using the SPSI, Sadowski and Kelly (1993) compared adolescent suicide attempters with psychiatric and nonpsychiatric controls. They found that the suicide attempters had lower problem-solving ability than both psychiatric and nonpsychiatric controls. Moreover, psychiatric controls had lower problem-solving ability than nonpsychiatric controls. More specific analyses indicated that negative problem orientation was primarily responsible for the difference between the suicide attempters and the controls. Both clinical groups were found to have poorer problem-solving skills than the nonpsychiatric controls, but they did not differ from each other on this measure.

SOCIAL PROBLEM SOLVING AND ANXIETY

Similar to the research regarding depression, researchers have used a variety of measures of social problem solving when investigating its relationship to anxiety. However, it appears that the MEPS was used much less frequently in these anxiety studies compared with research addressing depression. One study by Davey (1994) that used the MEPS (as well as the PSI) found no anxiety-related deficits in problem-solving performance among a group of college undergraduates, but the study did identify that worry was associated with lowered problem-solving confidence and perceived self-control. In contrast to this study regarding problem-solving performance deficits is the findings from Brodbeck and Michelson (1987). Focusing on a population of women diagnosed with agoraphobia and panic attacks, these researchers found that, compared to controls, such individuals evidenced lowered performance on a measure requiring respondents to generate alternatives and make decisions concerning a series of hypothetical real-life problems.

The Problem-Solving Inventory

Studies using the PSI provide substantial evidence of a significant association between problem solving and anxiety or worry. Although the majority of these investigations include college undergraduates as the sample population (e.g., Davey & Levy, 1999; Nezu, 1986c; Zebb & Beck, 1998), two studies were identified that did include clinical samples. Nezu and Carnevale (1987) evaluated the relationship between posttraumatic stress disorder (PTSD) and problem solving among a sample of Vietnam War veterans who fell into one of the following four categories: (a) combat veterans reliably diagnosed with PSTD; (b) combat veterans with significant adjustment problems (AP) but not PTSD-diagnosable; (c) combat veterans who were well-adjusted (WA), and (d) veterans with little or no combat exposure who served during the Vietnam War era (ERA). Results indicated that the PTSD group reported poorer problem solving than all three other groups, whereas the AP had higher total PSI scores (indicating poorer problem solving) than the WA and ERA participants.

Ladouceur, Blais, Freeston, and Dugas (1998) recently focused on patients diagnosed with generalized anxiety disorder and found such individuals, compared with "moderate worriers," to endorse a more negative problem orientation as measured by scales of both the PSI and SPSI, although no differences were identified regarding the Problem-Solving Skills scale.

The Social Problem-Solving Inventory—Revised

Investigators seeking to assess the relationship between problem solving and anxiety have also used the SPSI or SPSI–R. Of these studies, four have found *all* SPSI–R scales to be strongly associated with measures of state and trait anxiety across samples of college undergraduates (Belzer, D'Zurilla, & Maydeu-Olivares, 1998), adults living in the community (Bond, Lyle, Tappe, Seehafer, & D'Zurilla, 2002; Kant et al., 1997), and adult cancer patients (C. M. Nezu et al., 1999). In addition, Belzer et al. (1998) found the AS and ICS scales of the SPSI–R to be associated with measures of worry. Those studies that used the original SPSI tended to find strong correlations between anxiety or worry and problem orientation variables, but not with regard to the problem-solving skills scale (e.g., Haaga et al., 1995).

Summary of the Relationship Between Problem Solving and Distress

Overall, across several different population samples of both clinical (e.g., depressed patients, veterans diagnosed with PTSD) and nonclinical (e.g., college students, community residents) groups, and using various types of measures (e.g., self-report and behavioral performance tests), a large body of studies indicate strong associations between various social problem-solving variables and negative affect, specifically depression, suicide ideation, anxiety, and worry. In particular, a negative problem orientation appears to be an especially strong predictor of depression and anxiety across various samples and measures of problem solving (PSI, SPSI, SPSI–R). However, a closer look at this body of literature engenders somewhat contradictory findings regarding *problem-solving skills*. Both the Problem-Solving Skills scale of the original SPSI and the Rational Problem-Solving scale of the SPSI–R comprise items specifically related to four general problem-solving tasks: *problem definition, generation of alternatives, decision making, and solution implementation and verification*. Although several studies that used the SPSI–R did find a relationship between problem-solving skill factors with negative affect, several failed to find any significant association between problem-solving skills and the various measures of distress. Simply focusing on this group of studies would lend itself to the conclusion that the crucial problem-solving variables actually involve more cognitive–affective processes (orientation variables) rather than actual problem-solving tasks themselves (e.g., generating effective solutions to real-life problems). However, the majority of studies that used performance-based measures of problem solving (e.g., MEPS) found otherwise. More specifically, actual problem-solving skills deficits were associated with higher levels of both depression (e.g., Goodman et al., 1995; Nezu & Ronan, 1987) and anxiety (Brodbeck & Michelson, 1987) in these studies. How ought we to understand this set of findings?

A significant part of a negative orientation involves lowered self-evaluations regarding one's ability to competently solve life's problems. Therefore, it is curious as to why depressed or anxious individuals in certain investigations (e.g., Haaga et al., 1995) who do endorse a strong negative problem orientation do not go on to also judge their actual problem-solving skills as less effective than nondepressed or nonanxious people, especially when other studies do find a depression-associated deficit, for example, in generating alternative solutions or making decisions. Future research needs to conduct more fine-tuned analyses to better understand such contradictions. For example, studies evaluating differences in social problem solving between depressed and nondepressed individuals should incorporate a variety of problem-solving measures in the same investigation, where differences on a performance measure (e.g., MEPS) can be compared to differences (or lack of) regarding self-evaluations of one's orientation and rational problem-solving.

In addition, it is possible that because the MEPS and other performance-based measures of problem solving do not address two of the four problem-solving skills included in the Problem-Solving Skills scale of the SPSI and the Rational Problem-Solving scale of the SPSI–R that no differences actually exist as a function of negative affectivity regarding the two remaining skills—namely problem definition and solution verification. If this is true, then the lack of an association between RPS and negative affect found in some studies may have been overshadowed by the lack of differences in these particular skills that are not addressed by the MEPS. Therefore, future research should also include more microanalyses to conduct assessments of the various differences in all four problem-solving skills by comparing negative affect-related differences regarding the four subscales of the RPS scale of the SPSI–R.

SOCIAL PROBLEM SOLVING AS A MODERATOR OF STRESS

A second area of research related to problem solving and negative affect involve those studies that have evaluated the moderating role of problem solving regarding the deleterious effects of stressful life events. This type of question is best viewed within a problem-solving model of stress (Nezu, 2004; Nezu & D'Zurilla, 1989). The working assumption underlying such a model is that much of what is viewed as "psychopathology" can often be understood as ineffective and maladaptive coping behavior leading to various personal and social consequences, such as depression, anxiety, anger, interpersonal difficulties, and physical symptoms (Nezu & D'Zurilla, 1989). Within this problem-solving model, psychological stress is viewed as a function of the reciprocal relationships among two types of stressful life events (major negative life events and daily problems), negative emotional states, and problem-solving coping (Nezu & D'Zurilla, 1989; Nezu & Ronan, 1985, 1988). These four stress-related variables are seen as constantly interacting in a reciprocal manner (influencing and changing each other), and as such, are best considered as being a dynamic process that changes in intensity and in quality over time.

Major negative life events are those life occurrences that are appraised as negative by the person experiencing them and include events usually associated with dramatic life changes, such as divorce, death of a family member, or a serious medical condition. Decades ago, research addressing the effects of stressful events tended to define life stress primarily by such major events (Nezu & Ronan, 1985). However, subsequent research has demonstrated that the accumulation of minor life events or problems, such as those that occur on a daily basis, have an independent and potentially greater impact on psychological and physical well-being than major life events (e.g., Nezu, 1986b). As such, two sources of life stress, both requiring coping responses, can lead to psychological distress if such coping responses are ineffective.

In addition, this model suggests that major life events also serve to engender and increase the frequency of minor life events, hassles, or daily problems (Nezu, 1986b; Nezu & Ronan, 1985). For example, with regard to a major event such as being diagnosed and treated for cancer, in addition to the obvious medical issues, experiencing this disease can result in a myriad of significant problems such as financial difficulties, feelings of isolation, loneliness, family difficulties, depression, anxiety, sexual problems, and work difficulties (Nezu, Nezu, Felgoise, & Zwick, 2003).

Moreover, it should be noted that problems often develop independently from major life changes as a normal part of daily living. However, the accumulation of daily problems can often result in a major life change (e.g., continuous arguments with a spouse can engender a divorce), which in turn produces new additional daily problems (Nezu, 1986b; Nezu & Ronan, 1985). In this manner, major stressful life events and daily problems function to influence each other in a reciprocal fashion, potentially creating ever-increasing stressful effects.

Psychological distress, such as depression and anxiety, can occur concurrently with, or as a consequence of (a) particular conditions inherent in the problem (e.g., harm or pain, ambiguity, conflict, novelty, complexity),

(b) one's appraisal of the problem (e.g., perceived or actual threat) and of one's own ability to cope with the threat (e.g., uncertainty, perceived uncontrollability), and (c) the outcome of one's actual problem-solving coping attempts (e.g., ineffective attempts and the creation of new problems). Continued successful problem-solving attempts are likely to reduce or minimize one's immediate emotional distress (e.g., depressive *symptomatology*) in reaction to a stressful event, as well as to attenuate the probability of long-term negative affective outcomes (e.g., depressive *disorder*). However, if one's coping attempts are ineffective, or if extreme emotional distress negatively affects one's coping efforts, resulting in either reduced motivation, inhibition of problem-solving performance, or both, then the likelihood of long-term negative affective conditions would be increased. These negative outcomes then increases the number and severity of daily problems (e.g., depression reduces motivation for active attempts at solving a problem), which in turn may lead to another major life change (e.g., poor health outcome), and so on.

Thus, each of the four major stress-related variables (major negative life events, daily problems, negative emotional states, problem-solving coping) influences each other to either escalate the stress process and eventually produce clinically significant psychological disorders or to reduce the stress process and attenuate these negative long-term effects. The type of outcome that results depends on the nature of these four variables as they interact and change over time (see D'Zurilla & Nezu, 1999; Nezu, 1987; Nezu & D'Zurilla, 1989, for a more comprehensive discussion of these interaction effects). However, with reference to interventions, this model places key emphasis on strategies (PST) that are geared to facilitate or enhance problem-solving effectiveness as a means of reducing emotional distress, minimizing ineffective behavior, and improving overall quality of life (Nezu, Nezu, Friedman, Faddis, & Houts, 1998).

In part to determine the validity of this conceptualization, researchers have addressed the issue of whether the manner in which people cope with stressful events can affect the degree to which they will experience both acute and long-term psychological distress. For example, do continued successful attempts at problem resolution lead to a reduction or minimization of immediate emotional distress and a reduced likelihood of experiencing long-term negative affective states, such as depression or anxiety? In other words, does problem solving moderate the stress–distress relationship? Studies have been conducted to directly answer this question. Overall, several investigations provide strong evidence that problem solving is a significant moderator of the relationship between stressful events and consequent psychological distress. For example, under *similar* levels of high stress, individuals with poor problem-solving skills have been found to experience significantly *higher* levels of psychological distress, such as depression (Brack, LaClave,

& Wyatt, 1992; Cheng, 2001; Frye & Goodman, 2000; Goodman et al., 1995; Miner & Dowd, 1996; Nezu, Nezu, Faddis, DelliCarpini, & Houts, 1995; Nezu, Nezu, Saraydarian, Kalmar, & Ronan, 1986; Nezu & Ronan, 1988; Priester & Clum, 1993; Schotte & Clum, 1982) and anxiety (Miner & Dowd, 1996; Nezu, 1986c), as compared to individuals characterized by effective problem solving, strongly suggesting that effective problem solving serves to attenuate the negative effects of stress. This conclusion is particularly striking given that this group of studies provide converging evidence for this hypothesis across varying participant samples (e.g., college undergraduates, adolescent and child populations, clinically depressed patients, adult cancer patients) have incorporated both cross-sectional (Nezu et al. 1986) and prospective designs (Nezu & Ronan, 1988), and included different measures of problem solving (e.g., MEPS, PSI, SPSI–R).

In addition, consistent with the reciprocal nature of the problem-solving model of stress as it pertains specifically to depression, Dixon et al., 1993; Nezu, 1987; and Nezu et al., 1986, using a prospective design, found that ineffective problem solving was an important *antecedent* in predicting future depressive symptoms, as well as a *consequence*, in that the experience of depressive symptoms was also found to lead to temporary deficits in problem-solving ability. Moreover, Dixon (2000) provided evidence for a recovery function for problem solving in that effective problem solvers are more likely to recover from a depressive episode than ineffective problem solvers.

CONCLUSION

Social problem solving has been hypothesized to be an important general coping strategy that can reduce or prevent the negative effects of major and minor stressful life events on overall psychological well-being. To test the validity of this type of assumption, studies addressing (a) the relationship between various problem-solving variables and negative affect and (b) the moderating role of problem solving regarding stress-related depression and anxiety were briefly reviewed. In general, results of this body of literature provide strong evidence in support of the importance of problem solving regarding adaptation across a variety of differing participant samples and using differing measures of problem solving. However, much of this literature is correlational in nature, which therefore makes it difficult to determine conclusively the causal role that problem solving plays regarding psychological distress. Yet, some studies using prospective designs demonstrate, for example, a moderating function of problem solving regarding the stress-distress relationship (e.g., Nezu & Ronan, 1988). More specifically, individuals with problem-solving deficits may be particularly vulnerable to the deleterious effects of negative life events that serve as triggers for negative affect. According to the problem-solving model of stress (e.g., Nezu, 1987; Nezu & D'Zurilla, 1989), stressful events can also serve to impair one's problem-solving ability, highlighting the reciprocal nature among stressful events, problem solving, and emotional distress. Results of the Dixon et al. (1993) study found support for this notion in that problem-solving deficits were both an antecedent and a consequence of depression. Additional research is necessary before firm conclusions can be made. However, regardless of the actual direction of the relationship between problem solving and psychopathology, clinical interventions that teach effective problem solving should be useful treatment approaches because they can increase overall adaptive functioning, which in turn should improve a person's psychological well-being (Nezu, 2004). In fact, several prospective outcome studies provide strong support for the efficacy of such interventions for the treatment of major depressive disorder, as well as many other psychological disorders (Nezu, 2004).

REFERENCES

Beck, A. T., Ward, C. H., Mendelson, M., Mock, J., & Erbaugh, J. (1961). An inventory to measure depression. *Archives of General Psychiatry, 4*, 561–571.

Belzer, K. D., D'Zurilla, T. J., & Maydeu-Olivares, A. (1998, Nov.). *The relationships between problem-solving efficacy, worry, and trait anxiety.* Paper presented at annual meeting of the Association for Advancement of Behavior Therapy, Washington, DC.

Biggam, F. H., & Power, K. G. (1998). A comparison of the problem-solving abilities and psychological distress of suicidal, bullied, and protected prisoners. *Criminal Justice and Behavior, 25*, 177–197.

Biggam, F. H., & Power, K. G. (1999). Suicidality and the state–trait debate on problem-solving deficits: A re-examination with incarcerated young offenders. *Archives of Suicide Research, 5*, 27–42.

Blankstein, K. R., Flett, G. L., & Johnston, M. E. (1992). Depression, problem-solving ability, and problem-solving appraisals. *Journal of Clinical Psychology, 48*, 749–759.

Bond, D. S., Lyle, R. M. Tappe, M. K., Seehafer, R. S. & D'Zurilla, T. J. (2002). Moderate aerobic exercise, T'ai Chi, and social problem-solving ability in relation to psychological stress. *International Journal of Stress Management, 9*, 329–343.

Bonner, R. L., & Rich, A. (1988). Negative life stress, social problem-solving self-appraisal, and hopelessness: Implications for suicide research. *Cognitive Therapy and Research, 12*, 549–556.

Brack, G., LaClave, L., & Wyatt, A. S. (1992). The relationship of problem solving and reframing to stress and depression in female college students. *Journal of College Student Development, 33*, 124–131.

Brodbeck, C., & Michelson, I. (1987). Problem-solving skills and attributional styles of agoraphobics. *Cognitive Therapy and Research, 11*, 593–610.

Chang, E. C. (1998). Cultural differences, perfectionism, and suicidal risk in a college population: Does social problem solving still matter? *Cognitive Therapy and Research, 22*, 237–254.

Chang, E. C., & D'Zurilla, T. J. (1996). Relations between problem orientation and optimism, pessimism, and trait affectivity: A construct validation study. *Behaviour Research and Therapy, 34*, 185–195.

Cheng, S. K. (2001). Life stress, problem solving, perfectionism, and depressive symptoms in Chinese. *Cognitive Therapy and Research, 25*, 303–310.

Davey, G. C. L. (1994). Worrying, social problem-solving abilities, and problem-solving confidence. *Behaviour Research and Therapy, 32*, 327–330.

Davey, G. C. L., & Levy, S. (1999). Internal statements associated with catastrophic worrying. *Personality and Individual Differences, 26*, 21–32.

Dixon, W. A. (2000). Problem-solving appraisal and depression: Evidence for a recovery model. *Journal of Counseling and Development, 78*, 87–91.

Dixon, W. A., Heppner, P. P., & Anderson, W. P. (1991). Problem-solving appraisal, stress, hopelessness, and suicide ideation in a college population. *Journal of Counseling Psychology, 38*, 51–56.

Dixon, W. A., Heppner, P. P., Burnett, J. W., Anderson, W. P., & Wood, P. K. (1993). Distinguishing among antecedents, concomitants, and consequences of problem-solving appraisal and depressive symptoms. *Journal of Counseling Psychology, 40*, 357–364.

Dixon, W. A., Heppner, P. P., & Rudd, M. D. (1994). Problem-solving appraisal, hopelessness, and suicide ideation: Evidence for a mediational model. *Journal of Counseling Psychology, 41*, 91–98.

Dobson, D. J., & Dobson, K. S. (1981). Problem-solving strategies in depressed and nondepressed college students. *Cognitive Therapy and Research, 5*, 237–249.

D'Zurilla, T. J., Chang, E. C., Nottingham, E. J., IV, & Faccini, L. (1998). Social problem-solving deficits and hopelessness, depression, and suicidal risk in college students and psychiatric inpatients. *Journal of Clinical Psychology, 54*, 1–17.

D'Zurilla, T. J., & Goldfried, M. R. (1971). Problem solving and behavior modification. *Journal of Abnormal Psychology, 78*, 107–126.

D'Zurilla, T. J., & Nezu, A. M. (1990). Development and preliminary evaluation of the Social Problem-Solving Inventory (SPSI). *Psychological Assessment: A Journal of Consulting and Clinical Psychology, 2*, 156–163.

D'Zurilla, T. J., & Nezu, A. M. (1999). *Problem-solving therapy: A social competence approach to clinical intervention* (2nd ed.). New York: Springer.

D'Zurilla, T. J., Nezu, A. M., & Maydeu-Olivares (2002). *Social Problem-Solving Inventory—Revised (SPSI–R): Technical manual*. North Tonawanda, NY: Multi-Health Systems.

Elliott, T. R., Godshall, F., Herrick, S., Witty, T., & Spruell, M. (1991). Problem solving appraisal and psychological adjustment following spinal cord injury. *Cognitive Therapy and Research, 15*, 387–398.

Elliott, T. R., Sherwin, E., Harkins, S., & Marmarosh, C. (1995). Self-appraised problem-solving ability, affective states, and psychological distress. *Journal of Counseling Psychology, 42*, 105–115.

Elliott, T. R., Shewchuk, R. M., & Richards, J. S. (2001). Family caregiver social problem-solving abilities and adjustment during the initial year of the caregiving role. *Journal of Counseling Psychology, 48*, 223–232.

Evans, J., Williams, J. M. G., O'Loughlin, S., & Howells, K. (1992). Autobiographical memory and problem-solving strategies of parasuicide patients. *Psychological Medicine, 22*, 399–405.

Frye, A. A., & Goodman, S. H. (2000). Which social problem-solving components buffer depression in adolescent girls? *Cognitive Therapy and Research, 24*, 637–650.

Goodman, S. H., Gravitt, G. W., & Kaslow, N. J. (1995). Social problem solving: A moderator of the relation between negative life stress and depression symptoms in children. *Journal of Abnormal Child Psychology, 23*, 473–485.

Gosselin, M. J., & Marcotte, D. (1997). The role of self-perceived problem-solving skills in relation with depression during adolescence. *Science et Comportement, 25*, 299–314.

Haaga, D. A. F., Fine, J. A., Terrill, D. R., Stewart, B. L., & Beck, A. T. (1995). Social problem-solving deficits, dependency, and depressive symptoms. *Cognitive Therapy and Research, 19*, 147–158.

Hawton, K., Kingsbury, S., Steinhardt, K., James, A., & Fagg, J. (1999). Repetition of deliberate self-harm by adolescents: The role of psychological factors. *Journal of Adolescence, 22*, 369–378.

Heppner, P. P. (1988). *The Problem-Solving Inventory*. Palo Alto, CA: Consulting Psychologist Press.

Kant, G. L., D'Zurilla, T. J., & Maydeu-Olivares, A. (1997). Social problem solving as a mediator of stress-related depression and anxiety in middle-aged and elderly community residents. *Cognitive Therapy and Research, 21*, 73–96.

Ladouceur, R., Blais, F., Freeston, M. H., & Dugas, M. J. (1998). Problem solving and problem orientation in generalized anxiety disorder. *Journal of Anxiety Disorders, 12*, 139–152.

Linehan, M. M., Camper, P., Chiles, J. A., Strosahl, K., & Shearin, E. (1987). Interpersonal problem solving and parasuicide. *Cognitive Therapy and Research, 11*, 1–12.

Marx, E. M., & Schulze, C. C. (1991). Interpersonal problem-solving in depressed students. *Journal of Clinical Psychology, 47*, 361–367.

Marx, E. M., Williams, J. M. G., & Claridge, G. C. (1992). Depression and social problem solving. *Journal of Abnormal Psychology, 101,* 78–86.

Maydeu-Olivares, A., & D'Zurilla, T. J. (1996). A factor-analytic study of the Social Problem-Solving Inventory: An integration of theory and data. *Cognitive Therapy and Research, 20,* 115–133.

McCabe, R. E., Blankstein, K. R., & Mills, J. S. (1999). Interpersonal sensitivity and social problem-solving: Relations with academic and social self-esteem, depressive symptoms, and academic performance. *Cognitive Therapy and Research, 23,* 587–604.

Miner, R. C., & Dowd, E. T. (1996). An empirical test of the problem solving model of depression and its application to the prediction of anxiety and anger. *Counseling Psychology Quarterly, 9,* 163–176.

Nezu, A. M. (1985). Differences in psychological distress between effective and ineffective problem solvers. *Journal of Counseling Psychology, 32,* 135–138.

Nezu, A. M. (1986a). Cognitive appraisal of problem-solving effectiveness: Relation to depression and depressive symptoms. *Journal of Clinical Psychology, 42,* 42–48.

Nezu, A. M. (1986b). The effects of stress from current problems: Comparison to major life events. *Journal of Clinical Psychology, 42,* 847–852.

Nezu, A. M. (1986c). Negative life stress and anxiety: Problem solving as a moderator variable. *Psychological Reports, 58,* 279–283.

Nezu, A. M. (1987). A problem-solving formulation of depression: A literature review and proposal of a pluralistic model. *Clinical Psychology Review, 7,* 122–144.

Nezu, A. M. (2004). Problem solving and behavior therapy revisited. *Behavior Therapy, 35,* 1–33.

Nezu, A. M., & Carnevale, G. J. (1987). Interpersonal problem solving and coping reactions of Vietnam veterans with posttraumatic stress disorder. *Journal of Abnormal Psychology, 96,* 155–157.

Nezu, A. M., & D'Zurilla, T. J. (1989). Social problem solving and negative affective states. In P. C. Kendall & D. Watson (Eds.), *Anxiety and depression: Distinctive and overlapping features* (pp. 285–315). New York: Academic Press.

Nezu, A. M., & Nezu, C. M. (1987). Psychological distress, problem solving, and coping reactions: Sex-role differences. *Sex Roles, 16,* 205–214.

Nezu, A. M., Nezu, C. M., Faddis, S., DelliCarpini, L. A., & Houts, P. S. (1995, Nov.). *Social problem solving as a moderator of cancer-related stress.* Paper presented to the Association for Advancement of Behavior Therapy, Washington, DC.

Nezu, A. M., Nezu, C. M., Felgoise, S. H., & Zwick, M. L. (2003). Psychosocial oncology. In A. M. Nezu, C. M. Nezu, & P. A. Geller (Eds.), *Health psychology* (pp. 267–292). New York: Wiley.

Nezu, A. M., Nezu, C. M., Friedman, S. H., Faddis, S., & Houts, P. S. (1998). *Helping cancer patients cope: A problem-solving approach*. Washington, DC: American Psychological Association.

Nezu, A. M., Nezu, C. M., Saraydarian, L., Kalmar, K., & Ronan, G. F. (1986). Social problem solving as a moderating variable between negative life stress and depression. *Cognitive Therapy and Research, 10*, 489–498.

Nezu, A. M., & Ronan, G. F. (1985). Life stress, current problems, problem solving, and depressive symptoms: An integrative model. *Journal of Consulting and Clinical Psychology, 53*, 693–697.

Nezu, A. M., & Ronan, G. F. (1987). Social problem solving and depression: Deficits in generating alternatives and decision making. *Southern Psychologist, 3*, 29–34.

Nezu, A. M., & Ronan, G. F. (1988). Problem solving as a moderator of stress-related depressive symptoms: A prospective analysis. *Journal of Counseling Psychology, 35*, 134–138.

Nezu, C. M., Nezu, A. M., Friedman, S. H., Houts, P. S., DelliCarpini, L. A., Nemeth, C. B., et al. (1999). Cancer and psychological distress: Two investigations regarding the role of problem solving. *Journal of Psychosocial Oncology, 16*, 27–40.

Platt, J. J., & Spivack, G. (1975). *Manual for the Means–Ends Problem-Solving Procedures (MEPS): A measure of interpersonal cognitive problem-solving skills*. Philadelphia: Hahnemann Community Mental Health/Mental Retardation Center.

Pollock, L. R., & Williams, J. M. G. (2001). Effective problem solving in suicide attempters depends on specific autobiographical recall. *Suicide and Life-Threatening Behavior, 31*, 386–396.

Pretorius, T. B., & Diedricks, M. (1994). Problem-solving appraisal, social support and stress-depression relationship. *South African Journal of Psychology, 24*, 86–90.

Priester, M. J., & Clum, G. A. (1993). Perceived problem-solving ability as a predictor of depression, hopelessness, and suicide ideation in a college population. *Journal of Counseling Psychology, 40*, 79–85.

Reinecke, M. A., DuBois, D. L., & Schultz, T. M. (2001). Social problem solving, mood, and suicidality among inpatient adolescents. *Cognitive Therapy and Research, 25*, 743–756.

Sacco, W. P., & Graves, D. J. (1984). Childhood depression, interpersonal problem solving, and self-ratings of performance. *Journal of Clinical Child Psychology, 13*, 10–15.

Sadowski, C., & Kelly, M. L. (1993). Social problem-solving in suicidal adolescents. *Journal of Consulting and Clinical Psychology, 61*, 121–127.

Sadowski, C., Moore, L. A., & Kelley, M. L. (1994). Psychometric properties of the Social Problem-Solving Inventory (SPSI) with normal and emotionally-disturbed adolescents. *Journal of Abnormal Child Psychology, 22*, 487–500.

Schotte, D. E., & Clum, G. A. (1982). Suicide ideation in a college population: A test of a model. *Journal of Consulting and Clinical Psychology, 50*, 690–696.

Schotte, D. E., & Clum, G. A. (1987). Problem-solving skills in suicidal psychiatric patients. *Journal of Consulting and Clinical Psychology, 55*, 49–54.

Sidley, G. L., Whitaker, K., Calam, R. M., & Wells, A. (1997). The relationship between problem-solving and autobiographical memory in parasuicide patients. *Behavioural and Cognitive Psychotherapy, 25*, 195–202.

Zebb, B. J., & Beck, J. G. (1998). Worry versus anxiety: Is there really a difference? *Behavior Modification, 22*, 45–61.

4

SOCIAL PROBLEM SOLVING AND SUICIDE RISK

GEORGE A. CLUM AND GREG A. R. FEBBRARO

Various constructs have been proposed to explain the development of suicidal behavior. One such construct is social problem solving (D'Zurilla & Goldfried, 1971). This chapter examines the construct of social problem solving and the utility of social problem solving in explaining suicidal behavior, reviews common measures of social problem solving, evaluates the current status of social problem-solving research in regard to suicidal behavior, and suggests future directions for research.

EPIDEMIOLOGY OF SUICIDE

Suicide, or self-intentioned death, is an increasing concern in U.S. society as indicated by recent statistics. The extent of this problem is reflected in the 29,199 suicide deaths in the United States in 1999, a rate of 10.7 per 100,000 (Hoyert, Smith, Murphy, & Kochenek, 2001). Suicide was the eighth leading cause of death for males of all ages, who were four times more likely to commit suicide than females; the third leading cause of death for adolescents and young adults (ages 15–24 years); and the fourth leading cause of death for young adults (ages 25–44). It is estimated that 8 to 20 nonfatal suicide attempts occur for every completed suicide (Maris, 1998). Much more common than attempted suicide or suicide is suicidal ideation. Various studies have estimated lifetime prevalence as extant in from 40 to 80% of the general population.

Given the seriousness of suicide and suicidal behavior, a number of different models have been offered to explain these phenomena, although none has achieved preeminent status. Each of these models has proposed a specific diathesis that is identified as increasing vulnerability to life stressors. One diathesis that increasingly has been examined as a diathesis for suicidal behavior is deficits in social problem solving (see chap. 1, this volume, for a discussion of this construct).

SOCIAL PROBLEM-SOLVING MEASURES USED IN SUICIDE RESEARCH

Although a number of measures exist for assessing problem-solving skills, only a handful of these have been used to test the problem-solving deficit hypothesis of suicidal behavior. Of these measures, three assess the process of problem solving and three assess the outcome (D'Zurilla & Maydeu-Olivares, 1995). Process measures assess the attitudes, skills, and abilities that make it possible for an individual to discover effective or adaptive solutions to specific, everyday problems. Outcome measures assess problem-solving performance, or the ability to apply problem-solving skills effectively to specific problem situations. An outcome measure is viewed as an overall global indicator of problem-solving ability. Research relating social problem solving to suicidal behavior have used the Social Problem-Solving Inventory (SPSI; D'Zurilla & Nezu, 1990), the Social Problem-Solving Inventory—Revised (SPSI–R; D'Zurilla, Nezu, & Maydeu-Olivares, 2002), and the Problem-Solving Inventory (PSI; Heppner & Petersen, 1982) as process measures; and the Means–Ends Problem-Solving Procedure (MEPS; Platt & Spivack, 1975) and other versions of it—the Modified MEPS (Schotte & Clum, 1987) and the Personal Problem Solving Evaluation (Clum et al., 1997) as outcome measures.

ROLE OF THEORY IN UNDERSTANDING SUICIDAL BEHAVIOR

Theoretical models aimed at explaining the development of suicidal behavior are essential. Our current level of understanding of factors related to the development of suicidal behavior and the relationships among these etiological factors, however, is rudimentary. One problem is that little knowledge exists of the ways suicide ideation, suicide attempts, and suicide overlap and of the ways in which they are distinct. In addition, no other viable taxonomy of suicidal behavior exists. Given the complexity of suicidal behavior, it is likely that other distinguishable typologies will be identified that will, in turn, lead to the identification of additional etiological factors. At the simplest level, for example, etiological differences have been found between single and multiple suicide attempters (Rudd, Joiner, & Rajab, 1996). The possibility that different processes exist that result in either a single attempt or in a series of attempts has implications for the ways problem-solving deficits play a role in the etiology of suicidal behavior. Stable, trait-like problem-solving deficits are likely to characterize multiple attempters, with links to early childhood environments. Acute problem-solving deficits are more likely to develop in response to transient stressors in individuals with single attempts. Thus, for single attempters, recent stressful events may play a more significant role.

One direction from which to approach an understanding of suicidality is to see it as part of an ongoing process, beginning in childhood, where intrafamilial events and processes lead to learned vulnerability. This vulnerability may include deficits in self-esteem, problem-solving, and the ability to identify and use others as supports in times of stress. In adolescence and early adulthood, when self-awareness increases and individuals face the task of negotiating the world on their own, these deficits become more pronounced. The most difficult tasks involve the development of skills that allow individuals to identify and satisfy their needs and skills that allow individuals to recognize and effectively deal with environmental stressors.

ROLE OF STRESS IN SUICIDAL BEHAVIOR

Historically, evidence has linked stressful events, particularly those associated with loss, to suicidal behavior. These initial links were provided by a number of studies that demonstrated that life changes were more pronounced in suicide attempters than in the general population (Cochrane & Robertson, 1975), hospitalized patients (Luscomb, Clum, & Patsiokas, 1980) or depressed patients (Paykel, Prusoff, & Myers, 1975). Scant information, however, existed that explained why some individuals under stress became suicidal while others did not. In this context, Clum, Patsiokas, and Luscomb (1979) suggested that problem-solving deficits moderated the stress–suicidality relationship, with the former acting as a diathesis to the effects of stress.

In addition to the link between acute stressful events and suicidal behavior, chronic stressors, as measured by daily hassles (Dixon, Rumford, Heppner, & Lips, 1992), and remote stressors, such as physical and sexual abuse (van der Kolk, Perry, & Herman, 1991), have been found to be related to suicidality. Clearly, the construct of stress is multidimensional and is itself a factor in suicidal behavior. In the diathesis–stress model, however, stress is most often considered a proximate causal factor, with more recent events playing a larger role than more remote events. However, Yang and Clum (1996) established in a review of the literature that remote stressful events play an important role in the development of later suicidal behavior. Yang and Clum (2000) found that cognitive deficits, including problem-solving deficits, mediated the effects of early life stressors on suicidal behavior. Although further evidence linking early abuse to suicidal behavior via cognitive deficits is needed, the possibility exists that a subset of suicidal individuals develops chronic cognitive deficits as a consequence of early abuse. These individuals, in turn, may develop a more chronic pattern of suicidal behavior in adulthood.

It appears likely that stressful events, both remote and near, produce an increase in stress-reducing behavior, including problem-solving behaviors. When these behaviors are inadequate to the task and the stress is high, increased suicidality is a likely consequence. Understanding the interplay between stressors and problem-solving deficits is critical to understanding suicidal behavior. Requisite to such understanding is an appreciation of the mechanisms by which vulnerability develops.

ROLE OF PROBLEM SOLVING IN SUICIDAL BEHAVIOR

Problem solving has long been thought to play an important role in understanding the phenomena of suicide and suicidality. Various aspects of problem solving (e.g., problem-solving appraisal, problem-solving skills) have been viewed as both a predictor and moderator of the stress–suicide behavior relationship (e.g., Bonner & Rich, 1987, 1988; Chang, 1998; Clum & Febbraro, 1994; Clum et al., 1979, 1997; Dixon, Heppner, & Anderson, 1991; Priester & Clum, 1993b; Sadowski & Kelly, 1993; Schotte & Clum, 1982, 1987). One model, which attempts to explain the role of problem solving in suicidality, is the diathesis–stress model of Clum and colleagues (Clum et al., 1979; Schotte & Clum, 1982, 1987). Clum et al. (1979) proposed a diathesis–stress model of suicidal behavior in which problem-solving deficits moderated the relationship between life stress and suicidal behavior. Specifically, individuals deficient in the capacity for flexible divergent thinking and problem solving are cognitively unprepared to generate effective alternative solutions necessary for adaptive coping when under naturally occurring conditions of high life stress. This in turn may result in a state of hopelessness, which places the individual at heightened risk for suicidal behavior. Deficits in problem-solving appraisal, problem-solving ability, or both are thought to be associated with increased hopelessness and suicidal behavior.

EMPIRICAL DATA LINKING SOCIAL PROBLEM SOLVING AND SUICIDAL BEHAVIOR

Social problem-solving deficits were linked to suicidal behavior in a number of studies. Schotte and Clum (1982, 1987) demonstrated that problem-solving deficits as measured by the MEPS predicted both suicidal status and suicidal ideation. In the first of these studies, suicide-ideating college students failed to generate as many relevant alternatives as did nonideating students to a series of vignettes that required them to link alternative courses of action to the attainment of identified goals. In addition, high stress was a significant factor in suicidal ideation only for the subgroup of the poorest problem solvers. A second study (Schotte & Clum, 1987) compared hospitalized suicidal individuals with hospitalized nonsuicidal patients using both the MEPS and the Modified MEPS (MMEPS), designed to tap various stages of D'Zurilla and Goldfried's (1971) social problem-solving model. On the MMEPS, suicidal patients identified more negative consequences for their identified solutions, identified more irrelevant alternative solutions, and were less likely to attempt to use their identified solutions. This was one of the first studies to link deficits in several stages of problem solving to suicidal behavior.

A number of studies have shown a connection between D'Zurilla and Goldfried's first stage of problem solving with regard to problem orientation and suicidal behavior. Two measures have been used to measure problem orientation, the PSI and the SPSI. Evidence exists using both measures that link problem appraisal and suicidality. Several of these studies (Clum & Febbraro, 1994; Dixon et al., 1991; Rudd, Rajeb, & Dahm, 1994) have reported connections between poor problem appraisal and increased suicide ideation and attempts. The majority of these studies found that problem-solving confidence is the factor most consistently related to suicidality. Given that problem-solving confidence has been identified with the problem-appraisal dimension, these studies provide support for the importance of deficits in this dimension to suicidal behavior. Apparently, low self-assurance while engaged in a variety of problem-solving activities increases vulnerability to stressful situations.

Problem orientation as measured by the SPSI and SPSI—Revised (SPSI–R) has also been examined with regard to both suicide ideation and suicide attempts. In the first such study, Sadowski and Kelley (1993) compared adolescent suicide attempters with both psychiatric and nonpsychiatric controls using the SPSI. Individuals attempting suicide had a poorer problem orientation than individuals in either control group. Clum, Yang, and Febbraro (1996) compared a group of depressed, high-ideating young adults to a group of depressed, low-ideating young adults on both the SPSI and SPSI–R. In this study, only orientation as measured by the SPSI differentiated between the two groups. Because a number of items had been dropped from the SPSI in developing the SPSI–R, the authors speculated that it was those items that were important in predicting suicidal ideation. Recently, Chang (2002) used a global score of a shortened version of the SPSI–R to predict suicidal ideation in a group of high school students.

Because problem orientation as measured by the PSI has been consistently related to depression (Bonner & Rich, 1987, 1988; Nezu, 1987; Priester & Clum, 1993a), it is important to determine whether deficits in problem orientation are related to suicidal behavior independent of depression. Such a determination would establish a unique connection between deficits in problem solving and suicidal behavior. Clum et al. (1997) controlled for depression and found problem orientation total score as measured by the PSI unrelated to suicidal ideation. A reported tendency to avoid as opposed to approach problems, however, did uniquely predict suicidal ideation beyond that afforded by level of depression. Given the identification of the approach–avoidance subscale with problem-solving skills, this study supports the importance of deficits in problem-solving skills as uniquely predictive of suicidal ideation. Dieserud (2000) also concluded that depression fully mediated the effect of early life stress on suicidal attempts, overshadowing the relationship between problem orientation to suicidality. The finding by Clum et al. (1997) suggests the possibility that deficits in problem-solving skills uniquely predispose to suicidal behavior. Deficits in a more general construct of problem orientation, however, appear to exert their influence on suicidality via their effects on depression. This conclusion was supported in another study by Clum et al. (1996) that used the SPSI to measure problem orientation. When depression was statistically controlled in a regression analysis to predict suicidal ideation, neither measure of problem orientation was related to suicidal ideation. In still another study that examined the relationships among problem solving, depression, and suicide attempts, Dieserud (2000) reported that depression and problem-solving deficits contributed independently to predicting attempts. In this case, deficits were a composite measure of both problem-solving skills and orientation.

The vast majority of studies in this area assess suicidal behavior and problem-solving deficits concurrently. This approach leaves open the question of whether problem-solving deficits cause suicidal behavior or vice versa, or whether some third variable such as stress increases both. Longitudinal studies are needed to help answer this question. In a study by Dieserud (2000) in his monograph on suicidal behavior, problem orientation as well as a measure of general self-efficacy for dealing with stress predicted subsequent attempts during an 18-month follow-up period among a group of individuals who had made a first attempt. This relationship existed independently of depression, hopelessness, self-esteem, and suicide intent.

Some evidence exists that links problem orientation and problem-solving skills independently to suicidal behavior. Sadowski and Kelley (1993) found that both problem orientation and problem-solving skills independently differentiated suicide attempters and psychiatric inpatients from a group of normal adolescents. Skill deficits, however, did not differentiate between the suicide attempters and psychiatric inpatients, a comparison possibly complicated by the stress of hospitalization. Priester and Clum (1993b) reported that orientation to solving problems and skill in solving them predicted suicidal ideation in a longitudinal analysis of this phenomenon. Similarly, Clum et al. (1997) reported that both an avoidance style of solving problems and deficits in being able to generate relevant alternatives to specified problem situations as measured by the Personal Problem Solving Evaluation (PPSE) independently predicted severe suicidal ideation after controlling for depression in a sample of college students. Given the low level of relationship between these two types of problem-solving skills (Clum et al., 1997), this independence is not surprising. It does, however, point to the value of a complete assessment of problem-solving skills in estimating vulnerability to suicidal behavior.

MODELS EXPLAINING CONNECTIONS AMONG STRESS, PROBLEM-SOLVING, AND SUICIDE

Essentially, three models exist to explain the relationships among stressors, problem-solving deficits, and suicidal behavior. In the first of these, stressors and problem-solving deficits are thought to contribute uniquely and independently to the development of suicidal behavior. Thus, the probability of suicidal behavior increases linearly as a function of increased stressors and problem-solving deficits. In the second model, the diathesis-stress model of suicidal behavior (Clum et al., 1979), deficits in problem solving are thought to precede and increase vulnerability to stressful life events. Both stress and problem-solving deficits are viewed on a continuum with extremes of either able to produce suicidal behavior, but with interactions of both the more common scenario. When stressful life events occur, inadequate problem-solving skills are strained, and increased levels of suicidal behavior are the consequence. Developmentally, problem-solving deficits were thought related to inadequate modeling of appropriate problem-solving skills and the existence of overwhelming stressors in early life that interfered with the acquisition of such skills. In this model, faulty family modeling, family pathology, and early stressors increased the likelihood that adaptive problem-solving skills were not learned. If other moderating influences do not exist, such as extrafamilial sources of effective skill modeling or social support, problem-solving deficits stabilize, and the individual becomes vulnerable to small fluctuations in stressful events. In the third model, life stressors are thought to reduce effective problem-solving behavior that, in turn, increases the likelihood that suicidal behavior will develop. These life stressors could be either proximate to the development of suicidal behavior or remote, as in the case of childhood abuse. Problem-solving deficits are related to the existence of stressors and are proportionate to the level of these stressors. This model postulates that problem-solving deficits mediate, rather than moderate, the relationship between stressors and suicidal behavior. None of these models are necessarily mutually exclusive. Rather, it is possible that stress and problem-solving deficits have both main effects and interact to increase suicidal behavior. Evidence for these multiple relationships is provided when regression analysis yields both main and interaction effects in predicting suicidal behavior. It is also possible that problem-solving deficits mediate the effects of stress on suicidal behavior, but only partially, with stress level or problem-solving deficits continuing to exert some direct effect on suicidal behavior. Finally, it is possible that the relationship between stress and problem-solving deficits is bidirectional. Problem-solving deficits might lead to increased stress, as is the case when such deficits lead to the loss of a job or of a significant relationship. Likewise, cumulative stress places a load on problem-solving skills, breaking down a person's ability to access extant skills.

Evidence exists for each of these models. The independent contributions of stressors and problem-solving deficits to suicidal behavior are well-established. The importance of each to suicide becomes comprehensible when one considers the likely effects of extremes of either variable. Thus, extreme stress by itself leads to a breakdown in coping resources and an increased likelihood that suicide will become a viable option. Likewise, extreme deficits in problem solving render the individual vulnerable to small fluctuations in stress or, alternatively, lead to an increased probability that the individual will generate his or her own stress. The more common scenario, however, is that moderate deficits on both these dimensions combine to increase vulnerability to suicide.

The moderator hypothesis does not negate the possibility that stress and problem-solving deficits act independently to increase the likelihood of suicidal behavior. It does state, however, that each can potentiate the other. Moreover, this hypothesis recognizes the possibility that at least in some cases problem-solving deficits can develop early in life and antedate suicidal behavior. When learned early in life, problem-solving deficits are likely to be stable over time and, therefore, more trait-like. When stressors occur, the vulnerable individual is likely to exhibit suicidal behavior. In addition, because of this increased vulnerability, relatively small increases in stressors can lead to suicidal behavior, with a pattern of multiple attempts more likely to develop. Acute problem-solving deficits can also moderate the relationship between stress and suicide. Thus, an increase in stressors can compromise fragile problem-solving skills, with the combination leading to increased suicidality.

The mediator hypothesis links the relationship between stressors and suicidal behavior through the mediating effect of problem-solving deficits. Again, the independent effect of either stress or problem solving on suicidal behavior is not denied. Rather, one mechanism by which stress leads to increased suicidality is via its effect on producing deficits in problem solving. This model has found empirical support in work by Chang (2002), who reported that general problem-solving deficits mediated the relationship between stress and suicidal ideation. Chang speculated that increased levels of stress may result in individuals becoming more careless in considering their options to a particular situation. This carelessness leads to decrements in problem solving and increased emotional distress, which may include suicidal ideation and suicidal behavior. Chang (2002) pointed out that the role of social problem solving as a potential mediator of the relationship between life stress and suicide ideation has not yet been fully examined. For example, it is unclear whether social problem solving should best be thought of as a process variable (i.e., a factor that limits an individual's ability to implement problem solving) or as an outcome variable (i.e., deficits in problem solving and generation of alternative solutions).

In addition to the mediational role that problem-solving deficits play in the relationship between immediate stressors and suicidal behavior, problem-solving deficits may also mediate the more remote association between early traumatic or chronically stressful events and suicidality. To address this question, Yang and Clum (2000) examined four sets of variables: (a) early life stress in the form of physical and sexual abuse, loss, and neglect; (b) cognitive variables, including problem-solving confidence; (c) social support in childhood and adulthood; and (d) a composite score of suicidal ideation and suicidal behavior. Mediating models were examined. These analyses revealed that cognitive variables, including confidence in problem-solving ability, fully mediated the relationship between early life stress and suicidal behavior. Dieserud (2000), however, failed to support this mediating effect when predicting suicide attempts, primarily because of low relationships between early stressors and problem-solving confidence, a discrepancy that might be partially explained by variations between the measures of early life stress in the two studies.

PROBLEM-SOLVING TREATMENT AND SUICIDAL BEHAVIOR

Given the relationship between problem-solving deficits and suicidal behavior, research clinicians have devised psychological interventions aimed at improving problem-solving skills, with the idea that the acquisition of such skills would improve individuals' ability to deal with stress and, in turn, reduce suicidal behavior. Basing their recommendations on a review of factors that predicted suicidal behavior, Clum et al. (1979) proposed that interventions be developed based on D'Zurilla and Goldfried's (1971) social problem-solving model.

Treatments based on this approach aimed to help individuals (a) link unresolved life problems to suicidal thoughts, impulses, and actions; (b) increase their motivation to view such problems as issues to be resolved and managed effectively; and (c) use problem-solving skills to solve these problems. Treatments that used such an approach were predicted to produce differential reductions in suicidal behavior. In addition, improvements in problem-solving skills were expected to be associated with reductions in suicidal behavior. These problem-solving skills could in turn be differentiated from skills in implementing identified solutions. The problem-solving skills taught in such interventions were cognitive skills as distinguished from behavioral skills used to implement the identified solutions.

Several studies (Allard, Marshall, & Plante, 1992; McLeavey, Daly, Ludgate, & Murry, 1994; Salkovskis, Atha, & Storer, 1990; van der Sande, van Roojin, Buskins, & Allart, 1997) have used problem-solving treatments to target frequency of suicide attempts in samples of individuals with previous attempts. Salkovskis et al. (1990) compared a problem-solving treatment of five sessions to a "treatment as usual" control group. At posttreatment, individuals in the problem-solving group had lower levels of depression, hopelessness, and suicidal ideation than did individuals in the control group. In addition, individuals receiving the problem-solving treatment took a longer time to engage in repeat suicidal behavior than did individuals receiving treatment as usual. After 18 months, however, no differences were found between the two groups. Patsiokas and Clum (1985) compared an individually administered problem-solving intervention with both cognitive restructuring and nondirective support in an inpatient sample of suicide attempters. Although individuals who were taught problem-solving skills did better on measures of problem-solving ability and were less hopeless, no differences between the two groups were found on a measure of suicidal ideation. These results were similar to those reported by Lerner and Clum (1990). These researchers found that suicidal college students who were taught problem-solving skills in a group format had lower levels of loneliness, depression, and hopelessness than did individuals in social support groups.

As in the Patsiokas and Clum study, suicide ideation was reduced by both interventions.

Recently, Rudd et al. (1996) demonstrated that an intensive outpatient treatment program, of which learning problem-solving skills was a part, produced outcomes equivalent to an intensive inpatient program. Comparable improvements between the two programs were found on depression, hopelessness, and suicidal ideation, with improvements maintained over a year. Clum et al. (2004) compared a group-administered social problem-solving treatment to group social support and group functional analysis on measures of problem solving, depression, hopelessness, and suicidal ideation. The sample was a group of severely ideating college students, many of whom had made a previous suicide attempt. All three groups improved significantly on measures of depression, hopelessness, and suicidal ideation, gains that continued and were extended over a one-year follow-up. Suicide ideators in the problem-solving and social support groups improved significantly more than those in the functional analysis (FA) group on a measure of problem-solving confidence. Moreover, when the percentage of individuals achieving a "clinically significant" level of improvement in each treatment were compared, individuals in both the problem-solving (PS) and social support (SS) interventions were more likely to show significant improvement on a self-report measure of suicidal ideation than were individuals in the FA intervention.

To further establish the therapeutic validity of interventions that emphasize problem-solving skills for reducing suicidal behavior, it is necessary to show that individuals who actually learn the problem-solving skills are the ones who improve most on measures of suicidal behavior. Clum et al. (2004) carried out these analyses and found that improvement on measures of problem-solving from pre- to posttreatment were predictive of posttreatment and one-year follow-up levels of depression, hopelessness, and suicidal ideation only for individuals in the PS treatment. No such relationships were found within either the SS or FA intervention. These results suggest that learning problem-solving skills was related to improvement as predicted by the theory.

Taken together, the studies that have examined the effectiveness of problem-solving interventions on suicidal behavior support the validity of this approach. Nevertheless, demonstrating consistent differential improvement when comparing problem-solving interventions to other viable psychological interventions is difficult. One reason for this difficulty is that suicidal behavior fluctuates and suicidal individuals likely enter treatment during the acute phase of such behavior. Any intervention is therefore likely to produce reductions in suicidal behavior. When one compares the effectiveness of problem-solving interventions to other treatments on factors associated with suicidality, such as depression and hopelessness, some studies (Lerner & Clum, 1990; Patsiokas & Clum, 1985) have shown problem-solving interventions are superior. In addition, Rudd et al.'s (1996) finding that an outpatient treatment featuring problem-solving techniques was equivalent to traditional inpatient therapy underscores both the power and efficiency of this approach for suicidal individuals. It appears that problem-solving skills are learned in brief interventions that emphasize their acquisition (Patsiokas & Clum, 1985) and that individuals who acquire more confidence in their problem-solving skills are more likely to experience reductions in suicidal behavior, depression, and hopelessness.

CONCLUSION

It is important to be mindful of the goals for linking problem-solving deficits to suicidal behavior. Primary among several goals is understanding the process by which suicidal behavior develops. Given that our understanding of problem-solving behavior is dependent both on our models of problem solving and on the measures used to evaluate relevant constructs, additional work in each of these areas is required. D'Zurilla and Goldfried (1971) advanced the field significantly with their development of a problem-solving model, the examination of which was enhanced by the development of research instruments (the SPSI and SPSI–R) designed to measure it (D'Zurilla & Nezu, 1990; D'Zurilla et al., 2002). These instruments, however, measure an individual's own appraisal of their problem-solving behavior rather than the behavior itself. Given the definition of problem solving as a conscious process aimed at resolving life problems, it is assumed but largely unproven that such a process is in fact engaged in differentially by both suicidal and nonsuicidal individuals. Equally important is determining whether the instruments used to measure problem solving predict the actual process when individuals come under stress. With such concurrent validity established, conclusions linking problem-solving deficits to suicidal behavior could be made more confidently.

The issue of how best to assess problem solving is likewise unclear, especially as it relates to suicidality. Although some measures of problem solving have been consistently used in the area of predicting suicidality, and although there has been some consistency in the demonstrated relationships, there is little known about how the extant measures relate to each other and what constructs within the problem-solving model are actually being measured. Because there is also variability in the methodology used to measure problem solving, with both objective and self-report measures in use, the relationships among these measures need to be established. Only then will researchers be able to determine if the conclusions reached using these various measures are consistent.

Another area in need of research is concerned with the question of whether problem-solving deficits cause, or are otherwise linked to, suicidal behavior. This question relates to the issue of whether problem-solving deficits are trait or state phenomena as well as to whether problem-solving deficits cause or are caused by stressors. Longitudinal studies that evaluate problem-solving skills and suicidal behavior before the occurrence of major stressors are needed to answer this question. Repeated assessments of problem-solving behavior over short, intermediate, and long intervals are needed to establish the stability of both the construct and the methods used to assess the construct. It may well be that self-report measures of problem solving are more variable than more objective assessment methods. Along these lines, it is important to determine whether subgroups of individuals exist who are chronically deficient in their problem-solving skills, while others become deficient in response to either generic or idiosyncratic stressors. If this information were known, interventions could be tailored to either reviving problem-solving skills or teaching them to individuals who are stably deficient.

REFERENCES

Allard, R., Marshall, M., & Plante, M. (1992). Intensive follow-up does not decrease the risk of suicide attempts. *Suicide and Life-Threatening Behavior, 22,* 303–314.

Bonner, R. L., & Rich, A. R. (1987). Concurrent validity of stress-vulnerability model of suicidal ideation and behavior. A follow-up study. *Suicide and Life-Threatening Behavior, 17,* 265–271.

Bonner, R. L., & Rich, A. (1988). Negative life stress, social problem-solving self-appraisal, and hopelessness: Implications for suicide research. *Cognitive Therapy and Research, 12,* 549–556.

Chang, E. C. (1998). Cultural differences, perfectionism, and suicide risk in a college student population: Does social problem solving still matter? *Cognitive Therapy and Research, 22,* 237–254.

Chang, E. C. (2002). Predicting suicide ideation in an adolescent population: Examining the role of social problem solving as a moderator and a mediator. *Personality and Individual Differences, 32,* 1279–1291.

Clum, G. A., Canfield, D., Van Arsdel, M., Yang, B., Febbraro, G. A. R., & Wright, J. (1997). An expanded etiological model for suicide behavior in adolescence: Evidence for its specificity relative to depression. *Journal of Psychopathology and Behavioral Assessment, 19,* 207–223.

Clum, G. A., & Febbraro, G. A. R. (1994). Stress, social support, and problem-solving appraisal/skills: Prediction of suicide severity within a college sample. *Journal of Psychopathology and Behavioral Assessment, 16,* 69–83.

Clum, G. A., Patsiokas, A., & Luscomb, R. (1979). Empirically based comprehensive treatment program for parasuicide. *Journal of Consulting and Clinical Psychology, 47,* 937–945.

Clum, G. A., Yang, B., & Febbraro, G. A. R. (1996). An investigation of the validity of the SPSI and SPSI–R in differentiating suicidal from depressed, non-suicidal college students. *Journal of Psychopathology and Behavioral Assessment, 18,* 119–132.

Clum, G. A., Yang, B., Febbraro, G. A. R., Pickett, C. Weaver, T., Wright, J., et al. (2004). *A comparison of three treatments for a group of severely ideating suicidal college students* Manuscript under review.

Cochrane, R., & Robertson, A. (1975). Stress in the lives of parasuicides. *Social Psychiatry, 10,* 161–172.

Diesurud, G. (2000). *Suicide attempt: Unsolvable lives?* Doctoral dissertation, University of Oslo, Norway.

Dixon, W. A., Heppner, P. P., & Anderson, W. P. (1991). Problem-solving appraisal, stress, hopelessness, and suicide ideation in a college population. *Journal of Counseling Psychology, 38,* 51–56.

Dixon, W. A., Rumford, K. G., Heppner, P. P., & Lips, B. J. (1992). Use of different sources of stress to predict hopelessness and suicide ideation in a college population. *Journal of Counseling Psychology, 39,* 342–349.

D'Zurilla, T. J., & Goldfried, M. (1971). Problem-solving and behavior modification. *Journal of Abnormal Psychology, 78,* 104–126.

D'Zurilla, T. J., & Maydeu-Olivares, A. (1995). Conceptual and methodological issues in social problem-solving assessment. *Behavior Therapy, 26,* 409–432.

D'Zurilla, T. J., & Nezu, A. M. (1990). Development and preliminary evaluation of the Social Problem-Solving Inventory. *Psychological Assessment, 2,* 156–163.

D'Zurilla, T. J., Nezu, A. M., & Maydeu-Olivares, A. (2002). *Social Problem-Solving Inventory—Revised (SPSI–R): Technical manual.* North Tonawanda, NY: Multi-Health Systems.

Heppner, P. P., & Petersen, C. H. (1982). The development and implications of a personal problem-solving inventory. *Journal of Counseling Psychology, 29,* 166–175.

Hoyert, D. L., Smith, B. L., Murphy, S. L., & Kochanek, M. A. (2001). *Deaths: Final data for national vital statistics reports, 49.* Hyattsville, MD: National Center for Health Statistics.

Lerner, M., & Clum, G. A. (1990). A problem-solving approach for treating adolescent suicide behavior. *Behavior Therapy, 21,* 403–413.

Luscomb, R., Clum, G. A., & Patsiokas, A. T. (1980). Mediating factors in the relationship between life stress and suicide attempting. *Journal of Nervous and Mental Disease, 168,* 644–649.

Maris, R. W. (1998). Suicide. In H. S. Friedman (Ed.), *Encyclopedia of mental health, Vol. 3* (pp. 417–430). San Diego, CA: Academic Press.

McLeavey, B. C., Daly, R. J., Ludgate, J. W., & Murray, C. M. (1994). Interpersonal problem-solving skills training in the treatment of self-poisoning patients. *Suicide and Life-Threatening Behavior, 24,* 382–394.

Nezu, A. M. (1987). A problem-solving formulation of depression: A literature review and proposal of a pluralistic model. *Clinical Psychology Review, 7,* 121–144.

Patsiokas, A. T., & Clum, G. A. (1985). Effects of psychotherapeutic strategies in the treatment of suicide attempters. *Psychotherapy, 22,* 281–290.

Paykel, E., Prusoff, B., & Myers, J. (1975). Suicide attempts and recent life events. *Archives of General Psychiatry, 32,* 327–333.

Platt, J. J., & Spivack, G. (1975). *Manual for the Means–Ends Problem-Solving Procedure (MEPS): A measure of interpersonal cognitive problem-solving skills.* Philadelphia: Hahnemann Community Mental Health/Mental Retardation Center.

Priester, M. J., & Clum, G. A. (1993a). Perceived problem-solving ability as a predictor of depression, hopelessness, and suicidal ideation in a college population. *Journal of Counseling Psychology, 40,* 79–85.

Priester, M. J., & Clum, G. A. (1993b). The problem-solving diathesis in depression, hopelessness, and suicide ideation: A longitudinal analysis. *Journal of Psychopathology and Behavioral Assessment, 15,* 239–254.

Rudd, M. D., Joiner, T., & Rajab, M. H. (1996). Relationships among suicide ideators, attempters, and multiple attempters in a young-adult sample. *Journal of Abnormal Psychology, 105,* 541–550.

Rudd, M. D., Rajab, M. H., & Dahm, P. F. (1994) Problem-solving appraisal in suicide ideators and attempters. *American Journal of Orthopsychiatry, 64,* 136–149.

Rudd, M. D., Rajab, M. H., Orman, D. T., Stulman, D. H., Joiner, T., & Dixon, W. (1996). Effectiveness of an outpatient intervention targeting suicidal young adults: Preliminary results. *Journal of Consulting and Clinical Psychology, 64,* 179–190.

Sadowski, C. & Kelley, M. L. (1993). Social problem-solving in suicidal adolescents. *Journal of Consulting and Clinical Psychology, 61,* 121–127.

Salkovskis, P. M., Atha, C., & Storer, D. (1990) Cognitive–behavioural problem solving in the treatment of patients who repeatedly attempt suicide: A controlled trial. *British Journal of Psychiatry, 157,* 871–876.

Schotte, D. E., & Clum, G. A. (1982). Suicide ideation in a college population: A test of a model. *Journal of Consulting and Clinical Psychology, 50,* 690–696.

Schotte, D. E., & Clum, G. A. (1987). Problem-solving skills in suicidal psychiatric patients. *Journal of Consulting and Clinical Psychology, 55,* 49–54.

van der Kolk, B. A., Perry, C., & Herman, J. L. (1991). Childhood origins of self destructive behavior. *American Journal of Psychiatry, 148,* 1665–1671.

Van der Sande, R., van Roojen, L., Buskins, E., & Allart, E. (1997). Intensive inpatient and community intervention versus routine care after attempted suicide: A randomized, controlled intervention study. *British Journal of Psychiatry, 171*, 35–41.

Yang, B., & Clum, G. A. (1996). Effects of early negative life experiences on cognitive functioning and risk for suicide: A review. *Clinical Psychology Review, 16*, 177–195.

Yang, B., & Clum, G. A. (2000). Childhood stress leads to suicidality via its effect on cognitive functioning. *Suicide and Life-Threatening Behavior, 30*, 183–198.

5

SOCIAL PROBLEM SOLVING AND SCHIZOPHRENIA

SARAH E. MORRIS, ALAN S. BELLACK, AND WENDY N. TENHULA

Schizophrenia is a severe, chronic mental disorder characterized by various behavioral, emotional, and cognitive disturbances. Although the phenomenology of the disorder is highly heterogeneous, common characteristics of the illness can generally be classified into four domains: positive symptoms, negative symptoms, cognitive impairment, and social dysfunction. The positive–negative classification may be used to group symptoms as well as subtypes of the disorder (Andreasen, 1985). Positive symptoms are those things that schizophrenia patients experience that nonpatients generally do not. Some of the most frequently observed positive symptoms are hallucinations, most commonly in the auditory modality; delusions, often of persecution or reference; and disorganization of thinking, speech, and behavior. The negative symptom cluster consists of deficiencies compared to nonpatients. These frequently include restriction in the range of emotional

Preparation of this manuscript was supported by the Department of Veterans Affairs Capitol Health Care Network MIRECC (Alan S. Bellack, director), by National Institutes of Health Grants DA11753 and DA12265 from NIDA to ASB, and a Merit Review Entry Program grant from the Department of Veterans Affairs, Veterans Health Administration, Medical Research Service to Wendy N. Tenhula.

experience and expressivity, social withdrawal, and reduction in the initiation of goal-directed behavior.

Another prominent feature of the disorder is a profound disruption of
social behavior. Social dysfunction, often manifested as a decline in the
amount and quality of social interactions, or, in individuals in whom the
disorder developed in childhood or adolescence, a failure to achieve expected
levels of interpersonal and occupational functioning, is a diagnostic criteria
of schizophrenia according to the *Diagnostic and Statistical Manual*, 4th
edition (*DSM–IV*; American Psychiatric Association, 1994). Social withdrawal and isolation have been identified as common prodromal symptoms,
warning of the onset of the illness or of an episode (American Psychiatric
Association, 1994), but social impairment frequently persists during periods
of remission (Bellack, Morrison, Mueser, Wade, & Sayers, 1990). Social
deficits in schizophrenia patients include difficulty initiating and sustaining
conversations and inability to achieve goals or have needs met in situations
requiring social interactions (Morrison & Bellack, 1987). Ultimately, these
impairments manifest themselves in profound difficulties in role functioning.
For many schizophrenia patients, poor social functioning, odd interpersonal
behavior, and stigmatizing experiences, in combination with social anxiety,
contribute to isolation, inadequate social support, and vocational impairment, which, in an unfortunate cycle, diminish schizophrenia patients'
opportunities to develop and improve their social skills.

Finally, a large literature documents that schizophrenia patients exhibit
impairments in a diverse array of neurocognitive domains, including attention, working, and episodic memory and "executive" processes such as planning, self-monitoring, and problem solving (Heinrichs & Zakzanis, 1998).
Deficits in social problem solving, as defined by D'Zurilla and colleagues
(D'Zurilla & Goldfried, 1971; D'Zurilla & Nezu, 1999), may be considered
a manifestation of a unique combination of positive or negative symptoms,
chronic social disability, and cognitive impairment observed in schizophrenia. In this chapter, we discuss the social problem-solving model as it applies
to schizophrenia and present issues related to assessment and treatment that
are specific to social problem solving in this disorder.

SOCIAL PROBLEM SOLVING IN SCHIZOPHRENIA

In their seminal 1971 article, D'Zurilla and Goldfried placed social
problem solving into the realm of consideration of mental health practitioners and researchers. The influence of their model can be observed in
the subsequent decades of work attempting to understand and remediate
social problem-solving deficits in schizophrenia and other psychiatric disorders. The model was developed at a time when behavioral models were

innovative and in conflict with the prevailing "medical" view of psychiatric disorders. Although it was formulated with less severe psychiatric problems as its focus, and it would be difficult to argue that the psychotic symptoms observed in schizophrenia are a result of social problem-solving impairment, the characterization of social problem solving as a key contributor to psychological well-being and a legitimate target for psychosocial interventions is highly relevant to schizophrenia.

Although extensive empirical work supports the primary tenets of the D'Zurilla and Goldfried social problem-solving model (1971) and its later refinements (D'Zurilla, Nezu, & Maydeu-Olivares, 2002) in various populations (D'Zurilla, Chang, Nottingham, & Faccini, 1998; also see review by D'Zurilla & Nezu, 1999), little attention has been given to establishing the validity of the model for patients with psychotic disorders. Although it is informative to use constructs developed through research with healthy populations to describe variations observed in clinical samples for the purposes of making comparisons, it is also important to have a model that is specific for understanding social problem solving in schizophrenia rather than attempting to classify and describe patients solely using categories and characteristics that may not reflect primary patterns of thinking and behaving in this population. Although the evidence of a relationship between poor social functioning and positive symptoms is mixed (Bellack, Morrison, Wixted, & Mueser, 1990; Bellack, Sayers, Mueser, & Bennett, 1994), delusional thoughts experienced by some patients may introduce inaccurate or irrelevant information into the development of a problem orientation and interfere with judgment. Individuals with schizophrenia may exhibit problem orientation dimensions and problem-solving styles that differ from those observed in nonpatients. For example, problem orientation in schizophrenia patients may be based on delusional thinking about one's abilities (e.g., grandiose delusions of control, paranoid delusions of sabotage) that may wax and wane over time. Thus, patients with schizophrenia may also have difficulty maintaining a stable problem orientation. Patients with schizophrenia also may be predisposed to a negative problem orientation because of many failure experiences as a result of their illness.

The *impulsivity/carelessness style* describes the response style of many patients with schizophrenia, specifically those with a disorganized subtype, as well as many patients who are not adequately medicated. In addition, however, many schizophrenia patients experience persistent, pervasive thought disorder and cognitive impairment. The problem-solving style exhibited by these patients can be described as irrational, characterized by bizarre and illogical solutions, anticipation of consequences based on delusional or unreasonable thought processes, haphazard implementation of solutions, and gross errors in evaluating outcomes. The evaluation of solutions requires the ability to make ongoing judgments about the advantages and disadvantages of different choices, which requires a level of attention, introspection, and organized thinking that many schizophrenia patients do not possess.

The D'Zurilla model is based on the assumption that if an individual is taught the skills to systematically evaluate situations and outcomes, the likelihood that they will choose the most appropriate response is maximized. For individuals with schizophrenia, the relationship between problem-related information and selection of an optimal response can be assumed to be weakened because of disordered thinking and cognitive deficits. The impact of negative symptoms also threatens the applicability of the model. Specifically, symptoms such as affective flattening, avolition–apathy, anhedonia–asociality, and inattention have been reported to be associated with poor social, work, and family adjustment (Bellack et al., 1990), suggesting that symptom-related deficits may interfere with schizophrenia patients' ability to attend to social interactions, become emotionally involved in interpersonal situations, and engage important expressive facial and motor behaviors to implement responses. These types of symptoms may introduce a moderating effect on the relationship between problem orientation and effective problem solving.

Although D'Zurilla and colleagues' model primarily addresses two levels of cognitive–behavioral processes, specifically problem orienting and problem-solving skills, the model also incorporates the role of basic cognitive abilities that are necessary for individuals to learn and apply the attitudes and skills described in the first two levels (D'Zurilla & Nezu, 1999). The model of cognitive dysfunction in schizophrenia proposed by Jonathan Cohen and colleagues is relevant to this third level of functioning. In this model (Braver, Barch, & Cohen, 1999), a single mechanism, the failure to exert control over thoughts and actions, underlies core cognitive deficits. These authors proposed that for an individual to selectively attend to stimuli, ignore extraneous sensory input, manipulate information, access relevant stored memories, and select appropriate actions, one must maintain an adequate mental context. Context is defined as task-relevant information that promotes selective activation of neural pathways that are necessary for task performance. Cohen and colleagues proposed that the dopamine (DA) neurotransmitter system in the prefrontal cortex (PFC) modulates the availability of context-related information to active memory. In this system, DA serves to provide ongoing updating and maintaining of context information and protects the system against interference from irrelevant, disrupting stimuli, memories, and thoughts. It is proposed that the pathophysiology of schizophrenia lies in a disturbance of the DA system, resulting in deficits in maintenance of timely context information.

Although Cohen and colleagues do not specifically apply their model to social problem-solving impairment, it provides a framework for considering the possible underlying causes as well as potential strategies for rehabilitation of such deficits in schizophrenia. Many problems encountered in everyday life require frequent updating of context information via social perception and judgment, reliance on memory and reward systems, and the maintenance of goal representations that are often in flux. Insufficient gating of irrelevant information would activate pathways, resulting in behavior that is dissociated from the social situation and, depending on the ineffectiveness of the gating, could range from odd to profoundly disordered. For example, a schizophrenia patient may make a verbal response in a conversation that is based on an insufficiently gated, irrelevant thought that is only loosely associated with something said by the conversational partner. If the phasic DA activity that is hypothesized to accompany task-relevant stimuli is underactivated, important social information such as facial expressions, gestures, and spoken words will not be incorporated into the internal representation of the context of the social interaction, resulting in solutions to social problems that are disconnected from the situation and likely to be confusing to others. Poor maintenance of context information would further contribute to ineffective social problem solving by interfering with patients' ability to sustain a constant, updated representation of the situation with the possible result of perseverative, stereotypic social behavior. For example, in an interpersonal situation that requires persistence, such as asking for assistance in a store, a schizophrenia patient may not be able to maintain the goal of the interaction over a long enough period of time to activate him- or herself to repeat the request and then ask to speak with a manager. This model suggests that, in addition to efforts aimed at developing a positive problem orientation and enhancing problem-solving skills, remediation of neurocognitive deficits could have beneficial effects on social problem solving.

RELATIONSHIPS BETWEEN SOCIAL PROBLEM SOLVING AND COGNITIVE FUNCTIONING IN SCHIZOPHRENIA

The integration of D'Zurilla and colleagues' model of social problem solving and Cohen and colleagues' schizophrenia-specific model of basic cognitive functioning provides a useful framework for considering the role of cognition in social problem solving among individuals with schizophrenia. The model suggests that there would be a link between the memory, perceptual, and attentional impairments in schizophrenia and deficits in the processing of social information. This link may in turn underlie or mediate social problem-solving difficulties. It has been hypothesized (e.g., Green, 1996) that cognitive deficits in schizophrenia may serve as "rate limiting" factors in social problem solving.

Bellack and colleagues (1994) reported that IQ and verbal memory were significantly correlated with social problem solving. Addington and Addington (1999) found that verbal ability, verbal memory, and cognitive flexibility were related to the three phases of social problem solving that they measured: problem identification ("receiving"), solution generation ("processing"), and role-played execution of a solution ("sending"). However, in another study, Addington, McCleary, and Munroe-Blum (1998) reported that auditory attention on a continuous performance test predicted "processing" and "sending" skills on a measure of social problem solving (the Assessment of Interpersonal Problem-Solving Skills, described later), whereas verbal and nonverbal intelligence, visual and verbal memory, verbal fluency, and executive function did not predict social problem-solving performance. Similarly, Corrigan and Toomey (1995) reported that social problem solving was not associated with performance on a neurocognitive test of problem solving and abstract reasoning, the Wisconsin Card Sorting Test. Penn, Mueser, Spaulding, Hope, and Reed (1995) reported that early information processing (reaction time, span of apprehension, vigilance) was related to global ratings of social competence on a role-play task.

The literature in this area has focused on links between cognition and social *perception* rather than on the links between cognition and social *problem solving*. Although a thorough review of the literature on social perception is beyond the scope of this chapter, there is evidence (Toomey, Wallace, Corrigan, Schuldberg, & Green, 1997) that the perception and interpretation of nonverbal social cues are important for the identification and processing of social problems. Thus, it is worth noting that the neurocognitive deficits in schizophrenia, particularly "early" information-processing functions such as vigilance and span of apprehension, have been associated with sensitivity to social cues (e.g., Corrigan, Green, & Toomey, 1994).

Taken together, these findings provide preliminary support for the notion that attention–vigilance and memory may serve as rate-limiting factors in social problem solving but do not clearly delineate the specific relationships between which cognitive factors are related to various aspects of social problem solving. Additional delineation of specific cognitive rate-limiting factors will help guide future approaches to cognitive remediation and increase the probability that such remediation will benefit social behavior and functioning.

ASSESSING SOCIAL PROBLEM SOLVING IN INDIVIDUALS WITH SCHIZOPHRENIA

A variety of techniques have been developed to assess social problem solving; however, their validity and reliability often have not been evaluated for use with individuals with schizophrenia. Self-report instruments are problematic because schizophrenia patients may have difficulty grasping the abstract concepts necessary to reflect on and report their social problem-solving abilities. Ratings may be derived from structured interactions with clinicians, but this type of observation is not likely to be representative of a patient's social behavior across situations encountered in daily life, and such procedures are difficult to standardize. Alternatively, naturalistic observation allows the assessment of social behavior under routine circumstances, but the cost and effort associated with this method are often prohibitive. Situational analogue methods, primarily using role-play techniques, allow direct observation of patients' responses in various social situations while allowing standardization through consistency in the scenarios and in the responses of the individual administering the measure. Studies of the validity of analogue measures of social skills have found good to moderate correspondence between role-play performance and naturalistic observation in psychiatric and nonpsychiatric populations, with some evidence of superior performance during role-plays compared to naturalistic behavior (see Norton & Hope, 2001, for a review).

Many of the instruments developed to measure social problem-solving ability in the general population include topics and situations that are largely irrelevant to many schizophrenia patients and neglect those that are particularly salient for patients. For example, work and marital situations are relevant to fewer schizophrenia patients than the general population. Interactions with physicians, case managers, and family members on illness- and treatment-related topics occur frequently for many patients and are an appropriate area for assessment. Also, performance by schizophrenia patients on measures that rely heavily on memory, speed of information processing and responding, and attention will tend to be negatively affected by deficits that are not specific to social problem solving.

Three standardized measures of social problem solving that have been widely used in studies of schizophrenia patients illustrate these issues. These measures are the Social Problem Solving Assessment Battery (SPSAB; Sayers & Bellack, 1995), the Assessment of Interpersonal Problem-Solving Skills (AIPSS; Donahoe et al., 1990), and the Means–Ends Problem-Solving battery (MEPS; Platt & Spivack, 1975). The SPSAB was designed specifically to measure the functional ability of chronically psychiatrically ill individuals to solve social problems. The battery was created using empirical methods to maximize the validity of the items for evaluating real-world problem solving. Problem scenarios were generated by interviewing schizophrenia patients, family members, and mental health workers and then rated by a group of patients on the dimensions of difficulty and likelihood that the situation would happen to them. Problems that were rated as moderately difficult and at least somewhat familiar to the patients was selected for use in the test battery (see Sayers et al., 1995, for a description of the test development). The battery consists of three components: the Role-Play Test (RPT), the Response Generation Test (RGT), and the Response Evaluation Test (RET). The RPT is intended to measure the patient's ability to resolve interpersonal conflict through conversation. It consists of role plays that elicit assertion, conversation initiation, and compromise–negotiation. The RPTs are rated on six dimensions in two categories: (a) verbal content, consisting of clarity, negotiation, and persistence; and (b) noncontent behavior, consisting of interest, fluency, and affect.

The purpose of the RGT is to measure patients' ability to identify social problems and generate solutions. Participants read a description of a problem situation, watch a videotaped narrator read the same description, and watch a videotape of actors enacting the scene. The enacted scenes end before a solution is reached, and after each scene, patients are asked to define the problem, identify the goals of one of the actors, and to generate three possible solutions. Problem definitions and goal identifications are rated for accuracy. Each suggested solution is rated on the basis of appropriateness, the degree to which it could be carried out, likelihood that it would be effective, adequate assertiveness, and absence of hostility.

The RET was developed to assess the individual's ability to discriminate between effective and ineffective social problem-solving behavior. Participants listen to an audiotape of 12 dyadic interactions, half of which present effective problem solutions and the other half of which portray ineffective solutions. After listening to each interaction and identifying the target person in the interaction, participants rate the effectiveness of the target person's behavior.

This battery allows flexibility for the assessment of social behavior in various situations that may be of interest for different clinical or research applications. For example, the effectiveness of an intervention designed to help schizophrenia patients resist pressure to use illegal drugs could be assessed by evaluating patient's responses in role-play scenes in which the patient is confronted with such pressure from friends, family members, or drug dealers. In another clinical research setting, employment-related behavior may be of interest and a role-played job interview and conversation with a supervisor could be included in the assessment.

In a study comparing the performance of schizophrenia patients, patients with bipolar disorder, and nonpatient controls on the SPSAB (Bellack et al., 1994), both patient groups performed worse than controls on each of the three tests in the battery. The two patient groups, however, did not differ in their social problem-solving abilities. This finding suggests that social problem-solving difficulties are not specific to schizophrenia and that the SPSAB is effective in discriminating populations in which social problem solving is impaired and intact.

The AIPSS (Donahoe et al., 1990) was developed on the basis of Liberman, Wallace, and colleagues' model of social problem solving (Wallace et al., 1980). In this measure, participants view videotaped vignettes, some of which present social problems. The patient is then asked to identify with a specific actor and to describe the problem illustrated in the video clip. If a problem is identified, the client is asked to generate solutions, choose an alternative, and role play the solution with the examiner. The patient's performance is rated on six scales within three domains: receiving (identification and description of the problem), processing (describing solutions to the problem), and sending (content, performance, and overall role-play performance). Donahoe and colleagues (1990) reported adequate levels of interrater and test–retest reliability for schizophrenic and nonschizophrenic participants. Several studies (Bowen et al., 1994; Donahoe et al., 1990; Toomey et al., 1997) report discriminative validity between these groups, with schizophrenia patients performing worse than nonpatients on each of the six scales of the AIPSS. These group differences may be attributable, however, to group differences in age (Donahoe et al., 1990) and intellectual ability (Donahoe et al., 1990; Toomey et al., 1997).

The MEPS measure (Platt & Spivak, 1975) is based on the hypothesis that the ability to perform an analysis of alternative methods for reaching a goal is central to social problem solving. Participants are presented with the beginning and ending of 10 problem situations and are instructed to make up ways in which the actor in each story can reach the stated goals. Responses are scored on a variety of dimensions, including the number of relevant and irrelevant means. Studies of chronic psychiatric patients suggest that patients generate fewer solutions to problems than nonpatients (Platt & Spivack, 1972, 1974), and the solutions they propose are qualitatively different than those proposed by controls (Platt & Spivak, 1975). Unfortunately, there are significant problems with this measure that threaten the conclusions that may be drawn from the work (Bellack, Morrison, & Mueser, 1989). The MEPS was not developed using empirical methods and has poor psychometric properties (Butler & Meichenbaum, 1981). The content is neither representative of the range of social problem situations nor relevant to the situations encountered by most chronic patients. Scoring focuses on the number, not the quality, of solutions generated. Platt and Spivack (1975) found that although psychiatric patients generated fewer solutions to MEPS stories, they were not deficient in the ability to recognize effective solutions. This suggests that other MEPS findings might represent diminished effort by patients or difficulty generating multiple responses spontaneously, rather than an inability to solve the problems.

INTERVENTIONS FOR SOCIAL PROBLEM-SOLVING DEFICITS IN SCHIZOPHRENIA PATIENTS

Interventions targeting social functioning in individuals with schizophrenia may be grouped into two general categories. First, there are methods that address social problem-solving skills directly with the goal of enhancing social functioning. Second, there are interventions that attempt to improve neurocognitive impairment that may underlie social problem-solving deficits.

BEHAVIORALLY ORIENTED SOCIAL SKILLS TRAINING INTERVENTIONS

Behaviorally oriented social skills training interventions have in common a focus on behavioral strategies for teaching skills related to social functioning. These strategies generally include breaking down problems into simple steps, learning via observation and role play, and shaping of behavior through positive reinforcement and coaching. Positive feedback from therapists and group members is used to provide reinforcement and to shape behavior on role plays. Handouts and written prompts are used to minimize demand on memory and maximize success on the skill. The use of homework assignments is encouraged to maximize opportunities for generalization of newly acquired skills. Curricula have been developed for a variety of skills within the domains of conversation, assertiveness, conflict management, romantic relationships, medication management, HIV prevention, and employment, but the method may be adapted and used to teach any social skill.

Several parallel versions of social skills training have been developed and manualized. Bellack, Mueser, Gingerich, and Agresta (1997) described an approach that was designed to *compensate* for cognitive impairment by teaching patients a relatively small set of critical skills that can be used relatively automatically. Training entails repeated rehearsal to produce *overlearning*. Bellack and colleagues argued that patients have difficulty engaging in higher level reasoning, especially in stressful social situations. Although they may be able to use a problem-solving mnemonic in the clinic, there is no evidence that they are able to translate that behavior to the environment. This hypothesis was supported in a study by Bellack, Weinhardt, Gold, and Gearon (2001) in which patients learned to improve their performance on one of two parallel problem-solving tasks in the laboratory but were unable to transfer what they learned to the other task.

Liberman and colleagues (Liberman, Eckman, & Marder, 2001) developed what is probably the most widely disseminated approach to social skills training. It includes a series of modules in which patients are taught to use the following steps to solve social problems: (a) identify the problem, (b) generate alternative solutions, (c) weigh the pros and cons of each solution, (d) select a feasible solution, and (e) make a plan to implement the selected alternative. Videotaped vignettes are used to demonstrate both good and poor examples of social problem solving and participants use role plays and coaching to increase their mastery of the material.

There have been eight major narrative reviews and four meta-analyses of the social skills literature published in peer reviewed journals since 1990, including recent comprehensive reviews by Dilk and Bond (1996) and Heinssen, Liberman, and Kopelowicz (2000). The literature documents that people with schizophrenia can learn new social behaviors and retain them for up to two years and that the training has a beneficial impact on diverse aspects of functioning (Liberman et al., 2001; Liberman, Wallace, Blackwell, et al., 1998). It has yet to be demonstrated that patients perform the skills in the community or that training has a reliable impact on role functioning. In one study (Wallace & Liberman, 1985), ratings on activities such as work, church, and recreation made by patients' parents were more positive for patients who had intensive social problem-solving training compared to patients who completed an intervention focused on increasing patients' physical and emotional well-being. This is a promising result but the magnitude of the difference is not clear and the ratings may have been biased by the parents having participated in family therapy sessions that were conceptually and operationally congruent with the patients' treatment. A recent report by Glynn and colleagues (Glynn et al., 2002) provides encouraging evidence for the effectiveness of community-based support in addition to clinic-based social skills training in increasing patients' social functioning.

COGNITIVE REMEDIATION

In light of the hypothesized relationship between neurocognitive functioning and social problem-solving deficits, cognitive remediation may prove to be an effective intervention for social problem-solving deficits. Cognitive remediation may affect social functioning via two routes: indirectly, by potentiating patients' ability to engage in and benefit from social skills training, or directly, by enhancing cognitive processes that underlie social problem solving.

The publication of several reviews of the research on cognitive training and remediation in schizophrenia (Bellack, Gold, & Buchanan, 1999; Twamley, Jeste, & Bellack, 2003; Wykes & van der Gaag, 2001) is indicative of the increasing attention being paid to this area, but few of the studies included in these reviews addressed the relationship between cognitive remediation and social problem solving or social functioning. Brenner and colleagues (Brenner, Hodel, Roder, & Corrigan, 1992; Brenner et al., 1994) have developed a treatment program that allows examination of the effects of cognitive remediation on social skills training and social functioning. Integrated Psychological Therapy (IPT) is a comprehensive, highly structured group therapy program. Early sessions target basic cognitive skills, later sessions focus on shaping cognitive skills into verbal and social behaviors, and the final section is directed at interpersonal skills training. Although the effects of IPT on elementary cognitive processes appear promising (see Brenner et al., 1992, for a review), it is difficult to determine the independent contributions of the cognition- and skills-focused units.

Spaulding, Reed, Sullivan, Richards, and Weiler (1999) compared social competence, cognitive functioning, and clinical status in patients who completed social skills training following either a U.S. version of the cognitively focused units of IPT or standard treatment. Patients in the cognitive program showed greater improvement on the AIPSS articulation subscale, tests of skill-training module content, attention and concept manipulation, and depression ratings than patients in the standard treatment. Although this study provides promising findings of the potentially beneficial effects of cognition-focused interventions on social problem solving and skills training, the evidence of generalization is circumscribed because only laboratory-based measures of social problem solving were used and the cognitive training was primarily focused on social interactions. It remains to be seen whether cognitive interventions conducted in a nonsocial context (e.g., computer-administrated cognitive rehabilitation) may affect social functioning. In that regard, van der Gaag, Kern, van den Bosch, and Liberman (2002) developed a three-month intervention to enhance neurocognition. Although the treatment produced gains on some measures of executive function, there was no evidence that it had a significant effect on social cognition or that the effects of training generalized to other areas of functioning.

CONCLUSION

Several important issues warrant further study if we are to understand the role of social problem-solving deficits in schizophrenia and develop techniques to improve patients' social functioning. A fundamental question is whether the social problem-solving model developed by D'Zurilla and colleagues is valid for schizophrenia patients. One possible starting point for addressing this issue would be to repeat the factor analytical work previously completed with responses from healthy individuals (e.g., Maydeu-Olivares

& D'Zurilla, 1996) using responses from schizophrenia patients. It may be that a substantially different factor structure would emerge that would allow more valid study of social problem solving in this population. If the resulting factors are similar to those that were obtained in studies of healthy individuals, the model could be used with more confidence in studies of schizophrenia patients.

The possible relationship between basic cognitive functions as modeled by Cohen and colleagues and higher order problem-solving dimensions awaits additional examination. It will be important to consider the aspects of problem solving that are common in everyday situations and to assess whether the model of dopamine and PFC functioning is useful in explaining the deficits observed in schizophrenia when these factors are incorporated. For example, social problems often involve the perception of affect in facial expressions, body posture, and voice tone. It remains to be seen whether this type of context information is subject to the same disruptive impact of poor dopamine regulation as other, nonsocial context information. Considering the evidence of poor affect recognition by schizophrenia patients (Feinberg, Rifkin, Schaffer, & Walker, 1986), the inclusion of affective and social content may have minimal effect on context representation. Alternately, including such content may have the effect of increasing the "gain" of social information so that it is incorporated into the context representation and increases the likelihood that responses will be appropriate to the social context. Finally, in light of suggestions of hypersensitivity to negative affect (Rabin, Doneson, & Jentons, 1979), the impact of social information may vary according to its valence such that negative information is selectively processed and has undue impact on social problem solving, which could lead to paranoid, hostile, or isolative behavior. It would be of tremendous value if this promising model could be adapted to improve understanding of the consequences of social information on behavior and integrated with the D'Zurilla model of metacognitive and performance-related abilities.

Another important issue in need of additional examination is the relative importance of developmental social experiences versus neurobiological anomalies as contributors to social problem-solving deficits. Are disruptions in social information processing resulting from infrequent and impoverished social interactions more important to the etiology of social problem-solving deficits than structural or functional brain abnormalities? Alternately, there may be an interaction between experience and neurobiology such that neurodevelopmental anomalies contribute to abnormal social information processing from an early age and initiate long-standing patterns of social problem-solving difficulties. If social problem-solving deficits were found to be associated with functional (i.e., neurochemical) brain abnormalities, it would suggest a promising role for pharmacological interventions targeted at regulating relevant neurotransmitter systems. Such interventions, however, would likely benefit from supplementation with psychosocial techniques to maximize patients' development of new problem-solving skills.

REFERENCES

Addington, J., & Addington, D. (1999). Neurocognitive and social functioning in schizophrenia. *Schizophrenia Bulletin, 25,* 173–182.

Addington, J., McCleary, L., & Munroe-Blum, H. (1998). Relationship between cognitive and social dysfunction in schizophrenia. *Schizophrenia Research, 34,* 59–66.

American Psychiatric Association. (1994). *Diagnostic and statistical manual of mental disorders* (4th ed.) Washington, DC: Author.

Andreasen, N. C. (1985). Positive and negative schizophrenia: A critical evaluation. *Schizophrenia Bulletin, 11,* 380–389.

Bellack, A. S., Gold, J. M., & Buchanan, R. W. (1999). Cognitive rehabilitation for schizophrenia: Problems, prospects, and strategies. *Schizophrenia Bulletin, 25,* 257–274.

Bellack, A. S., Morrison, R., & Mueser, K. (1989). Social problem solving in schizophrenia. *Schizophrenia Bulletin, 15,* 101–116.

Bellack, A., Morrison, R., Mueser, K., Wade, J., & Sayers, S. (1990). Role play for assessing the social competence of psychiatric patients. *Psychological Assessment, 2,* 248–255.

Bellack, A. S., Morrison, R. L., Wixted, J. T., & Mueser, K. (1990). An analysis of social competence in schizophrenia. *British Journal of Psychiatry, 156,* 809–818.

Bellack, A. S., Mueser, K. T., Gingerich, S., & Agresta, J. (1997). *Social skills training for schizophrenia: A step-by-step guide.* New York: Guilford Press.

Bellack, A. S., Sayers, M., Mueser, K. T., & Bennett, M. (1994). Evaluation of social problem solving in schizophrenia. *Journal of Abnormal Psychology, 103,* 371–378.

Bellack, A. S., Weinhardt, L. S., Gold, J. M., & Gearon, J. S. (2001). Generalization of training effects in schizophrenia. *Schizophrenia Research, 48,* 255–262.

Bowen, L., Wallace, C., Glynn, S., Nuechterlein, K., Lutzker, J. R., & Kuehnel, T. G. (1994). Schizophrenic individuals' cognitive functioning and performance in interpersonal interactions and skills training procedures. *Journal of Psychiatric Research, 28,* 289–301.

Braver, T. S., Barch, D. M., & Cohen, J. D. (1999). Cognition and control in schizophrenia: A computational model of dopamine and prefrontal function. *Biological Psychiatry, 46,* 312–328.

Brenner, H. D., Hodel, B., Roder, V., & Corrigan, P. (1992). Treatment of cognitive dysfunctions and behavioral deficits in schizophrenia. *Schizophrenia Bulletin, 18,* 21–26.

Brenner, H., Roder, V., Hodel, B., Kienzle, N., Reed, D., & Liberman, R. (1994). *Integrated psychological therapy for schizophrenia patients*. Toronto, Ontario, Canada: Hogrefe & Huber.

Butler, L., & Meichenbaum, D. (1981). The assessment of interpersonal problem-solving skills. In P. C. Kendall & S. D. Hollon (Eds.), *Assessment strategies for cognitive–behavioral interventions* (pp. 197–221). New York: Academic Press.

Corrigan, P. W., Green, M. F., & Toomey, R. (1994). Cognitive correlates to social cue perception in schizophrenia. *Psychiatry Research, 53*, 141–151.

Corrigan, P., & Toomey, R. (1995). Interpersonal problem solving and information processing in schizophrenia. *Schizophrenia Bulletin, 21*, 395–403.

Dilk, M., & Bond, G. (1996). Meta-analytic evaluation of skills training research for individuals with severe mental illness. *Journal of Consulting and Clinical Psychology, 64*, 1337–1346.

Donahoe, C. P., Carter, M. J., Bloem, W. D., Hirsch, G. L., Laasi, N., & Wallace, C. J. (1990). Assessment of interpersonal problem-solving skills. *Psychiatry, 53*, 329–339.

D'Zurilla, T. J., Chang, E. C., Nottingham, E. J., & Faccini, L. (1998). Social problem-solving deficits and hopelessness, depression, and suicidal risk in college students and psychiatric inpatients. *Journal of Clinical Psychology, 54*, 1091–1107.

D'Zurilla, T. J., & Goldfried, M. R. (1971). Problem solving and behavior modification. *Journal of Abnormal Psychology, 78*, 107–126.

D'Zurilla, T. J., & Nezu, A. M. (1999). *Problem-solving therapy: A social competence approach to clinical intervention* (2nd ed.) New York: Springer.

D'Zurilla, T. J., Nezu, A. M., & Maydeu-Olivares, A. (2002). *Social Problem-Solving Inventory—Revised (SPSI–R): Technical manual*. North Tonawanda, NY: Multi-Health Systems.

Feinberg, T. E., Rifkin, A., Schaffer, C., & Walker, E. (1986). Facial discrimination and emotional recognition in schizophrenia and affective disorders. *Archives of General Psychiatry, 43*, 276–279.

Glynn, S., Marder, S. R., Liberman, R. P., Blair, K., Wirshing, W. C., Wirshing, D. A., et al. (2002). Supplementing clinic-based social skills training with manual-based community support sessions: Effects on social adjustment of patients with schizophrenia. *American Journal of Psychiatry, 159*, 829–837.

Green, M. F. (1996). What are the functional consequences of neurocognitive deficits in schizophrenia? *American Journal of Psychiatry, 153*, 321–330.

Heinrichs, R. W., & Zakzanis, K. K. (1998). Neurocognitive deficits in schizophrenia: A quantitative review of the evidence. *Neuropsychology, 12*, 426–445.

Heinssen, R. K., Liberman, R. P., & Kopelowicz, A. (2000). Psychosocial skills training for schizophrenia: Lessons from the laboratory. *Schizophrenia Bulletin, 26*, 21–46.

Liberman, R. P., Eckman, T., & Marder, S. R. (2001). Training in social problem solving among persons with schizophrenia. *Psychiatric Services, 52*, 31–33.

Liberman, R. P., Wallace, C. J., Blackwell, G., Kopelowicz, A., Vaccaro, J. V., & Mintz, J. (1998). Skills training vs. psychosocial occupational therapy for persons with persistent schizophrenia. *American Journal of Psychiatry, 155*, 1087–1091.

Maydeu-Olivares, A., & D'Zurilla, T. J. (1996). A factor-analytic study of the social problem-solving inventory: An integration of theory and data. *Cognitive Therapy and Research, 20*(2), 115–133.

Morrison, R., & Bellack, A. S. (1987). Social functioning of schizophrenic patients: Clinical and research issues. *Schizophrenia Bulletin, 13*, 715–725.

Norton, P. J., & Hope, D. A. (2001). Analogue observational methods in the assessment of social functioning in adults. *Psychological Assessment, 13*, 59–72.

Penn, D. L., Mueser, K. T., Spaulding, W., Hope, D. A., & Reed, D. (1995). Information processing and social competence in chronic schizophrenia. *Schizophrenia Bulletin, 21*, 269–281.

Platt, J. J., & Spivack, G. (1972). Problem-solving thinking of psychiatric patients. *Journal of Consulting and Clinical Psychology, 39*, 148–151.

Platt, J. J., & Spivack, G. (1974). Means of solving real-life problems: I. Psychiatric patients vs. controls and cross-cultural comparisons of normal females. *Journal of Community Psychology, 2*, 45–48.

Platt, J. J., & Spivack, G. (1975). Unidimensionality of the Means–Ends Problem-Solving (MEPS) procedure. *Journal of Clinical Psychology, 31*, 15–16.

Rabin, A. I., Doneson, S. L., & Jentons, R. L. (1979). Studies of psychological functions in schizophrenia. In A. S. Bellack (Ed.), *Disorders of the schizophrenic syndrome* (pp. 181–231). New York: Basic Books.

Sayers, M. D., & Bellack, A. S. (1995). An empirical method for assessing social problem solving in schizophrenia. *Behavior Modification, 19*, 267–289.

Spaulding, W., Reed, D., Sullivan, M., Richardson, C., & Weiler, M. (1999). Effects of cognitive treatment in psychiatric rehabilitation. *Schizophrenia Bulletin, 25*, 657–675.

Toomey, R., Wallace, C. J., Corrigan, P. W., Schuldberg, D., & Green, M. F. (1997). Social processing correlates of nonverbal social perception in schizophrenia. *Psychiatry: Interpersonal and Biological Processes, 60*, 293–300.

Twamley, E. W., Jeste, D. V., & Bellack, A. S. (2003). A review of cognitive training in schizophrenia. *Schizophrenia Bulletin, 29*(2), 359–383.

van der Gaag, M., Kern, R., van den Bosch, R.J., & Liberman, R. P. (2002). A controlled trial of cognitive remediation in schizophrenia. *Schizophrenia Bulletin, 28*, 167–176.

Wallace, C. J., & Liberman, R. P. (1985). Social skills training for patients with schizophrenia: A controlled clinical trial. *Psychiatry Research, 15*, 239–247.

Wallace, C. J., Nelson, C. J., Liberman, R. P., Altchison, R. A., Lukoff, D., Elder, J. P., et al. (1980). A review and critique of social skills training with schizophrenic patients. *Schizophrenia Bulletin, 6*, 42–63.

Wykes, T., & van der Gaag, M. (2001). Is it time to develop a new cognitive therapy for psychosis—Cognitive remediation therapy (CRT)? *Clinical Psychology Review, 21*, 1227–1256.

6

SOCIAL PROBLEM SOLVING AND POSITIVE PSYCHOLOGICAL FUNCTIONING: LOOKING AT THE POSITIVE SIDE OF PROBLEM SOLVING

EDWARD C. CHANG, CHRISTINA A. DOWNEY,
AND JENNI L. SALATA

A disciplined mind takes delight in the problematic, and cherishes it until a way out is found that approves itself upon examination.

John Dewey (1929, p. 228)

More than two centuries ago, in the *Nicomachean Ethics*, Aristotle attempted to address the question of what it meant for individuals to live the good life. Within the modern era, some Western psychologists have attempted to address this question by focusing on understanding ways that individuals may optimally develop and interact with their changing environments (e.g., Antonovsky, 1979; Jahoda, 1958; Maslow, 1954; Rogers, 1961).

POSITIVE PSYCHOLOGY: THE SCIENCE OF PURSUING A LIFE WORTH LIVING

Building on these important historical efforts, Seligman and Csikszentmihalyi (2000) and others (e.g., McCullough & Snyder, 2000;

Sheldon & King, 2001; cf. Chang & Sanna, 2003) have argued for the development of a positive psychology that involves as its aim "to catalyze a change in the focus of psychology from preoccupation only with repairing the worst things in life to also building positive qualities" (Seligman & Csikszenthihalyi, 2000, p. 5). Thus, from the standpoint of positive psychology, it is important not only to identify factors that are contemporaneously or causally related to psychological dysfunction, but it is important to also identify and study factors (e.g., optimism, flow, self-determination, love, gratitude, and creativity) that are related to positive psychological functioning. It may be worth noting that this renewed focus within psychology is quite consistent with the World Health Organization's (1948) earlier definition of health as more than simply the absence of disease or infirmity.

As mentioned earlier, much of the available research on social problem solving has resulted in telling us what and how specific problem-solving processes are related to psychological dysfunction and disorders (e.g., depressive symptoms, anxiety, suicide ideation). No doubt, these results are important in illuminating potential paths to prevent psychological dysfunction and distress. However, within a positive psychology framework, it would be important also to understand what and how specific problem-solving processes are related to positive psychological functioning in illuminating potential paths to promote positive psychological functioning.

A MULTIDIMENSIONAL MODEL OF SOCIAL PROBLEM SOLVING

Almost half a century ago, Allport (1955) noted that psychologists have seldom studied factors related to understanding how and why people may strive to attain a worthwhile and meaningful life, compared to factors related to understanding how and why people may become sick and ill. In that regard, it seems quite astonishing that little has changed over the past five decades. By and large, Western psychologists have placed, and continue to place, emphasis on studying factors related to health, defined typically as the absence of illness and disease (Seligman & Csikszentmihalyi, 2000). Not surprisingly, this emphasis is also present in modern research on social problem solving and social problem-solving training, which itself began with an emphasis on understanding how various problem-solving processes may relate to psychological dysfunctions and disorders (D'Zurilla & Goldfried, 1971). As a consequence, we have learned a great deal over the past several decades about how different problem-solving processes are related to a host of maladaptive conditions (for reviews, see chaps. 3 to 5, this volume). Therefore, our major focus in this chapter is to look at the positive side of problem solving. Specifically, we highlight and summarize the results of several recent studies based on the comprehensive social problem-solving model proffered by D'Zurilla and his associates (see chap. 1, this volume), which have begun to look at the relationship between social problem solving and positive psychological functioning.

SOCIAL PROBLEM SOLVING AND POSITIVE PSYCHOLOGICAL FUNCTIONING

As noted by Ryff and Keyes (1995; Keyes, Shmotkin, & Ryff, 2002), there have been two distinguishable approaches or traditions to the study of positive psychological functioning. These two approaches involve examining the potential antecedents and correlates of subjective well-being on the one hand and psychological well-being on the other.

Social Problem Solving and Subjective Well-Being: Life Satisfaction and Positive Affect

Subjective well-being has been defined by variations in life satisfaction and positive affect (see Diener, Suh, Lucas, & Smith, 1999, for a review). Life satisfaction, often measured by the Satisfaction With Life Scale (SWLS; Diener, Emmons, Larsen, & Griffin, 1985), refers to a person's positive appraisal of their life as a whole (e.g., "In most ways my life is close to my ideal"). Positive affect, often measured by the Positive Affect (PA) scale of the Positive and Negative Affect Scales (PANAS; Watson, Clark, & Tellegen, 1988), refers to a person's experience of various positive moods (e.g., "excited," "interested," "inspired"). Of the many studies conducted using the original Social Problem-Solving Inventory (D'Zurilla & Nezu, 1990), the Social Problem-Solving Inventory—Revised (SPSI–R; D'Zurilla, Nezu, & Maydeu-Olivares, 2002), and other related problem-solving process measures, only a handful have included an examination of what and how social problem-solving dimensions relate to subjective well-being.

With regard to life satisfaction, results from several studies have implicated the relevance of social problem solving to this central component of subjective well-being. However, results have varied across different studies based on the measure of social problem solving used and the population studied. In one recent study of college students, D'Zurilla et al. (2002) found that all five social problem-solving dimensions tapped by the SPSI–R were significantly associated with life satisfaction (absolute rs = .15 to .46). The largest of these associations involved negative problem orientation. In contrast, results (as reported in Chang, 2001) from examining the relations of the five social problem-solving dimensions with life satisfaction between a group of Asian American and European American college students indicated that only positive problem orientation (r = .46) and negative problem orientation ($r = -.41$) were associated with life satisfaction for the former group, whereas only negative orientation ($r = -.36$) and avoidance style ($r = -.44$) were associated with life satisfaction for the latter group. However, it is important to note that these results were based on relatively small samples ($ns < 50$).

In a study focusing on hope in a sample of middle-aged men and women, Chang (2003) found that global social problem solving was positively associated with life satisfaction for both adult groups (rs were .38 and .24 for middle-aged men and women, respectively). Unfortunately, because this study used a total SPSI–R score to assess for global social problem solving, it is impossible to identify the specific source or sources that accounted for the significant association found. In a recent study of young and middle-aged adults, Chang, Sanna, and Edwards (2003) found that, across both age groups, reactive and suppressive styles of problem solving, based on using Heppner, Cook, Wright, and Johnson's (1995) Problem-Focused Style of Coping (PF–SOC), had negative associations with life satisfaction (rs ranged from $-.31$ to $-.38$ across both age groups), whereas a reflective problem-solving style had a positive association with life satisfaction (rs were .21 and .30 for the young adult and middle-aged adult group, respectively). Insofar as reflective style, reactive style, and suppressive style are theoretically similar to D'Zurilla and colleagues' conceptualization of rational problem solving, impulsivity–carelessness style, and avoidance style, respectively, Chang et al.'s (2003) findings indicate that greater life satisfaction may involve the use of greater problem solving skills, more care and attention in solving problems, and a greater willingness to pursue and address problems directly. Unfortunately, the PF–SOC does not directly tap all aspects of the social problem-solving model developed by D'Zurilla and his colleagues. Specifically, the PF–SOC fails to assess for important variations in problem orientation.

In addition, in a study of adult caregivers of individuals who had suffered a stroke, Grant, Elliott, Giger, and Bartolucci (2001) found that only one problem-solving dimension, based on using Heppner's (1988) Problem Solving Inventory (PSI), was significantly associated with life satisfaction. Specifically, greater personal control was found to be associated with greater life satisfaction ($r = .38$). Unfortunately, insofar as personal control is believed to theoretically map onto D'Zurilla and colleagues' conceptualization of positive and negative problem orientation (Nezu & Perri, 1989), Grant et al.'s (2001) findings do not clarify if greater life satisfaction in this population is associated with greater positive problem orientation, lesser negative problem orientation, or with both. Finally, in a study in which cluster-analytical procedures were used on scores obtained on the SPSI–R, Elliott, Shewchuk, Miller, and Richards (2001) identified four groups that could be distinguished within a sample of individuals with diabetes. The group identified as having the lowest level of life satisfaction (cluster 1) was also found to have lower positive problem orientation, greater negative problem orientation, lower rational problem solving, greater impulsivity–carelessness style, and greater avoidance style, compared to the group identified as having the highest level of life satisfaction (cluster 4). Thus, Elliott et al.'s (2001) findings may be taken to suggest that all five dimensions of social problem solving may be involved in determining different levels of life satisfaction in this population.

With regard to positive affect, in a series of studies conducted on college students, Elliott, Sherwin, Harkins, and Marmarosh (1995) found that scores on two of the three scales composing the PSI were associated with positive affect and positive affectivity. Specifically, scores reflecting greater problem-solving confidence and personal control were found to be associated with greater (state and trait) positive affect (rs ranged from .15 to .40). Unfortunately, because both of these PSI scales are unidimensional and are believed to each map onto both positive and negative problem orientation, it is unclear how much of the association found may be a result of processes associated with positive problem orientation, negative problem orientation, or processes associated with both. Finally, in a study that attempted to examine the construct validity of positive and negative problem orientation from other conceptually related variables, Chang and D'Zurilla (1996) found that both problem orientations were significantly associated with positive affectivity (a trait form of positive affect). Specifically, positive problem orientation was positively associated with positive affectivity ($r = .42$), whereas negative problem orientation was negatively associated with positive affectivity ($r = -.34$). In sum, although different social problem-solving dimensions have been implicated, these findings for life satisfaction and positive affect indicate that, at the very least, a significant relationship exists between measures of social problem solving and subjective well-being.

Social Problem Solving and Psychological Well-Being: Ryff's Multidimensional Model

Although measures of life satisfaction have commonly been used to assess for subjective well-being over the past 20 years, Ryff and Keyes (1995) have argued that most conceptualizations of life satisfaction fail to provide a theory-based formulation of well-being (i.e., "What does it mean to be well psychologically?"). Drawing from points of convergence across the diverse and extensive conceptualizations of positive psychological functioning proffered in the extant life-span developmental, clinical, and mental health literatures, Ryff (1989, 1995) formulated a multidimensional model of psychological well-being comprising six theoretically distinguishable functions.

Self-acceptance involves positive evaluations of oneself and of one's past life and acknowledgment and acceptance of the multiple aspects of oneself, including good and bad qualities (e.g., "In general, I feel confident and positive about myself"). *Positive relations with others* involves the possession of quality relations with others, concern about the welfare of others, and an appreciation of the give and take of human relationships (e.g., "People would describe me as a giving person, willing to share my time with others"). *Autonomy* involves a sense of self-determination and the ability to resist social pressures to think and act in certain ways (e.g., "My decisions are not usually influenced by what everyone else is doing"). *Environmental mastery* involves the capacity to manage one's life and surrounding world effectively and the ability to create contexts suitable to one's needs and values (e.g., "In general, I feel I am in charge of the situation in which I live"). *Purpose in life* involves the belief that one's past and present life is purposeful and meaningful (e.g., "I have a sense of direction and purpose in life"). *Personal growth* involves a sense of continued growth and development as a person and an openness to new experiences for self-knowledge and improvement (e.g., "For me, life has been a continuous process of learning, changing, and growth").

To capture aspects of these six distinct theory-based dimensions, Ryff (1989) developed the Scales of Psychological Well-Being (SPWB), which comprises six separate scales that map directly onto the six theoretically distinct dimensions of psychological well-being just discussed. Empirical studies on the SPWB scales have shown that scores on the six scales demonstrate moderate to high intercorrelations (Ryff, 1989); relate to (but are not redundant with) traditional measures of psychological well-being (Ryff, 1989); differ considerably across young adults, middle-aged adults, and older adults (Ryff, 1989, 1991); and provide a good fit with a six-factor model (versus a one-factor model) based on using confirmatory factor-analytical techniques (Ryff & Keyes, 1995). Keyes et al. (2002) recently showed that the six constructs composing psychological well-being were related but empirically distinct from life satisfaction.

Social Problem Solving and Subjective Well-Being in College Students

After conducting an exhaustive review of the extant literature several years ago, the first author failed to find any published studies examining the relations between social problem solving and psychological well-being. (It is worth noting that in conducting a more recent review in writing this chapter, we obtained the same negative result.) Accordingly, Chang (1999) conducted a study to address this gap and to provide an initial effort to understand what and how different social problem-solving processes relate to psychological well-being. Specifically, in a study involving 238 (81 men and 157 women) college students attending a public university in the Midwest, Chang (1999) administered the SPSI–R, the SWLS, and the SPWB. The large majority of participants were White (88.2%). Ages ranged from 18 to 32 years, with a mean of 20.1 years.

The results of computing correlations involving the major social problem-solving dimensions (as well as subdimensions for rational problem solving) with life satisfaction and the six psychological well-being measures are presented in Table 6.1. Several patterns are worth noting in these correlational results. First, all of the significant associations were in the direction expected based on the model proffered by D'Zurilla and his colleagues. For example, positive problem orientation was positively associated with each measure of psychological well-being and with life satisfaction. Thus, the more an individual perceived problems as challenges that can be met or overcome, the more likely that individual also experienced greater life satisfaction, self-acceptance, positive relations with others, autonomy, environmental mastery, purpose in life, and greater personal growth. Similarly, negative problem orientation was negatively associated with each measure of psychological well-being and with life satisfaction. Therefore, in this case, the more an individual perceived problems as unsolvable or as a threat, the more likely that individual also experienced less life satisfaction, self-acceptance, positive relations with others, autonomy, environmental mastery, purpose in life, and less personal growth. Second, the involvement of each of the five social problem-solving processes appeared to differ between measures of life satisfaction and psychological well-being. For example, greater impulsivity–carelessness style was associated with less self-acceptance, positive relations with others, autonomy, environmental mastery, purpose in life, and less personal growth. In contrast, this problem-solving dimension was not significantly associated with life satisfaction. Similarly, although greater avoidance style was associated with less self-acceptance, positive relations with others, autonomy, environmental mastery, purpose in life, and less personal growth, this dimension was not associated with life satisfaction. Third, within the rational problem-solving subset (with regard to problem definition and formulation, generation of alternative solutions, decision making, and solution implementation and verification), we found that each of these specific problem-solving components of rational problem solving was significantly associated with greater self-acceptance, positive relations with others, autonomy, environmental mastery, purpose in life, and greater personal growth. However, only decision making and solution implementation and verification were found to be significantly associated with greater life satisfaction. In sum, these correlational results not only provide support for the social problem-solving model of D'Zurilla and his colleagues, but they also point to the potential greater involvement of social problem solving in psychological well-being than in life satisfaction.

Yet to further clarify our understanding of the associations of social problem solving with the various indexes of positive psychological functioning examined, we decided to analyze the available data using a different data-analytical strategy. This time, we conducted a series of multiple regression analyses in which all five social problem-solving dimensions were regressed on to each of the relevant dependent variables—namely, life satisfaction, self-acceptance, positive relations with others, autonomy, environmental mastery, purpose in life, and personal growth. We did this for at least two reasons. First, we wanted to see how much of the variance in each dependent variable could be accounted for by the social problem-solving model. For example, the correlational findings noted earlier suggest that the model may account for greater variance in measures of psychological well-being than in life satisfaction. Second, by regressing all five social problem-solving dimensions simultaneously, we hoped to identify the most unique predictors within the social problem-solving set. That is, because the five social problem-solving dimensions tapped by the SPSI–R are not orthogonal to each other, it is unclear which problem-solving dimensions are most uniquely involved in predicting variations in subjective and psychological well-being. Results of conducting these analyses are presented in Table 6.2.

As Table 6.2 shows, the social problem-solving model, as measured by all five scales from the SPSI–R, accounted for 11% of the variance in life satisfaction, $F(5, 232) = 6.01$, $p < .001$. Within the social problem-solving predictor set, positive problem orientation ($\beta = .16$, $p < .05$) and negative problem orientation ($\beta = .16$, $p < .05$) emerged as the only unique and significant predictors of life satisfaction. In predicting self-acceptance, the social problem-solving model was found to account for 41% of the variance, $F(5, 232) = 32.33$, $p < .001$. Within the predictor set, positive problem orientation ($\beta = .23$, $p < .01$), negative problem orientation ($\beta = -.45$, $p < .001$), and impulsivity–carelessness style ($\beta = -.19$, $p < .01$) emerged as the only unique and significant predictors of self-acceptance. In predicting positive relations with others, the social problem-solving model was found to account for 27% of the variance, $F(5, 232) = 17.84$, $p < .001$. Within the predictor set, negative problem orientation ($\beta = -.24$, $p < .01$), impulsivity–carelessness style ($\beta = -.33$, $p < .001$), and avoidance style ($\beta = -.17$, $p < .05$) emerged as the only unique and significant predictors of positive relations with others. In predicting autonomy, the social problem-solving model was found to account for 23% of the variance, $F(5, 232) = 13.94$, $p < .001$. Within the predictor set, positive problem orientation ($\beta = .31$, $p < .001$), negative problem orientation ($\beta = -.24$, $p < .001$), and impulsivity–carelessness style ($\beta = -.20$, $p < .05$) emerged as the only unique

TABLE 6.1
Zero-Order Correlations Between Social Problem Solving and Positive Psychological Functioning

SPSI–R scale	Life satisfaction	Self-acceptance	Positive relations with others	Autonomy	Environmental mastery	Purpose in life	Personal growth
PPO	.26***	.43***	.32***	.38***	.43***	.38***	.43***
NPO	-.30***	-.58***	-.40***	-.40***	-.58***	-.45***	-.35***
RPS	.23***	.34***	.34***	.25***	.36***	.42***	.41***
PDF	.10	.31***	.31***	.28***	.35***	.37***	.39***
GAS	.12	.28***	.22***	.17**	.26***	.30***	.28***
DM	.17**	.28***	.34***	.21***	.30***	.30***	.35***
SIV	.24***	.27***	.30***	.19**	.30***	.37***	.35***
ICS	-.12	-.43***	-.44***	-.31***	-.41***	-.53***	-.46***
AS	-.09	-.40***	-.29***	-.27***	-.46***	-.44***	-.36***

Note. N = 238. SPSI–R = Social Problem-Solving Inventory—Revised; PPO = Positive Problem Orientation; NPO = Negative Problem Orientation; RPS = Rational Problem Solving; PDF = Problem Definition and Formulation; GAS = Generation of Alternative Solutions; DM = Decision Making; SIV = Solution Implementation and Verification; ICS = Impulsivity/Carelessness Style; AS = Avoidance Style.
*p < .05. **p < .01. ***p < .001.

TABLE 6.2
Results of Regression-Analyses Predicting Scores on Measures of Positive Psychological Functioning Based on Social Problem-Solving Inventory—Revised (SPSI–R) Subscale Scores

Criterion and predictor	β	R	R²	df	F
Life satisfaction		.34	.11	5, 232	6.01***
PPO	.16*				
NPO	−.20*				
RPS	−.01				
ICS	−.02				
AS	−.03				
Self-acceptance		.64	.41	5, 232	32.33***
PPO	.23**				
NPO	−.45***				
RPS	.04				
ICS	−.19**				
AS	.08				
Positive relations with others		.52	.27	5, 232	17.48***
PPO	.13				
NPO	−.24**				
RPS	.12				
ICS	−.33***				
AS	−.17*				
Autonomy		.48	.23	5, 232	13.94***
PPO	.31***				
NPO	−.24***				
RPS	−.05				
ICS	−.20*				
AS	.11				
Environmental mastery		.63	.40	5, 232	30.76***
PPO	.16*				
NPO	−.43***				
RPS	.10				
ICS	−.07				
AS	−.04				
Purpose in life		.61	.37	5, 232	27.20***
PPO	.14				
NPO	−.14				
RPS	.14				
ICS	−.34***				
AS	−.03				
Personal growth		.57	.33	5, 232	22.42***
PPO	.32***				
NPO	−.01				
RPS	.05				
ICS	−.37***				
AS	.02				

Note. N = 283. PPO = Positive Problem Orientation; NPO = Negative Problem Orientation; RPS = Rational Problem Solving; ICS = Impulsivity/Carelessness Style; AS = Avoidance Style.
*$p < .05$. **$p < .01$. ***$p < .001$.

and significant predictors for autonomy. In predicting environmental mastery, the social problem-solving model was found to account for 40% of the variance, $F(5, 232) = 30.76$, $p < .001$. Within the predictor set, positive problem orientation ($\beta = .16$, $p < .05$) and negative problem orientation ($\beta = -.43$, $p < .001$) emerged as the only unique and significant predictors of environmental mastery. In predicting purpose in life, the social problem-solving model was found to account for 37% of the variance, $F(5, 232) = 27.20$, $p < .001$. Within the predictor set, impulsivity–carelessness style ($\beta = -.34$, $p < .001$) emerged as the only unique and significant predictor of purpose in life. Finally, in predicting personal growth, the social problem-solving model was found to account for 33% of the variance, $F(5, 232) = 22.42$, $p < .001$. Within the predictor set, positive problem orientation ($\beta = .32$, $p < .001$) and impulsivity–carelessness style ($\beta = -.37$, $p < .001$) emerged as the only unique and significant predictors of personal growth. It is worth noting that based on computing for effect size, estimated by f^2 (Cohen, 1977), and using the convention for small ($f^2 = .02$), medium ($f^2 = .15$), and large effects ($f^2 = .35$), a prediction model that included all five social problem-solving dimensions accounted for a modest amount of the variance in life satisfaction ($f^2 = .12$) but accounted for a large amount of the variance in each of the six measures of psychological well-being (f^2s ranged from .30 to .69) examined in this study.

Overall, the results of this preliminary study point to a number of important considerations. First, the social problem-solving model proposed by D'Zurilla and his colleagues appears to have important, if not greater, relevance for understanding the various dimensions involved in psychological well-being than in subjective well-being. For example, whereas the social problem-solving model was found to account for 11% of the variance in life satisfaction, it was found to account for more than twice the amount of variance across the six dimensions of psychological well-being examined. Second, in contrast to the commonly found robust involvement of negative problem orientation in maladjustment, these results indicate that negative problem orientation may not always be the most robust predictor of positive psychological functioning. For example, these regression results indicated that negative problem orientation did not play an important and unique role in predicting purpose in life and personal growth. Third, these findings also suggest that (at least when global measures of positive psychological functioning are considered), rational problem solving may not be critically or consistently associated with some measures. For example, the present results indicate that rational problem solving, compared to other social problem-solving dimensions, is not a unique predictor of life satisfaction, self-acceptance, positive relations with others, autonomy, environmental mastery, purpose in life, and personal growth. Fourth, insofar as different social problem-solving dimensions were involved to varying degrees for predicting subjective and psychological well-being, these findings also provide important additional support for the distinction between life satisfaction and dimensions of psychological well-being, as well as support for the distinctions believed to exist within the latter. For example, although positive problem orientation, negative problem orientation, and impulsivity–carelessness style were all uniquely involved in the prediction of both positive relations with others and with autonomy, impulsivity–carelessness style was found to be the strongest predictor of positive relations with others, whereas positive problem orientation was found to be the strongest predictor of autonomy. However, despite these findings and observations, it remains important to await the results of additional studies conducted on different populations to draw useful conclusions regarding the generalizability and reliability of these preliminary findings.

SOCIAL PROBLEM SOLVING AND POSITIVE PSYCHOLOGICAL FUNCTIONING: SOME UNRESOLVED ISSUES AND DIRECTIONS FOR FUTURE RESEARCH

One thing that should become most clear from our brief review of empirical studies examining the relation of social problem solving with positive psychological functioning is how little research has been done on this topic. As a consequence, our understanding of how social problem solving relates to positive psychological functioning is limited to a scattering of findings that are sometimes inconsistent across different studies. As we noted, there have not been many studies looking at social problem solving and positive psychological functioning. However, we believe this lacking represents an opportunity for more exciting research rather than a reason to maintain the status quo. Likewise, more research examining how social problem solving relates to positive behavioral functioning (e.g., interpersonal skills and competencies, test performance; see D'Zurilla et al., 2002, p. 62) seems warranted. As Seligman and Csikszentmihalyi (2000) have rightfully observed, too much past and present research has focused on how psychological variables relate to deficiencies and negative functioning. So it may indeed take some time before we see the fruits of more programmatic research examining the role of social problem solving in positive functioning. In a constructive vein, we briefly note a few issues and considerations for future research examining social problem solving and positive psychological functioning.

First, although conducting studies looking at the simple relations between social problem solving and positive psychological functioning remain important and fundamental to this area of research, the study of more complex models should also be examined. Conceptually, some dimensions of social problem solving may have greater proximal or causal status than other social problem-solving dimensions, depending on the particular index of psychological functioning examined. Specifically, although past studies have typically looked at how other variables (e.g., negative life stress) may mediate or moderate the associations of social problem solving with psychological functioning (see chap. 2, this volume), it may be worth considering how some social problem-solving dimensions themselves mediate the link between other social problem-solving dimensions and psychological functioning. For example, despite our finding indicating that positive problem orientation does not have a unique association with purpose in life, it may be that this dimension of psychological well-being has an indirect association through impulsivity–carelessness style. Or put another way, impulsivity–carelessness style may serve to mediate the association of positive problem orientation with purpose in life. Such possibilities seem to at least warrant empirical examination in future investigations.

Because a number of other variables have been identified in the general psychological literature as potentially important correlates or determinants of positive psychological functioning, including optimism (Scheier & Carver, 1985), hope (Snyder et al., 1991), self-esteem (Rosenberg, 1965), self-efficacy (Bandura, 1977), and adaptive perfectionism (Chang, Watkins, & Banks, 2004), it would be important to determine how D'Zurilla and colleagues' social problem-solving model relates to other positive psychological variables. Indeed, recent findings have shown that positive and negative problem orientation are associated with optimism and pessimism, respectively (Chang & D'Zurilla, 1996), and that other dimensions of the social problem-solving model are associated with hope (Chang, 2003) and self-esteem (D'Zurilla, Chang, & Sanna, 2003). Moreover, it would be important to determine if and how social problem solving adds to the prediction of positive psychological functioning beyond other positive variables. On that note, recent findings obtained by D'Zurilla et al. (2003) looking at the link between social problem solving, self-esteem, and psychological functioning in a college student population indicate that social problem solving is related to self-esteem and that both social problem solving and self-esteem can predict unique variance on important dimensions of aggression. Although these investigators did not include indexes of positive psychological functioning in their study, their findings and those of others (e.g., McCabe, Blankstein, & Mills, 1999) do suggest that a model involving other positive psychological variables is useful for obtaining a better understanding of how multiple psychological variables, including social problem solving, can uniquely and collectively contribute to the prediction of psychological functioning.

As noted recently by Chang (2001), most studies on social problem solving have to date been based largely on either White or European

Americans. Accordingly, we know little to nothing about how inclusive or exclusive psychological theories and research findings involving social problem solving are to diverse cultural and racial populations. Indeed, as findings from some studies have shown, it may be important to consider cultural and racial variations in social problem solving. In one study focusing on the relations between social problem solving, perfectionism, and suicidal risk in a sample of 69 Asian and 79 European Americans, Chang (1998) found that Asian Americans, compared to European Americans, reported greater negative problem orientation and impulsivity–carelessness style. No differences were found between the two ethnic groups on positive problem orientation, rational problem solving, and avoidance style. Thus, there appears to be normative differences between different cultural groups on some dimensions of social problem solving. Alternatively, Chang and Banks (in press) found that Black Americans, compared to White Americans, reported greater positive problem orientation. No racial differences were found on the remaining four social problem-solving dimensions between Black and White Americans. Although no race difference was found on impulsivity–carelessness style between Black and White Americans, impulsivity–carelessness style was strongly and negatively associated with agentic thinking (a component of hope; Snyder et al., 1991) in Black Americans, but it was not related to agentic thinking in White Americans. Accordingly, beyond a consideration of normative differences on social problem solving between different cultural and racial groups, it remains important to examine for cultural and racial differences in how different social problem-solving dimensions relate to external variables. Relatedly, it may be important to note that most measures of positive psychological functioning have been based on Western or Eurocentric ideals that have tended to emphasize self-enhancement and independence from others (e.g., autonomy, environmental mastery), compared to Eastern or Asian ideals that tend to emphasize interdependence and self-criticism (Markus & Kitayama, 1991). Accordingly, it would be important to examine how social problem solving relates to indexes of positive psychological functioning that may be more meaningful and indigenous to different racial or cultural groups.

Finally, it seems appropriate to consider potential variations in how social problem solving may relate to positive psychological functioning at different levels of adulthood. For example, as Ryff (1989) has shown, there appear to be significant normative differences across several different dimensions of psychological well-being across young adults, middle-aged adults, and older adults. Because most of the studies conducted in psychology continue to be based largely on young adults (Sears, 1986), we again have a limited understanding of how social problem solving relates to positive psychological functioning in more mature adult populations.

CONCLUSION

It is apparent that research examining the relations of social problem solving with various indexes of positive psychological functioning has yet to fully emerge. With the exception of the study conducted by Chang (1999), no other study to date has focused specifically on the link between social problem solving and positive psychological functioning. Thus, we urge researchers to not only focus on how social problem solving may relate to important indexes of negative psychological functioning but also to important indexes of positive psychological functioning as well. Just as findings from studies conducted examining how social problem solving relates to negative psychological functioning have helped to identify and to develop useful interventions to abate or resolve negative functioning among distressed and disordered individuals (e.g., D'Zurilla & Nezu, 1999; Nezu, Nezu, & Perri, 1989), we hope that researchers may one day reach a similar point in looking at the relationship between social problem solving and positive psychological functioning. As researchers who study social problem solving, we believe that the promise and challenge to social problem-solving theory, research, and training will be determined by the ability, or inability, to one day find ways to enhance or optimize positive functioning for each individual interested in finding a path to living a life worth living.

REFERENCES

Allport, G. W. (1955). *Becoming: Basic considerations for a psychology of personality.* New Haven, CT: Yale University Press.

Antonovsky, A. (1979). *Health, stress and coping.* San Francisco: Jossey-Bass.

Bandura, A. (1977). Self-efficacy: Toward a unifying theory of behavior change. *Psychological Review, 84,* 191–215.

Chang, E. C. (1998). Cultural differences, perfectionism, and suicidal risk: Does social problem solving still matter? *Cognitive Therapy and Research, 22,* 237–254.

Chang, E. C. (1999). [Social problem solving and psychological well-being in a college student population]. Unpublished raw data.

Chang, E. C. (2001). A look at the coping strategies and styles of Asian Americans: Similar and different? In C. R. Snyder (Ed.), *Coping with stress: Effective people and processes* (pp. 222–239). New York: Oxford University Press.

Chang, E. C. (2003). A critical appraisal and extension of hope theory in middle-aged men and women: Is it important to distinguish agency and pathways components? *Journal of Social and Clinical Psychology, 22,* 121–143.

Chang, E. C., & Banks, K. H. (in press). The color and texture of hope: Some preliminary findings and implications for hope theory and counseling among diverse racial/ethnic groups. *Cultural Diversity and Ethnic Minority Psychology*.

Chang, E. C., & D'Zurilla, T. J. (1996). Relations between problem orientation and optimism, pessimism, and trait affectivity: A construct validation study. *Behaviour Research and Therapy, 34*, 185–194.

Chang, E. C., & Sanna, L. J. (2003). Beyond virtue and vice in personality: Classical themes and current trends. In E. C. Chang & L. J. Sanna (Eds.), *Virtue, vice, and personality: The complexity of behavior* (pp. xix–xxvi). Washington, DC: American Psychological Association.

Chang, E. C., Sanna, L. J., & Edwards, M. C. (2003). *Relations between problem-solving styles and psychological outcomes: Is stress a mediating variable for young adults and middle-aged adults?* Unpublished manuscript, Department of Psychology, University of Michigan.

Chang, E. C., Watkins, A. F., Banks, K. H., & Hudson, H. (2004). How adaptive and maladaptive perfectionism relate to positive and negative psychological functioning: Testing a stress-mediation model in Black and White female college students. *Journal of Counseling Psychology, 51*, 93–102.

Dewey, J. (1929). *The quest for certainty: A study of the relation of knowledge and action*. New York: Minton, Balch.

Diener, E., Emmons, R. A., Larsen, R. J., & Griffin, S. (1985). The Satisfaction With Life Scale. *Journal of Personality Assessment, 49*, 71–75.

Diener, E., Suh, E. M., Lucas, R. E., & Smith, H. L. (1999). Subjective well-being: Three decades of progress. *Psychological Bulletin, 125*, 276–302.

D'Zurilla, T. J., Chang, E. C., & Sanna, L. J. (2003). Self-esteem and social problem solving as predictors of aggression in college students. *Journal of Social and Clinical Psychology, 22*, 424–440

D'Zurilla, T. J., & Goldfried, M. (1971). Problem solving and behavior modification. *Journal of Abnormal Psychology, 78*, 104–126.

D'Zurilla, T. J., & Nezu, A. M. (1990). Development and preliminary evaluation of the Social Problem-Solving Inventory (SPSI). *Psychological Assessment, 2*, 156–163.

D'Zurilla, T. J., & Nezu, A. M. (1999). *Problem-solving therapy: A social competence approach to clinical intervention*. New York: Springer.

D'Zurilla, T. J., Nezu, A. M., & Maydeu-Olivares, A. (2002). *Social Problem-Solving Inventory—Revised (SPSI–R): Technical manual*. North Tonawanda, NY: Multi-Health Systems.

Elliott, T. R. Sherwin, E., Harkins, S. W., & Marmarosh, C. (1995). Self-appraised problem-solving ability, affective states, and psychological distress. *Journal of Counseling Psychology, 42*, 105–115.

Elliott, T. R., Shewchuk, R. M., Miller, D. M., & Richards, J. S. (2001). Profiles in problem solving: Psychological well-being and distress among persons with diabetes mellitus. *Journal of Clinical Psychology in Medical Settings, 8*, 283–291.

Grant, J. S., Elliott, T. R., Giger, J. N., & Bartolucci, A. A. (2001). Social problem-solving abilities, social support, and adjustment among family caregivers of individuals with a stroke. *Rehabilitation Psychology, 46*, 44–57.

Heppner, P. P. (1988). *The Problem-Solving Inventory*. Palo Alto, CA: Consulting Psychologist Press.

Heppner, P. P., Cook, S. W., Wright, D. M., & Johnson, W. C., Jr. (1995). Progress in resolving problems: A problem-focused style of coping. *Journal of Counseling Psychology, 42*, 279–293.

Jahoda, M. (1958). *Current concepts of positive mental health*. New York: Basic Books.

Keyes, C. L., M., Shmotkin, D., & Ryff, C. D. (2002). Optimizing well-being: The empirical encounter of two traditions. *Journal of Personality and Social Psychology, 82*, 1007–1022.

Markus, H. R., & Kitayama, S. (1991). Culture and the self: Implications for cognition, emotion, and motivation. *Psychological Review, 98*, 224–253.

Maslow, A. H. (1954). *Motivation and personality*. New York: Harper & Row.

McCabe, R. E., Blankstein, K. R., & Mills, J. S. (1999). Interpersonal sensitivity and social problem-solving: Relations with academic and social self-esteem, depressive symptoms, and academic performance. *Cognitive Therapy and Research, 23*, 587–604.

McCullough, M. E., & Snyder, C. R. (2000). Classical sources of human strength: Revisiting an old home and building a new one. *Journal of Social and Clinical Psychology, 19*, 1–10.

Nezu, A. M., Nezu, C. M., & Perri, M. G. (1989). *Problem-solving therapy for depression: Therapy, research, and clinical guidelines*. New York: Wiley.

Nezu, A. M., & Perri, M. (1989). Social problem solving therapy for unipolar depression: An initial dismantling investigation. *Journal of Consulting and Clinical Psychology, 57*, 408–413.

Rogers, C. R. (1961). *On becoming a person*. Boston: Houghton Mifflin.

Rosenberg, M. (1965). *Society and the adolescent self-image*. Princeton, NJ: Princeton University Press.

Ryff, C. D. (1989). Happiness is everything, or is it?: Explorations on the meaning of psychological well-being. *Journal of Personality and Social Psychology, 57*, 1069–1081.

Ryff, C. D. (1991). Possible selves in adulthood and old age: A tale of shifting horizons. *Psychology and Aging, 6*, 286–295.

Ryff, C. D. (1995). Psychological well-being in adult life. *Current Directions in Psychological Science, 4*, 99–104.

Ryff, C. D., & Keyes, C. L. M. (1995). The structure of psychological well-being revisited. *Journal of Personality and Social Psychology, 69*, 719–727.

Scheier, M. F., & Carver, C. S. (1985). Optimism, coping, and health: Assessment and implications of generalized outcome expectancies. *Health Psychology, 4*, 219–247.

Sears, D. O. (1986). College sophomores in the laboratory: Influences of a narrow data base on social psychology's view of human nature. *Journal of Personality and Social Psychology, 51,* 515–530.

Seligman, M. E. P., & Csikszentmihalyi, M. (2000). Positive psychology: An introduction. *American Psychologist, 55,* 5–14.

Sheldon, K. M., & King, L. A. (2001). Why positive psychology is necessary. *American Psychologist, 56,* 216–217.

Snyder, C. R., Harris, C., Anderson, J. R., Holleran, S. A., Irving, L. M., Sigmon, S. T., et al. (1991). The will and the ways: Development and validation of an individual-differences measure of hope. *Journal of Personality and Social Psychology, 60,* 570–585.

Watson, D., Clark, L. A., & Tellegen, A. (1988). Development and validation of brief measures of positive and negative affect: The PANAS scales. *Journal of Personality and Social Psychology, 54,* 1063–1070.

World Health Organization. (1948). *Constitution of the World Health Organization.* Geneva, Switzerland: Author.

7

SOCIAL PROBLEM-SOLVING ABILITIES AND BEHAVIORAL HEALTH

TIMOTHY R. ELLIOTT, JOAN S. GRANT, AND DOREEN M. MILLER

Personal health is an aspect of everyday life that typifies both the commonplace and the stressful in the course of a lifetime. Many social–cognitive variables have been associated with indicators of behavioral health and with the adjustment and recovery of individuals facing health-related problems, and these characteristics are important factors in providing interventions (Auerbach, 1989). Therefore, it is important to consider the relations between social problem-solving abilities and indicators of behavioral health.

This chapter was supported by grants to the first author from the National Institute on Child Health and Human Development (1 R01 HD37661-01A3), from the National Institute on Disability and Rehabilitation Research, Office of Special Education and Rehabilitative Services, U.S. Department of Education (Grant nos. H133B90016 and H133A021927), and by Grant no. R49/CCR403641, U.S. Department of Health and Human Services, Centers for Disease Control and Prevention, National Center for Injury Prevention and Control to the University of Alabama at Birmingham. Its contents are solely the responsibility of the authors and do not necessarily represent the official views of the funding agencies.

HOW AND WHY WOULD SOCIAL PROBLEM-SOLVING ABILITIES RELATE TO BEHAVIORAL HEALTH?

The prevailing model stipulates that social problem-solving abilities may be best conceptualized in terms of two major components: problem orientation and problem-solving skills (see chap. 1, this volume). This conceptual framework may be used to evaluate the extant research concerning social problem-solving abilities and behavioral health. In this chapter we first discuss the documented associations between problem-solving abilities and different dimensions of behavioral health (distress, health-related behaviors, health outcomes, etc.) and with social dynamics often implicated in personal health. We then discuss the available intervention research, conclude with a comment about the limitations of the research to date and the merits of our conceptualization, and consider avenues for expanding the research scope to appreciate the full breadth of social problem-solving abilities as they pertain to personal health.

SOCIAL PROBLEM-SOLVING ABILITIES AND DIMENSIONS OF BEHAVIORAL HEALTH

Social problem-solving abilities have been studied in individuals with a variety of health-related issues. In this section we discuss this research as it pertains to distress and adjustment associated with health conditions, perceptions of health and physical symptoms, ill health and secondary complications, health-promotive and health-compromising behaviors, interpersonal relations and social support, and family dynamics.

Distress and Emotional Adjustment Accompanying Health Conditions

Before 1991 there were few studies concerning the relationship of social problem solving to physical health, generally, and no published studies of social problem solving and adjustment among individuals with health-related problems, specifically. The first study to examine this issue found that individuals who had incurred a spinal cord injury (SCI) and who varied tremendously in the amount of time since the onset of the injury (1 to 490 months) were more likely to report greater depression and psychosocial disability if they had more negative appraisals of their problem-solving abilities (Elliott, Godshall, Herrick, Witty, & Spruell, 1991).

It is particularly informative to note that in this study (a) the relationship of social problem-solving abilities to both adjustment measures was not mediated by either the severity of the disability or the duration of the condition, (b) the degree of handicap associated with the injury was related to social problem-solving abilities and beyond the variance attributable to the actual condition, and (c) elements of the problem orientation component were significantly associated with the self-report measures of adjustment. This provided the first evidence that social problem-solving abilities may operate in a theoretically consistent fashion among people with acute and chronic health problems and that the problem orientation component may influence the development of distress associated with health. Subsequent research has found that similar processes occur in the relationship of social problem-solving abilities to anxiety and depression among individuals recently diagnosed with cancer and among women recovering from breast cancer surgeries (Nezu, Nezu, Friedman, & Houts, 1999).

In the first study linking social problem solving with pain behavior, a low sense of control when solving problems was significantly predictive of premenstrual and menstrual pain complaints of undergraduate women, regardless of oral contraception usage (Elliott, 1992). Later research found social problem-solving abilities were predictive of psychosocial impairment and distress among patients entering a pain rehabilitation program (Witty, Heppner, Bernard, & Thoreson, 2001) and prospectively predictive of functional impairment among individuals with chronic pain who had returned to work (Shaw, Feuerstein, Haufler, Berkowitz, & Lopez, 2001).

The presumed mood-regulatory properties of the problem-orientation component were supported in a study of social problem solving, affectivity, and postpartum depression (Elliott, Shewchuk, Richardson, Pickelman, & Franklin, 1996). This scenario provided a conservative and rigorous test, given the expected high correlations between affectivity and depression and between peripartum and postpartum depression. The final model revealed that elements on the Problem-Solving Inventory (Heppner, 1988) representing positive and negative problem orientation—the problem-solving confidence and personal control factors, respectively—were significantly associated with trait positive and negative affect during the eighth month of pregnancy, and significant indirect paths were then associated with postpartum depression.

Perceptions of Health and Physical Symptoms

Social problem-solving ability operates as a metacognitive construct, influencing the way an individual perceives, processes, and uses information relevant to the self (Heppner & Krauskopf, 1987). Social–cognitive processes also operate in the ways people make inferences about their physiological status and sensations (Pennebaker, 1982), and some people tend to be aware of and pessimistically interpret physical sensations as symptomatic of illness whereas others are more circumscribed and benign in their interpretations (Pennebaker, 1982). Elliott and Marmarosh (1994) found ineffective problem solvers reported significantly more physical symptoms in the three week before assessment, at the time of assessment, and three months later than effective problem solvers. Ineffective problem solvers also reported a lower sense of personal control over their health and believed their health was influenced by chance, in comparison with the effective problem solvers.

Ill Health and Secondary Complications

In times of stress, individuals with ineffective problem-solving abilities often rely on emotion-focused and avoidant coping (MacNair & Elliott, 1992). Cross-sectional research has revealed that the problem-orientation component is instrumental in the problems people under duress experience with decreased vitality and impaired social functioning because of poor health (Elliott & Shewchuk, 2003; Grant, Elliott, Giger, & Bartolucci, 2001). Prospective research using trajectory modeling techniques has further revealed that a negative problem orientation is predictive of increasing levels of ill health over the course of a year (Elliott, Shewchuk, & Richards, 2001).

Individuals who live with chronic disease (e.g., diabetes) and physical disability (e.g., spinal cord injury) are responsible daily for maintaining personal health by observing regimens for self-care, therapy, diet, monitoring symptoms, and integrity of bodily functions (e.g., skin inspections); failure to adhere to these regimens can result in complications that can lead to expensive episodes of care (e.g., emergency room visits, inpatient hospitalizations) and intensive interventions (e.g., amputations, skin-flap surgeries). Secondary complications are mediated largely by behavioral and social mechanisms that either prevent or facilitate the development of these conditions.

An initial foray into this area found people with SCI who were diagnosed with at least one pressure sore one year after completing a measure of problem-solving abilities were characterized in part by avoidant tendencies (with 84.91% accuracy; Herrick, Elliott, & Crow, 1994). Individuals in this sample varied considerably in the amount of time they had lived with SCI. Recent work suggests that all elements of social problem solving—as measured by the Social Problem-Solving Inventory—Revised (SPSI–R; D'Zurilla, Nezu, & Maydeau-Olivares, 2002)—contribute to the prediction of pressure sore occurrence in the first three years of SCI (Elliott & Bush, 2003).

Available data suggest this may be a complex—if not convoluted—issue, not easily explained by our existing models. For example, in a study of treatment outcomes among people with dual-disorder diagnoses (e.g., substance abuse and personality disorders), a higher positive orientation was significantly predictive of fewer positive alcohol and illicit drug screens during inpatient treatment (with 70% accuracy; Herrick & Elliott, 2001). This finding implied that individuals with a positive orientation were motivated to observe treatment expectations for therapeutic behavior. However, the treatment program also stipulated that graduates of the program would keep their first scheduled outpatient visit following their discharge into the community. A predictive model found that individuals with a lower positive orientation were more likely to keep this scheduled appointment and those with a higher positive orientation were more likely to miss it (with 64.15% accuracy). These paradoxical results essentially highlight a fundamental shortcoming in these correlational analyses: We ultimately do not know what was important and of value to these participants, and we do not know what problems were of immediate concern. Once discharged into the community, did those with a positive orientation feel little need to keep this appointment? Did they have other problems of greater importance? Did they attend to a personal problem higher on their priority list—in other words, had they relapsed? When we do not know the actual problems people experience and the subjective valence of these problems, we are at a loss to understand the full impact and influence of social problem-solving abilities in everyday life.

Health-Promotive and Health-Compromising Behaviors

College students classified as ineffective problem solvers have reported more alcohol use than effective problem solvers (Heppner, Hibel, Neal, Weinstein, & Rabinowitz, 1982; Williams & Kleinfelter, 1989). These differences have not been found among clinical samples, however (Larson & Heppner, 1989), and there is some evidence that gender differences might be related to the reporting of substance use and problem-solving abilities (Elliott, Johnson, & Jackson, 1997). Cross-sectional data relying on self-report measures of health behaviors suggest that avoidant tendencies are associated with a greater likelihood to take risks when operating an automobile among undergraduates, and a positive problem orientation is associated with accident-prevention behaviors among undergraduates and people with acquired disabilities (Dreer, Elliott, & Tucker, in press; Elliott et al., 1997).

In the only prospective study to date on this topic, logged diaries of alcohol ingestion were used to assess undergraduate drinking behavior. Greater avoidant tendencies were predictive of greater alcohol intake over a two-week period (Godshall & Elliott, 1997). Moreover, this study also examined logged accounts of exercise and sedentary behavior (defined as hours watching television). Although no significant associations were found with exercise, avoidant tendencies were associated with more sedentary behavior. Incidentally, alcohol use was positively correlated with sedentary behavior as well. It appears that avoidant tendencies may be characterized by an unstructured lifestyle, marked by a lack of goal-directed behavior.

INTERPERSONAL RELATIONS AND SOCIAL SUPPORT

In the seminal Heppner et al. (1982) study, ineffective problem solvers reported more relationship problems than the effective problem solvers and interviewers observed rated the effective problem solvers more interpersonally skilled than the ineffective problem solvers. Effective assertiveness skills are thought to be crucial in adjusting to chronic and disabling health conditions, and effective problem-solving abilities were significantly predictive of assertion skills among individuals with spinal cord injuries in the Elliott et al. (1991) study.

It seems logical to assume that effective problem-solving abilities would be associated with higher levels of social support. Social problem-solving abilities and social support might share considerable statistical overlap and a common, underlying social dimension that conceptual differences may not be of real importance. Social support did not mediate the relationship between social problem-solving abilities and depression, nor did it mediate the problem-solving–personal health relationship (Grant et al., 2001). More important, social problem-solving abilities accounted for more variance in depression and health than social support. A negative orientation may be a better predictor of depression status than social support (Grant, Weaver, Elliott, Bartolucci, & Giger, in press).

There is evidence that problem-solving abilities *moderate* the social support–adjustment relationship among individuals with health conditions. In a study of individuals with spinal cord injuries, effective problem-solving ability was associated with less psychosocial impairment when support offering material assistance was low; in contrast, ineffective problem solving was associated with greater impairment when this support was high (Elliott, Herrick, & Witty, 1992). A second interaction revealed that effective problem solving was associated with less impairment when support offering advice and guidance was low; under conditions of high guidance and advice, effective problem solving was associated with greater impairment. A recent study found ineffective problem solving was associated with higher depression scores when support for pain behavior was low among individuals admitted into a pain management program (Kerns, Rosenberg, & Otis, 2002). Effective problem solvers may experience greater benefit from some types of social support than ineffective problem solvers, but effective problems solvers may encounter difficulties with support systems that provide direct advice and guidance (which may be characteristic of many health professions).

Family Dynamics

Observational studies indicate that families differ considerably in their ability to identify and solve problems that affect its members. Effective problem-solving skills have been observed in the interactions between parents of children who have been compliant with dietary regimens for a chronic disease (Fehrenbach & Peterson, 1989), and families with adolescents who abuse substances often display deficits in family problem solving and in coping with everyday problems (Hops, Tildesley, Lichtenstein, & Ary, 1990). Effective problem-solving abilities are associated with lower distress among mothers of children with disabilities (Noojin & Wallander, 1997), family caregivers of older individuals in stroke rehabilitation (Grant et al., 2001), and individuals assuming a caregiver role for a loved one with a recent-onset spinal cord injury (Elliott & Shewchuk, 2003). A negative orientation in particular is predictive of the subsequent trajectories of caregiver depression, anxiety, and ill health during the first year of assuming the caregiver role (Elliott, Shewchuk, & Richards, 2001).

The ability to manage the rigors and demands of caregiving may be directly related to the health and well-being of the care recipient. Individuals who incur a severe disability, for example, may have restricted mobility and disruptions in sensory perception; these individuals require routine assistance in adhering to therapeutic regimens for self-care, movement, diet, skin inspections, and toileting. The responsibility for adhering to these regimens usually resides with the family caregiver. If a caregiver lacks the problem-solving abilities necessary to observe the expected rituals—while simultaneously attending to the other tasks essential to family functioning and daily life, with a minimum of preparation, training, and formal support—nonadherence will likely ensue and the care recipient will be at risk for secondary complications (such as pressure sores among individuals with paralysis). Caregiver impulsive–careless problem-solving styles have been associated with care recipient difficulties with disability acceptance before discharge from an inpatient spinal cord injury rehabilitation program, and this association was independent of previous levels of care recipient depression during the program (Elliott, Shewchuk, & Richards, 1999). Moreover, caregiver impulsive–careless styles significantly contributed to the prediction of the occurrence of a pressure sore among individuals evaluated in the outpatient clinic one year later (with 87.88% accuracy).

PROBLEM-SOLVING INTERVENTIONS IN BEHAVIORAL HEALTH

Cognitive–behavioral therapies have been used in health care settings for some time, and problem-solving training (PST) has documented effectiveness in a variety of settings in lowering depression among older adults (Arean et al., 1993). PST has been described in detail for individuals with cancer (Nezu, Nezu, Friedman, & Faddis, 1998), and it is effective in promoting weight management over time among women with obesity (Perri et al., 2001). A recent study indicates that the benefits of PST in lowering distress among cancer patients may be evident a year after treatment (Nezu, Nezu, Felgoise, McClure, & Houts, 2003).

Other health-related interventions can be framed in problem-solving perspectives. Problem-solving principles can be incorporated into family education and caregiver preparation programs, and these can be delivered in community sites (Houts, Nezu, Nezu, & Bucher, 1996) and in the home (Kurylo, Elliott, & Shewchuk, 2001). Distressed caregivers may receive greater benefit from PST than those with less distress (Toseland, Blanchard, & McCallion, 1995); similarly, caregivers who exhibit poor problem-solving skills may be more responsive to training (Roberts et al., 1995).

Manualized PST has demonstrated limited effects in helping mothers of children with cancer over an eight-week period (Sahler et al., 2002). Another clinical trial using three groups—PST, a sham intervention, and a control group—examined the efficacy of PST in telephone sessions with family caregivers of stroke survivors on their return to the community (Grant, Elliott, Weaver, Bartolucci, & Giger, 2002). Caregivers were trained over a series of eight contacts during a 12-week period (including initial training in the home followed by weekly telephone contacts for the first month and biweekly contacts through the second and third months) to use social problem-solving skills in managing stressors that were identified at each contact. Trajectory modeling revealed that participants in the training group had better problem-solving skills over time, and they reported less depression and improvements in personal vitality, social functioning, mental health, and preparation for the caregiver role.

Implications and Future Directions

The extant literature and clinical experience have advanced our understanding of social problem solving, and it is evident that these abilities are meaningfully related to the ways people may sense and interpret physical symptoms, to the development of certain health conditions, and to the distress and impairment experienced by people who live with chronic conditions. There is evidence to support the utility of PST in health care settings. Nevertheless, several overarching issues in this literature temper the understanding of social problem-solving abilities in behavioral health.

What Is the Problem?

People who face acute health problems and those who live with chronic conditions encounter many potential stressors that can complicate their adjustment and well-being. These problems may relate to some aspect of the condition, but they may also stem from other roles and activities of daily life (e.g., parenting, budgeting finances). Unfortunately, determinations about what is stressful and what is a problem are often made by clinicians and theorists, who then typically design interventions in a top-down fashion based on clinical and research needs. As we have seen, we are at loss to explain some findings in the literature when we make assumptions about what problems participants experience without consulting them (cf. Herrick & Elliott, 2001). Individuals who live with chronic conditions are articulate about the problems that cause them stress (Miller, Shewchuk, Elliott, & Richards, 2000). A manualized approach to PST that does not actively attend first to the subjective, immediate concerns of the individual may be of little benefit to those living with a chronic health condition (Shanmugham, Elliott, & Palmatier, in press). In contrast, interventions that have documented effectiveness began each session with a discussion with the participant to address specific problems of concern at that time (Grant et al., 2002).

In some situations, individuals may be overwhelmed with many problems, or they may be reticent to share their problems with an interviewer. We have found that participants are more willing to consider problems that have been obtained from a group of peers; in some cases, this information might serve to stimulate discussion about other problems experienced by the participant that might not be identified by the group (Elliott & Shewchuk, 2000). Providing a list of problems identified by a peer group can normalize an individual's experience and may also be used to augment basic problem-identification skills. This kind of an approach can be used to tailor PST to the unique needs of a person. Individuals who sense greater relevance in training will have more motivation for learning and using problem-solving skills.

Some researchers have opted for condition-specific assessments of problem-solving abilities, arguing that the multifaceted aspects of a disease imposed many problems that required strategies to address these specific concerns (e.g., cancer; Sahler et al., 2002). The ability to solve problems specific to diabetes, for example, has been associated with more optimal adjustment (Toobert & Glasgow, 1991). It is often assumed that a condition constitutes the major focus of everyday life for people who live with a chronic disease or disability. Yet people vary considerably in the degree to which they attend to other aspects of life and as they find meaning and pursue fulfilling activities independent of their condition. Individuals who adjust optimally following the onset of chronic disease or disability do not regard the condition as the centerpiece of their life; conversely, individuals who have greater difficulty coming to terms with their condition often demonstrate difficulties coping with other aspects of life (Elliott, Kurylo, & Rivera, 2002). Thus, if a person has difficulty solving problems that accompany the routines of daily life, it is probable that they will have similar difficulty tending to the tasks, regimens, and symptoms prerequisite for optimal adjustment while living with a chronic disease or disability.

There are situations in which condition-specific assessments are pertinent, but these should not be administered with a general disregard for the impact of problem solving on the life experience, and assumptions about the nature of stress and problems (and the relative valence of these) should be anchored to the individual's experience. Problem-solving interventions that are tailored to the individual experience will be more relevant and elicit more motivation than standardized protocols. Furthermore, this kind of an approach is conducive to fostering a partnership with individuals who live with chronic conditions, and in doing so, they are trained to operate as active participants in their health and its care.

Emphasizing the Negative, Ignoring the Positive?

The tendency to assume the existence of problems—a result in no small part to the theoretical underpinnings and clinical focus of the social problem-solving model—unfortunately contributes to a rather pessimistic and unbalanced view of individuals who live with many health conditions. But there is ample evidence that effective problem solvers possess favorable opinions about their abilities, have good self-concepts, and have a fair amount of motivation to handle minor problems with dispatch, and thus carry a good deal of confidence to the business of solving major problems. When facing a major health event, individuals with effective problem-solving abilities will likely process available information in an adaptive manner, maintain their sense of motivation, and engage in goal-directed behavior that has served them well in the past. In one direct study of this issue, effective social problem-solving abilities were associated with disability acceptance among individuals with a recent-onset spinal cord injury (Elliott, 1999). These data indicate that social problem-solving abilities are associated with adaptive beliefs, values, and sense of purpose and meaning that characterizes acceptance of disability. These findings raise other intriguing questions: Do ineffective problem solvers have persistent problems with ruminations about their condition? Do they perceive the chronic health condition to be the centerpiece of their lives? Do they have recurrent interpersonal or social problems that reflect their inability to handle the minor, routine tasks of life? In contrast, do effective problem solvers report a different cluster of problems altogether, perhaps related to their goals and aspirations, or do they report fewer stressors of any type?

Studies relevant to this issue have explored the relationship of problem-solving abilities to life satisfaction among individuals with diabetes (Elliott, Shewchuk, Miller, & Richards, 2001) and caregivers of stroke survivors (Grant et al., 2001). In the Elliott, Shewchuk, Miller, et al. (2001) study, social problem solving was associated with satisfaction with life in a theoretical direction, and it should be noted that participants of this study had lived with their condition for some time. In the Grant et al. (2001) study, problem solving was not significantly correlated with life satisfaction; these caregivers were assessed before their family members' discharge from the rehabilitation unit. A cross-sectional study of caregivers of individuals with SCI found an effective problem orientation was significantly associated with greater mental health and happiness (Elliott & Shewchuk, 2003). There is also some promising evidence that PST can enhance quality of life: Grant et al. (2002) found PST significantly improved reports of mental health and happiness among family caregivers.

Piecemeal Publication and the Big Picture

The bulk of the extant literature has addressed basic theoretical questions or targeted specific adjustment issues in need of treatment. In many studies, statistical techniques were used to isolate the separate components of problem solving to test specific theoretical properties and clarify the role of the separate components in the prediction of adjustment, behavior, or some other relevant outcome. However, this approach does not instruct us in the ways the different components of social problem solving might operate in tandem, or if there are subgroups or profiles of individuals who have varying levels of adjustment at any point in time. The reliance on tests of specific theoretical tenets contributes to a rather piecemeal view of social problem-solving abilities and their role in the adjustment of an individual in a given day. We simply do not know how the various components of problem solving work together to influence adjustment among individuals who live with chronic health conditions. We could assume that the full array of social problem-solving abilities would be instrumental in facilitating personal health and quality of life, particularly among people who live with chronic health concerns, and perhaps among those who face acute and severe health problems.

In one of the few studies that attempted to identify subgroups of individuals based on their problem-solving profiles, Elliott, Shewchuk, Miller, et al. (2001) found four distinct problem-solving clusters among individuals with diabetes that varied significantly in depression and life satisfaction. Two of the groups mirrored the theoretical extremes of the model, but the other two groups presented a more complicated picture. One group clearly had the skills requisite for adjustment: They had the second highest positive orientation average and the second highest average on rational problem-solving skills. Yet this group also had the second highest average depression score and the second lowest in life satisfaction. Participants in this group then appeared skilled but nonetheless frustrated, pessimistic, and embattled, because their negative orientation and avoidance scores were also high.

Another intriguing group—which had the most members, it is interesting to note—had very low scores on practically all problem-solving scales. They also had the second lowest average depression score and they were the second highest in life satisfaction (although this average score was still rather low). These low-key individuals were not necessarily motivated or feeling competent, but it was apparent that they were not distressed or frustrated either. Perhaps there are times in chronic disease when individuals find it adaptive to rein in their goals and aspirations and find some sense of adjustment in lowered expectations (or, at least, a less aggressive approach to solving problems). These profiles are inconsistent with the presumed linear relationship between problem solving and adjustment among individuals with health conditions, as perpetuated in most cross-sectional studies.

Low-Cost Providers and Efficacious Service Delivery

The research to date germane to behavioral health suggests that PST can be a cost-effective approach to treating individuals with depression (and presumably, other emotional disorders) that are seen in primary care (Mynors-Wallis, Gath, Lloyd-Thomas, & Tomlinson, 1995). PST can be effectively provided by colleagues from other health professions (Grant et al., 2002; Roberts, et al., 1995). The use of low-cost service providers is particularly attractive in the delivery of services to individuals who have chronic health conditions and who may have daily, ongoing issues in daily living. These individuals are also likely to have decreased coverage for health care services, are more likely to be on public health care programs, and they are also more likely to have mobility and transportation difficulties. In sum, these individuals are at risk for complications that tax public-supported health care systems, but their needs are not logically or reasonably addressed by traditional programs of care centered in fee-for-service models and outpatient clinics. Additional research should explore the effectiveness of PST provided in innovative approaches such as Internet bulletin boards (Bucher & Houts, 1999) and in-home videoconferencing devices (Rivera, Shewchuk, & Elliott, 2003).

CONCLUSION

Social problem-solving abilities are related to several broad areas in behavioral health. Research concerning the relation of social problem-solving abilities to acute care needs has been lacking in general. Social problem-solving abilities appear to be particularly germane to the adjustment of individuals who live with chronic health conditions, because these individuals simultaneously cope with tasks and symptoms associated with their condition and perform roles essential to the function of everyday life. Available research supports this position. However, there is a remarkable lack of PST research among individuals with other chronic conditions. We should expect to see studies of PST in the treatment of chronic low-back pain, rheumatoid arthritis, cardiac rehabilitation, asthma, and AIDS/HIV (to name but a few examples). The social problem-solving model and its supportive literature base offers clear directives for assessment and intervention in these areas.

Similarly, a problem-solving perspective can provide a powerful vantage point for assessment and triage. Available evidence suggests that individuals with poor skills are at greater risk to develop secondary complications and incur greater expense to health care service delivery systems. More research is needed to demonstrate the prospective predictive ability of the model in identifying individuals who are in fact at risk for adverse outcomes and greater health care expenditures across many health conditions (such as those listed earlier). Information about individual deficits will then be pivotal in tailoring strategic, community-based training programs for individuals who are known to be susceptible and vulnerable to complications when left on their own recognizance.

REFERENCES

Arean, P. A., Perri, M., Nezu, A., Schein, R., Christopher, F., & Joseph, T. (1993). Comparative effectiveness of social problem-solving therapy as treatments of depression in older adults. *Journal of Consulting and Clinical Psychology, 61*, 1003–1010.

Auerbach, S. M. (1989). Stress management and coping research in the health care setting: An overview and methodological commentary. *Journal of Consulting and Clinical Psychology, 57*, 388–395.

Bucher, J. A., & Houts, P. S. (1999). Problem-solving through electronic bulletin boards. *Journal of Psychosocial Oncology, 16*, 85–91.

Dreer, L., Elliott, T., & Tucker, E. (in press). Social problem-solving abilities and health behaviors among persons with recent-onset spinal cord injury. *Journal of Clinical Psychology in Medical Settings*.

D'Zurilla, T. J., Nezu, A. M., & Maydeu-Olivares, A. (2002). *Social Problem-Solving Inventory—Revised (SPSI–R): Technical manual.* North Tonawanda, NY: Multi-Health Systems.

Elliott, T. (1992). Problem-solving appraisal, oral contraceptive use, and menstrual pain. *Journal of Applied Social Psychology, 22,* 286–297.

Elliott, T. (1999). Social problem solving abilities and adjustment to recent-onset physical disability. *Rehabilitation Psychology, 44,* 315–332.

Elliott, T., & Bush, B. (2003, April). *Social problem-solving abilities and pressure sore occurrence among persons with spinal cord injury.* Paper presented at the mid-winter conference of the Division of Rehabilitation Psychology/American Psychological Association and the American Board of Rehabilitation Psychology, Tucson, AZ.

Elliott, T., Godshall, F., Herrick, S., Witty, T., & Spruell, M. (1991). Problem-solving appraisal and psychological adjustment following spinal cord injury. *Cognitive Therapy and Research, 15,* 387–398.

Elliott, T., Herrick, S., & Witty, T. (1992). Problem solving appraisal and the effects of social support among college students and persons with physical disabilities. *Journal of Counseling Psychology, 39,* 219–226.

Elliott, T., Johnson, M., & Jackson, R. (1997). Social problem solving skills and health behaviors of undergraduate students. *Journal of College Student Development, 38,* 24–31.

Elliott, T., Kurylo, M., & Rivera, P. (2002). Positive growth and adjustment following acquired physical disability. In C. R. Snyder & S. Lopez (Eds.), *Handbook of positive psychology* (pp. 687–699). London: Oxford University Press.

Elliott, T., & Marmarosh, C. (1994). Problem solving appraisal, health complaints, and health-related expectancies. *Journal of Counseling and Development, 72,* 531–537.

Elliott, T., & Shewchuk, R. (2000). Problem solving therapy for family caregivers of persons with severe physical disabilities. In C. Radnitz (Ed.), *Cognitive–behavioral interventions for persons with disabilities* (pp. 309–327). New York: Jason Aronson.

Elliott, T., & Shewchuk, R. (2003). Social problem solving abilities and distress in family members assuming a caregiver role. *British Journal of Health Psychology, 8,* 149–163.

Elliott, T., Shewchuk, R, Miller, D., & Richards, J. S. (2001). Profiles in problem solving: Psychological well-being and distress among persons with diabetes mellitus. *Journal of Clinical Psychology in Medical Settings, 8,* 283–291.

Elliott, T., Shewchuk, R., & Richards, J. S. (1999). Caregiver social problem solving abilities and family member adjustment to recent-onset physical disability. *Rehabilitation Psychology, 44,* 104–123.

Elliott, T., Shewchuk, R., & Richards, J. S. (2001). Family caregiver problem solving abilities and adjustment during the initial year of the caregiving role. *Journal of Counseling Psychology, 48,* 223–232.

Elliott, T., Shewchuk, R., Richeson, C., Pickelman, H., & Franklin, K. (1996). Problem-solving appraisal and the prediction of depression during pregnancy and in the post-partum period. *Journal of Counseling and Development, 74*, 645–651.

Fehrenbach, A., & Peterson, L. (1989). Parental problem-solving skills, stress, and dietary compliance in phenylketonuria. *Journal of Consulting and Clinical Psychology, 57*, 237–241.

Godshall, F., & Elliott, T. (1997). Behavioral correlates of self-appraised problem-solving ability: Problem-solving skills and health-compromising behaviors. *Journal of Applied Social Psychology, 27*, 929–944.

Grant, J., Elliott, T., Giger, J., & Bartolucci, A. (2001). Social problem-solving abilities, social support, and adjustment among family caregivers of individuals with a stroke. *Rehabilitation Psychology, 46*, 44–57.

Grant, J., Elliott, T., Weaver, M. Bartolucci, A., & Giger, J. (2002). A telephone intervention with family caregivers of stroke survivors after hospital discharge. *Stroke, 33*, 2060–2065.

Grant, J., Weaver, M., Elliott, T., Bartolucci, A., & Giger, J. (in press). Caregivers of stroke survivors: characteristics of caregivers at-risk for depression. *Rehabilitation Psychology*.

Heppner, P. P. (1988). *The Problem-Solving Inventory: Manual*. Palo Alto, CA: Consulting Psychologists Press.

Heppner, P. P., Hibel, J., Neal, G. W., Weinstein, C. L., & Rabinowitz, F. E. (1982). Personal problem solving: A descriptive study of individual differences. *Journal of Counseling Psychology, 29*, 580–590.

Heppner, P. P., & Krauskopf, C. J. (1987). An information processing approach to personal problem solving. *Counseling Psychologist, 15*, 371–447.

Herrick, S., & Elliott, T. (2001). Social problem solving abilities and personality disorder characteristics among dual-diagnosed persons in substance abuse treatment. *Journal of Clinical Psychology, 57*, 75–92.

Herrick, S., Elliott, T., & Crow, F. (1994). Self-appraised problem solving skills and the prediction of secondary complications among persons with spinal cord injury. *Journal of Clinical Psychology in Medical Settings, 1*, 269–283.

Hops, H., Tildesley, E., Lichtenstein, E., & Ary, D. (1990). Parent and adolescent problem solving interactions and drug use. *American Journal of Drug & Alcohol Abuse, 16*, 239–258.

Houts, P. S., Nezu, A. M., Nezu, C. M., & Bucher, J. A. (1996). The prepared family caregiver: A problem-solving approach to family caregiver education. *Patient Education and Counseling, 27*, 63–73.

Kerns, R. D., Rosenberg, R., & Otis, J. D. (2002). Self-appraised problem solving and pain-relevant social support as predictors of the experience of chronic pain. *Annals of Behavioral Medicine, 24*, 100–105.

Kurylo, M., Elliott, T., & Shewchuk, R. (2001). FOCUS on the family caregiver: A problem-solving training intervention. *Journal of Counseling and Development, 79*, 275–281.

Larson, L. M., & Heppner, P. P. (1989). Problem-solving appraisal in an alcoholic population. *Journal of Counseling Psychology, 36,* 73–78.

MacNair, R. R., & Elliott, T. (1992). Self-perceived problem solving ability, stress appraisal, and coping over time. *Journal of Research in Personality, 26,* 150–164.

Miller, D., Shewchuk, R., Elliott, T., & Richards, J. S. (2000). Nominal group technique: A process for identifying diabetes self-care issues among patients and caregivers. *Diabetes Educator, 26,* 305–314.

Mynors-Wallis, L. M., Gath, D. H., Lloyd-Thomas, A. R., & Tomlinson, D. (1995). Randomised controlled trial comparing problem solving treatment with amitriptyline and placebo for major depression in primary care. *British Medical Journal, 310,* 441–445.

Nezu, A. M., & D'Zurilla, T. J. (1989). Social problem solving and negative affect. In P. Kendall & D. Watson (Eds.), *Anxiety and depression: Distinctive and overlapping features* (pp. 285–315). San Diego, CA: Academic Press.

Nezu, A. M., Nezu, C. M., Felgoise, S., McClure, K. & Houts, P. (2003). Project Genesis: Assessing the efficacy of problem-solving therapy for distressed adult cancer patients. *Journal of Consulting and Clinical Psychology, 71,* 1036–1048.

Nezu, A. M., Nezu, C. M., Friedman, S. H., & Faddis, S. (1998). *Helping cancer patients cope: A problem-solving approach.* Washington, DC: American Psychological Association.

Nezu, C. M., Nezu, A., Friedman, S., & Houts, P. (1999). Cancer and psychological distress: Two investigations regarding the role of social problem-solving. *Journal of Psychosocial Oncology, 16*(3–4), 27–40.

Noojin, A. B., & Wallander, J. L. (1997). Perceived problem-solving ability, stress, and coping in mothers of children with physical disabilities: Potential cognitive influences on adjustment. *International Journal of Behavioral Medicine, 4,* 415–432.

Pennebaker, J. W. (1982). *The psychology of physical symptoms.* New York: Springer-Verlag.

Perri, M., Nezu, A., McKelvey, W., Shermer, R., Renjilian, D., & Viegener, B. (2001). Relapse prevention training and problem-solving therapy in the long-term management of obesity. *Journal of Consulting and Clinical Psychology, 69,* 722–726.

Rivera, P., Shewchuk, R., & Elliott, T. (2003). Project FOCUS: Using videophone to provide problem solving training to caregivers of persons with spinal cord injuries. *Topics in Spinal Cord Injury Rehabilitation, 9*(1), 53–62.

Roberts, J., Browne, G. B., Streiner, D., Gafni, A., Pallister, R., Hoxby, H., et al. (1995). Problem-solving counselling or phone-call support for outpatients with chronic illness: Effective for whom? *Canadian Journal of Nursing Research, 27,* 111–137.

Sahler, O., Varni, J. W., Fairclough, D., Butler, R., Noll, R., Dolgin, M., et al. (2002). Problem-solving skills training for mothers of children with newly diagnosed cancer: A randomized trial. *Journal of Developmental and Behavioral Pediatrics, 23,* 77–86.

Shanmugham, K., Elliott, T., & Palmatier, A. (in press). Social problem solving abilities and psychosocial impairment among individuals recuperating from surgical repair for severe pressure sores. *NeuroRehabilitation.*

Shaw, W. S., Feuerstein, M., Haufler, A., Berkowitz, S., & Lopez, M. (2001). Working with low back pain: Problem-solving orientation and function. *Pain, 93,* 129–137.

Toobert, D. J., & Glasgow, R. E. (1991). Problem solving and diabetes self-care. *Journal of Behavioral Medicine, 14,* 71–86.

Toseland, R. W., Blanchard, C. G., McCallion, P. (1995). A problem solving intervention for caregivers of cancer patients. *Social Science in Medicine, 40,* 517–528.

Williams, J. G., & Kleinfelter, K. J. (1989). Perceived problem solving skills and drinking patterns among college students. *Psychological Reports, 65,* 1235–1244.

Witty, T. E., Heppner, P. P., Bernard, C., & Thoreson, R. (2001). Problem solving appraisal and psychological adjustment of persons with chronic low back pain. *Journal of Clinical Psychology in Medical Settings, 8,* 149–160.

8

SOCIAL PROBLEM SOLVING AND MENTAL SIMULATION: HEURISTICS AND BIASES ON THE ROUTE TO EFFECTIVE DECISION MAKING

LAWRENCE J. SANNA, EULENA M. SMALL,
AND LYNNETTE M. COOK

All three boats passed under the lee of the pack edge when all of a sudden, almost before we realized it, the whole pack was in motion as if impelled by some mysterious force against the direction of the wind and as if descending upon us to once more engulph [sic] us in its awful grip.

—(Orde-Lees, 2002)

Trapped with Antarctic ice crushing their ship *Endurance*, Ernest Shackleton and crew took to the sea in three tiny lifeboats, a decision portrayed in the diary of Orde-Lees, the expedition's motor-sledge expert. They were to traverse the continent but their ships became frozen permanently in the ocean, turning the journey into a survival epic (see Alexander, 1998). After five months adrift, confronted with waiting out the winter, they paddled 180 miles over treacherous waters in open boats to the safety of Elephant Island, with only a sextant and chronometer for navigation. If

The writing of this chapter was supported in part by a Junior Faculty Development Award to L. J. Sanna from the University of North Carolina at Chapel Hill. We thank the Imagination, Goals, and Affect (IGoA) laboratory group members at the University of North Carolina at Chapel Hill for their comments on this chapter.

that was not remarkable enough, Shackleton and a smaller group spent 17 stormy days sailing another 800 miles to South Georgia Island, and traveled 36 hours by foot over rugged mountains to a whaling village after arriving. Amazingly, the multitude of decisions made along the way led to the rescue of every crew member, the entire ordeal lasting a little over two years.

Few will face circumstances like those of Shackleton's crew, but decision making and problem solving are no less crucial. Problems can run from critical to mundane. We may decide to marry for love or money, to buy for function or form, or simply whether to seed or sod. To account for this, D'Zurilla and Goldfried (1971) proposed their social problem-solving model, the foundation for this book; problem solving "(a) makes available a variety of potentially effective response alternatives for dealing with the problematic situation and (b) increases the probability of selecting the most effective response from among these various alternatives" (p. 108). It is this aspect of their model that is the focus of our chapter. We first discuss various cognitive heuristics that may underlie the availability of alternatives, and then discuss how mental simulations can serve a variety of social problem-solving functions. We next describe several biases that occur over time and that seem critical to a full understanding of social problem solving. We end by offering conclusions and by providing additional suggestions about how these ideas can inform social problem-solving theory, research, and training.

PLANNING THE JOURNEY: MENTAL SIMULATION AND COGNITIVE HEURISTICS

Mental simulations are imaginative cognitive constructions and reconstructions of events, including future forecasts, present assessments, and past retrospections (Sanna, 2000; Sanna, Stocker, & Clarke, 2003; Taylor, Pham, Rivkin, & Armor, 1998). Problem solvers attempt to "produce alternative solution possibilities for a particular problem" (D'Zurilla & Nezu, 1980, p. 67). Surprisingly, the extensive research on cognitive heuristics has yet to be incorporated into the social problem-solving model. However, an awareness of heuristics may allow researchers, theorists, and practitioners to determine *which* alternatives will be available.

Anchor and Adjustment

Einhorn and Hogarth (1981) proposed "that adjustments are based on a mental simulation in which 'what might be,' or 'what might have been,' is combined with 'what is' (the anchor)" (p. 456). Anchoring and adjustment starts with base values, from which changes are made in appropriate directions. Anchors may be established by personal experiences, but primed or randomly provided anchors influence judgments. For example, asked to consider the mean winter temperature of Antarctica (see Epley & Gilovich, 2001), participants' judgments were affected by a provided, but incorrect, anchor value of 1°F—a perhaps useless little tidbit of atmospheric information unless, of course, one plans on spending some time there. The trouble is that adjustments tend to be insufficient (Chapman & Johnson, 1994; Strack & Mussweiler, 1997), leaving people's final decisions biased toward the anchor. It may benefit social problem-solving models to recognize more fully that alternatives may be biased toward anchors.

Simulation

The simulation heuristic is relevant to social problem solving because it involves "running through" alternatives before responding (Kahneman & Tversky, 1982). The alternatives have several implications and play a role in affective states. Its role in decisions accrues from comparing reality with alternatives (Kahneman & Miller, 1986). Counterfactual research (Miller, Turnbull, & McFarland, 1990; Roese, 1997) exemplifies this. Upward counterfactuals compare reality with *better* alternatives (e.g., "If only we hadn't left so late; we might not be in a position of freezing to death here in this putrid place"); downward counterfactuals compare reality with *worse* alternatives (e.g., "At least we saved the seal blubber and crates of sardines; our food could have sunk with the ship"). Upward simulations are useful for future preparation; downward simulations are useful for affect repair (Sanna, Chang, & Meier, 2001). Research on the simulation heuristic begins to specify exactly how it is that people generate alternatives, and thus it might be incorporated into social problem-solving models.

Availability

The availability heuristic underlies both anchor and adjustment and simulation heuristics. Tversky and Kahneman (1973) proposed that people judge frequency, likelihood, and typicality on the basis of "the ease with which instances or associations come to mind" (p. 208). This is important to social problem solving because people conclude events are frequent, likely, or typical when examples are easy to bring to mind, but infer they are infrequent, unlikely, or atypical when examples are difficult to bring to mind (see also Schwarz, 1998). In particular, the social problem-solving model's " 'quantity' principle states that the more alternatives a person produces, the more high quality solutions he will discover" (D'Zurilla & Nezu, 1980, p. 68; see also Nezu & D'Zurilla, 1980). Although this may be true, the availability heuristic also indicates that ease or difficulty of generation needs to be accounted for. People might, for instance, simply choose the alternative(s) that come to mind most easily.

Summary: Integrating Cognitive Heuristics and Social Problem Solving

D'Zurilla and Goldfried (1971) proposed that people generate alternatives when arriving at correct, but still uncertain, solutions. Cognitive heuristics have not yet been explicitly incorporated into their model, but they seem especially relevant. Reality anchors likely futures or possible pasts in anchoring and adjustment. People predict the future and retrospect the past via the simulation heuristic, and direction influences affect. Availability underlies both of these; judgments are based on how easily information comes to mind.

MAPPING THE ROUTE: IMAGINATION, GOALS, AND AFFECT MODEL

What types of mental simulations can serve functions related to social problem-solving theory and research? We outline the imagination, goals, and affect model (IgoA; pronounced "ego") model to further this understanding (see also Sanna, 2000; Sanna, Chang, et al., 2001; Sanna, Turley-Ames, & Meier, 1999; Sanna et al., 2003). It builds on ideas about cognitive heuristics that were presented previously in this chapter, including a focus on temporal orientation, comparisons over time, and simulation direction. The model also explicitly recognizes people's motives or goals, and *ego* refers to the degree that self-motives or goals are activated. The IGoA model is illustrated in Figure 8.1. Some mental simulations may be useful for social problem solving; other mental simulations might even be disruptive to social problem solving. In addition to their theoretical interest, knowledge of different types of simulations might be useful to practitioners and therapists (e.g., training people in the more constructive use of mental simulations).

Classification of Mental Simulations

We propose three underlying dimensions to mental simulations (see also Sanna et al., 2003, for discussion of the IGoA model). Examples of prototypical mental simulations conforming to our classification scheme are presented.

Basic Elements: Mental Simulation Dimensions

First, mental simulations can be goal-based or reactive. Klinger (1977) divided thoughts into respondent and operant. The former occur without

Event outcome

| | T_{-2} | T_{-1} | T_0 | T_{+1} |

	Reactive simulations		Goal-based simulations	
	Retrospective	Prospective	Retrospective	Prospective
Acquisitive	Reminiscing (upward)	Indulging (upward)	Mood-maintenance (downward)	Self-improvement (upward)
Aversive	Rumination (downward)	Catastrophizing (downward)	Mood-repair (downward)	Self-protection (upward)

Figure 8.1. The IGoA model and timing of events related to temporal biases. The predominant simulation direction is indicated in parentheses. Reactive simulations involve mental assimilation, and goal-based simulations involve mental contrasting.

premeditation and involve shifts away from goal-directed tasks. The latter are goal-based (Sanna, Chang, et al., 2001; Taylor & Schneider, 1989). Second, mental simulations can be prospective or retrospective. Prospective simulations are exemplified by prefactuals of "what may be" (Sanna, 1996, 1999). One could forecast losing retirement savings or being ecstatic while playing shortstop for the New York Yankees. Retrospective simulations are exemplified by counterfactuals, as described. Third, simulations can be acquisitive or aversive. Acquisitive refers to obtaining or retaining positives; aversive refers to avoiding or protecting from negatives (Arkin & Shepperd, 1989; see also Higgins, 1998).

What Is, What Was, and What May Be:
Mental Assimilation and Contrasting

We suggest that mental assimilation and contrasting determine how life events influence mental simulations. Earlier research emphasized contrasting, following anchor and adjustment and simulation heuristics. For example, counterfactual and prefactual simulations involve comparing realities with alternatives. Oettingen, Pak, and Schnetter (2001) proposed that comparing futures with the present underlies goal-setting, a mental contrasting. We extend this reasoning to all goal-based mental simulations; each involves a contrast with reality. Reactive simulations do not involve contrasts with reality to the same degree. People instead "indulge" in free fantasies by focusing on the future, without regard to reality (see also McMullen, 1997; Oettingen, 1996). We extend this reasoning to all reactive mental simulations; each focuses on the future or past without reality contrasts, a mental assimilation.

Goal-Based Simulations: Potential Social Problem-Solving Functions

Goal-based mental simulations outlined to the right in Figure 8.1 are most closely allied with constructive and effective social problem solving as proposed in D'Zurilla and Goldfried's (1971) model. There are several types, and they can serve diverse functions.

Self-Improvement

Generating alternatives can be useful for goal-attainment. People can improve traits, abilities, health status, or well-being (Collins, 1996). For example, cancer patients focus on better alternatives to improve coping (Wood, Taylor, & Lichtman, 1985), and people mentally simulate better realities when preparing for the future (Sanna, 1996). We propose that self-improvement is prospective, acquisitive, and goal-based. It involves a contrast with present realties, as does the original view of mental contrasting (Oettingen et al., 2001).

Self-Protection

People generate alternatives prospectively to protect themselves from potential failure or to "brace for loss" (Shepperd, Findley-Klein, Kwavruck, Walker, & Perez, 2000; Shepperd, Ouelette, & Fernandez, 1996). Mentally simulating how the worst may transpire can mitigate the sting of failure should it occur. Upward prefactuals can help people brace for failure (Sanna, 1999; Sanna & Meier, 2000). We propose that self-protection is prospective, aversive, and goal-based; it also involves an explicit contrast with the present.

Mood-Maintenance

Happy people preserve positive affect mood-maintenance (Isen, 1987). People select information that propagates good moods (Wegener & Petty, 1994). Happy people also generate greater numbers of downward counterfactuals and report high enjoyment in doing so (Sanna, Meier, & Wegner, 2001). We propose that mood-maintenance is retrospective, goal-based, and that it involves contrasting pleasant realities with worse alternatives to perpetuate positive affective states.

Mood-Repair

People in bad moods try to regain positive affect, or mood-repair. They recall favorable information about the self (Parrott & Sabini, 1990) or help others (Schaller & Cialdini, 1990). People also generate downward counterfactuals to mood-repair (Sanna, Meier, & Turley-Ames, 1998; Sanna et al., 1999). We propose that mood-repair is retrospective, goal-based, and that it involves contrasting negative realities with worse alternatives to reinstate positive affective states.

Reactive Simulations: Less Purposeful Imaginings

Reactive mental simulations are to the left in Figure 8.1. The main focus of D'Zurilla and Goldfried's (1971) model is on how thinking about alternatives can be useful for social problem solving. However, in many cases, quite the opposite of being useful for solving problems, mental simulations can sometimes be problematic. There are several types.

Catastrophizing

Catastrophizing entails simulating a variety of negative "what if" scenarios (Kendall & Ingram, 1987) and "worry" about how bad things may transpire. Progress toward problem solving is unlikely as there is an internal dialogue characterized by problem-specific pessimism, feelings of inadequacy, despair, and hopelessness. Catastrophizing is linked through lifestyles to negative events (Peterson, Seligman, Yurko, Martin, & Friedman, 1998). We view catastrophizing as prospective, aversive, and reactive; it occurs via mental assimilation.

Rumination

Ruminations are persistent or reoccurring thoughts about past events that focus on negatives or are associated with bad moods (Nolen-Hoeksema, 1996): For instance, men who lost a partner to AIDS did not think about goals, nor about solving problems; they simply thought repeatedly about lost loved ones. Ruminations are respondent or intrusive (Klinger, 1977). We suggest that ruminations are retrospective, aversive, and do not entail a contrast with a present state—that is, they involve mental assimilation.

Indulging

Oettingen et al. (2001) found people can look to the future without specific goals, which they called indulging. They think about desired futures without contrasts with the present and "enjoy the desired future in the here and now" (Oettingen et al. 2001, p. 737; see also Oettingen, 1996). People can assimilate upward simulations (McMullen, 1997; Sanna, 1997, 2000) to indulge. We propose that indulging is prospective, acquisitive, reactive, and occurs via mental assimilation.

Reminiscing

People reminisce by thinking about positive aspects of their lives with a focus on past accomplishments, positive events, or successes (Strack, Schwarz, & Gschneidinger, 1985). People who reminisce and assimilate thoughts to their current state experience increased sense of well-being (Strack et al., 1985; see also McMullen, 1997; Sanna, 1997). We propose that reminiscing is retrospective, reactive, and involves assimilating upward, or positive, thoughts while focusing only on the past.

Summary: Various Mental Simulations and Social Problem Solving

People can use various types of mental simulations when generating alternatives while social problem solving, as outlined in the IGoA model. Goal-based mental simulations are closely allied with D'Zurilla and Goldfried's (1971) social problem-solving functions. There are several types. People can prepare for future events (self-improvement), brace for loss (self-protection), alleviate bad moods (mood-repair), or maintain good moods (mood-maintenance). Reactive simulations are less aligned with social problem solving, and can at times even be problematic. Knowledge of various types of simulations, including their functions, might be useful to theorists, researchers, and practitioners and therapists.

TIMING MATTERS: BIASES IN FORESIGHT AND HINDSIGHT

Shackleton's earlier led expedition, the *Nimrod,* attempted to reach the South Pole, but fell short by 97 miles. Two years later, Roald Amundsen accomplished that feat in 1911, and just days before a group headed by Robert Scott.

Timing matters. As depicted in Figure 8.1, timing is also important to social problem solving, and there are several biases and errors that may occur that should be accounted for in any model. T_0 indicates the real or expected occurrence of an event; T_{-2} and T_{-1} precede the event; T_{+1} follows the event.

Confidence Changes

People are less confident in success when events draw near (T_{-1}) than at a more distant time (T_{-2}). Participants taking an immediate test were less confident than those taking a test in four weeks (Nisan, 1972; see also Gilovich, Kerr, & Medvec, 1993). Similarly, college seniors were more muted in estimated first-job salaries than sophomores and juniors (Shepperd et al., 1996, 2000). From a social problem-solving perspective, it is important to recognize that people's confidence decreases as the "moment of truth" approaches. The blushing bride who was supremely confident in her partner at engagement may have "cold feet" on wedding day, or the student who was sure when choosing a university is not so sure at enrollment time.

Planning Fallacy

People underestimate time needed to complete tasks when predicting distally (T_{-2}) relative to the actual time of task completion (T_{-1} or T_0). This planning fallacy (Buehler, Griffin, & Ross, 1994; Kahneman & Tversky, 1979) is observed in settings ranging from household chores to school assignments. When estimating book and chapter completion, for example, the plan may have seemed easily doable back when the contract was signed more than two years earlier and perhaps not as easy as the deadlines approached (did we just say that?). The planning fallacy "involves a process of mental simulation that focuses on future planning but neglects past experience" (Buehler, Griffin, & MacDonald, 1997, p. 239). Misestimating completion time can have obvious impact on social problem solving.

Affective Forecasting

People at T_{-2} predict that emotional reactions to events will be more intense than actually turns out to be the case at T_{+1} (Gilbert, Pinel, Wilson, Blumberg, & Wheatley, 1998). Overpredicting future emotional impact is one of the most prevalent biases in affective forecasting (Wilson & Gilbert, 2003). Voters and students thought they would be happier or sadder after preferred candidates or teams won or lost, respectively; yet no differences in happiness were observed between supporters of winners and losers when asked afterward (Wilson, Wheatley, Meyers, Gilbert, & Axom, 2000; see also Loewenstein & Schkade, 1999). People do feel good when good things happen and bad when bad things happen, but the fact that actually experienced affective reactions do not have their anticipated impact may have important implications for social problem solving by directing people's choice of alternatives.

Hindsight Bias

People believe they "knew all along" what would happen once event outcomes are known (T_0 or T_{+1}), even though their pre-event predictions

(T_{-2}) indicate otherwise (Fischhoff, 1975). This hindsight bias has been documented in varied domains, including political events, medical diagnoses, and labor disputes (see Christensen-Szalanski & Willham, 1991). Moreover, the past may be viewed as particularly inevitable after successes compared to failures (Louie, 1999; Mark & Mellor, 1991). Event outcomes are judged more likely once outcomes are known than when outcome information is unknown; the implication for social problem solving is that people may be unable to effectively learn from past experiences (Fischhoff, 1982).

Summary: Temporal Biases and Social Problem Solving

Temporal biases similarly have not been related to the social problem-solving model, but they clearly deserve more attention. People change confidence as performances approach, are overly optimistic in estimated task completion, are unable to accurately predict emotional reactions, and believe they knew all along what would happen.

CONCLUSION

D'Zurilla and Goldfried (1971) described making available and generating alternatives as critical to their social problem-solving model. In this chapter, we connected this to work in the areas of cognitive heuristics, types of mental simulation, and temporal biases, each of which are concerned with the generation of alternatives. Somewhat surprisingly, these areas had not yet been related to the social problem-solving model. However, when viewed in a more consolidated light, researchers of these topics may achieve greater insights. We conclude by discussing a few other implications for theory, research, and training.

Social problem solvers use mental simulation, moving forward from present to future or backward from present to past. In this way, people navigate the route from current states to final states that are solutions to problems. Generating alternatives is a pivotal juncture on this course, which is necessary to move to later stages in the social problem-solving model— namely, decision making and verification (D'Zurilla & Goldfried, 1971; D'Zurilla & Nezu, 1980; D'Zurilla & Sheedy, 1992). Because few of us claim either the mystical prescience of Nostradamus or the wisdom of Solomon, we often use cognitive heuristics and mental simulation of alternatives, and we are subject to various temporal biases when deciding how to act. These can lead to effective or maladaptive decision making, depending on particular circumstances.

Can anything make effective decision making more likely? D'Zurilla and Goldfried (1971) argued that "a situation is considered problematic if no effective response alternative is immediately available to the individual confronted with the situation" (p. 108). We suspect that this happens in part because people are experiencing reactive simulations (catastrophizing, rumination, indulging, and reminiscing) as identified by the IGoA model. It would be the job of successful therapy to move people from these reactive simulations to more goal-based ones. The IGoA model also illustrates how social problem-solving functions, such as self-improvement, self-protection, mood-maintenance, and mood-repair, can be served by mental simulations (see also Sanna et al., 2003). These are most closely aligned with the social problem-solving model (D'Zurilla & Chang, 1996; D'Zurilla & Goldfried, 1971; D'Zurilla & Nezu, 1990) but go even further by identifying different problem-solving functions. Future research directly testing connections between these previously independent research areas should prove interesting.

Using mental simulations to test possible futures or scrutinize possible pasts can leave social problem solvers sailing through balmy waters or frozen at a dead end. This is because decision makers are subject to a variety of heuristics and biases. Relating these directly to the social problem-solving model is another avenue that appears particularly intriguing. People become less confident as performances approach (confidence changes), underestimate how long task completion will take (planning fallacy), overpredict emotional reactions to events (affective forecasting), and emphasize known outcomes in lieu of what might have happened (hindsight bias). We speculate that *availability* is an important part of the answer when debiasing people's decisions. Evidence consistent with this reasoning was found for the hindsight bias (Sanna, Schwarz, & Small, 2002; Sanna, Schwarz, & Stocker, 2002). Ease of thought generation may be similarly responsible for the other temporal biases, and availability is known to underlie anchor and adjustment and simulation heuristics. Incorporating these heuristics and biases into the social problem-solving model may allow for a more accurate prediction of behaviors, and may perhaps lead to more effective therapies.

Mental simulations are useful for social problem solving because they allow people to predict results of behaviors that could be implemented, develop expectations about how circumstances might evolve, detect barriers that may impede execution of actions, and assess how experiences might have transpired instead. Incorporating cognitive heuristics, mental simulation, and temporal biases into the social problem-solving model may help promote the state of scientific knowledge in this area, moving future theory, research, and training along in ways that are even more productive. We attempted to begin to make such connections in this chapter. Clearly, there is a lot more to be learned. However, if the journey is charted carefully, there is also much to be gained by explicitly connecting research in these areas. To paraphrase Neil Armstrong, another famous 20th-century explorer, even the smallest steps may eventually lead to giant leaps.

REFERENCES

Alexander, C. (1998). *The Endurance: Shackleton's legendary Antarctic expedition.* New York: Knopf.

Arkin, R. M., & Shepperd, J. A. (1989). Self-presentation styles in organizations. In R. A. Giacalone & P. Rosenfeld (Eds.), *Impression management in the organization* (pp. 125–139). Hillsdale, NJ: Erlbaum.

Buehler, R., Griffin, D., & MacDonald, H. (1997). The role of motivated reasoning in optimistic time predictions. *Personality and Social Psychology Bulletin, 23,* 238–247.

Buehler, R., Griffin, D., & Ross, M. (1994). Exploring the "planning fallacy": Why people underestimate their task completion times. *Journal of Personality and Social Psychology, 67,* 366–381.

Chapman, G. B., & Johnson, E. J. (1994). The limits of anchoring. *Journal of Behavioral Decision Making, 7,* 223–242.

Christensen-Szalanski, J. J. J., & Willham, C. F. (1991). The hindsight bias: A meta-analysis. *Organizational Behavior and Human Decision Processes, 48,* 147–168.

Collins, R. L. (1996). For better or worse: The impact of upward social comparison on self-evaluations. *Psychological Bulletin, 119,* 51–69.

D'Zurilla, T. J., & Chang, E. C. (1996). The relations between problem solving and coping. *Cognitive Therapy and Research, 19,* 547–562.

D'Zurilla, T. J., & Goldfried, M. R. (1971). Problem solving and behavior modification. *Journal of Abnormal Psychology, 78,* 107–126.

D'Zurilla, T. J., & Nezu, A. M. (1980). A study of the generation-of-alternatives process in social problem solving. *Cognitive Therapy and Research, 4,* 67–72.

D'Zurilla, T. J., & Nezu, A. M. (1990). Development and preliminary evaluation of the Social Problem-Solving Inventory. *Psychological Assessment, 2,* 156–163.

D'Zurilla, T. J., & Sheedy, C. F. (1992). Relations between social problem-solving ability and subsequent level of psychological stress in college students. *Journal of Personality and Social Psychology, 61,* 841–846.

Einhorn, H. J., & Hogarth, R. M. (1981). Behavioral decision theory: Processes of judgment and choice. *Annual Review of Psychology, 32,* 53–88.

Epley, N., & Gilovich, T. (2001). Putting adjustment back in the anchoring and adjustment heuristic: Differential processing of self-generated and experimenter provided anchors. *Psychological Science, 12,* 391–396.

Fischhoff, B. (1975). Hindsight–foresight: The effect of outcome knowledge on judgment under uncertainty. *Journal of Experimental Psychology: Human Perception and Performance, 1,* 288–299.

Fischhoff, B. (1982). Debiasing. In D. Kahneman, P. Slovic, & A. Tversky (Eds.), *Judgment under uncertainty: Heuristics and biases* (pp. 422–444). New York: Cambridge University Press.

Gilbert, D. T., Pinel, E. C., Wilson, T. D., Blumberg, S. J., & Wheatley, T. P. (1998). Immune neglect: A source of durability bias in affective forecasting. *Journal of Personality and Social Psychology, 59,* 617–638.

Gilovich, T., Kerr, M., & Medvec, V. H. (1993). Effect of temporal perspective on subjective confidence. *Journal of Personality and Social Psychology, 64,* 552–560.

Higgins, E. T. (1998). Promotion and prevention: Regulatory focus as a motivational principle. In M. P. Zanna (Ed.), *Advances in experimental social psychology* (Vol. 23, pp. 305–331). New York: Academic Press.

Isen, A. M. (1987). Affect, cognition, and social behavior. In L. Berkowitz (Ed.), *Advances in experimental social psychology* (Vol. 20, pp. 203–253). San Diego, CA: Academic Press.

Kahneman, D., & Miller, D. T. (1986). Norm theory: Comparing reality to its alternatives. *Psychological Review, 93,* 136–153.

Kahneman, D., & Tversky, A. (1979). Intuitive prediction: Biases and corrective procedures. *Management Science, 12,* 313–327.

Kahneman, D., & Tversky, A. (1982). The simulation heuristic. In D. Kahneman, P. Slovic, & A. Tversky (Eds.), *Judgment under uncertainty: Heuristics and biases* (pp. 201–208). New York: Cambridge University Press.

Kendall, P. C., & Ingram, R. E. (1987). The future for cognitive assessment of anxiety: Let's get specific. In L. Michaelson & L. M. Ascher (Eds.), *Anxiety and stress disorders: Cognitive–behavioral assessment and treatment* (pp. 89–104). New York: Guilford Press.

Klinger, E. (1977). *Meaning and void: Inner experience and the incentives in people's lives.* Minneapolis: University of Minnesota Press.

Loewenstein, G. F., & Schkade, D. (1999). Wouldn't it be nice? Predicting future feelings. In D. Kahneman, E. Diener, & N. Schwarz (Eds.), *Well-being: The foundations of hedonic psychology* (pp. 85–105). New York: Russell Sage Foundation.

Louie, T. A. (1999). Decision makers' hindsight bias after receiving favorable and unfavorable feedback. *Journal of Applied Psychology, 84,* 29–41.

Mark, M. M., & Mellor, S. (1991). Effect of self-relevance of an event on hindsight bias: The foreseeability of a layoff. *Journal of Applied Psychology, 76,* 569–577.

McMullen, M. N. (1997). Affective assimilation and contrast in counterfactual thinking. *Journal of Experimental Social Psychology, 33,* 77–100.

Miller, D. T., Turnbull, W., & McFarland, C. (1990). Counterfactual thinking and social perception: Thinking about what might have been. In M. P. Zanna (Ed.), *Advances in experimental social psychology* (Vol. 23, pp. 305–331). New York: Academic Press.

Nezu, A., & D'Zurilla, T. J. (1980). Effects of problem definition and formulation on the generation of alternatives in the social problem-solving process. *Cognitive Therapy and Research, 5,* 265–271.

Nisan, M. (1972). Dimension of time in relation to choice behavior and achievement orientation. *Journal of Personality and Social Psychology, 21,* 175–182.

Nolen-Hoeksema, S. (1996). Chewing the cud and other ruminations. In R. S. Wyer (Ed.), *Ruminative thoughts: Advances in social cognition* (Vol. 9, pp. 135–144). Mahwah, NJ: Erlbaum.

Oettingen, G. (1996). Positive fantasy and motivation. In P. M. Gollwitzer & J. A. Bargh (Eds.), *The psychology of action: Linking cognition and motivation to behavior* (pp. 236–259). New York: Guilford Press.

Oettingen, G., Pak, H., & Schnetter, K. (2001). Self-regulation and goal-setting: Turning free fantasies about the future into binding goals. *Journal of Personality and Social Psychology, 80,* 736–753.

Orde-Lees, T. (2002). *Diary of a survivor.* Retrieved July 3, 2002, from http://www.pbs.org/wgbh/nova/shackelton/1914/diary/htm

Parrott, W. G., & Sabini, J. (1990). Mood and memory under natural conditions: Evidence for mood incongruent recall. *Journal of Personality and Social Psychology, 59,* 321–336.

Peterson, C., Seligman, M. E. P., Yurko, K. H., Martin, L. R., & Friedman, H. S. (1998). Catastrophizing and untimely death. *Psychological Science, 9,* 127–130.

Roese, N. J. (1997). Counterfactual thinking. *Psychological Bulletin, 121,* 133–148.

Sanna, L. J. (1996). Defensive pessimism, optimism, and simulating alternatives: Some ups and downs of prefactual and counterfactual thinking. *Journal of Personality and Social Psychology, 71,* 1020–1036.

Sanna, L. J. (1997). Self-efficacy and counterfactual thinking: Up a creek with and without a paddle. *Personality and Social Psychology Bulletin, 23,* 654–666.

Sanna, L. J. (1999). Mental simulations, affect, and subjective confidence: Timing is everything. *Psychological Science, 10,* 339–345.

Sanna, L. J. (2000). Mental simulation, affect, and personality: A conceptual framework. *Current Directions in Psychological Science, 9,* 168–173.

Sanna, L. J., Chang, E. C., & Meier, S. (2001). Counterfactual thinking and self-motives. *Personality and Social Psychology Bulletin, 27,* 1023–1034.

Sanna, L. J., & Meier, S. (2000). Looking for clouds in a silver lining: Self-esteem, mental simulations, and temporal confidence changes. *Journal of Research in Personality, 34,* 236–251.

Sanna, L. J., Meier, S., & Turley-Ames, K. J. (1998). Mood, self-esteem, and counterfactuals: Externally attributed moods limit self-enhancement strategies. *Social Cognition, 16,* 267–286.

Sanna, L. J., Meier, S., & Wegner, E. C. (2001). Counterfactuals and motivation: Mood as input to affective enjoyment and preparation. *British Journal of Social Psychology, 40,* 235–256.

Sanna, L. J., Schwarz, N., & Small, E. M. (2002). Accessibility experiences and the hindsight bias: I knew it all along versus it could never have happened. *Memory and Cognition, 30,* 1288–1296.

Sanna, L. J., Schwarz, N., & Stocker, S. L. (2002). When debiasing backfires: Accessible content and accessibility experiences in debiasing hindsight. *Journal of Experimental Psychology: Learning, Memory, and Cognition, 28,* 497–502.

Sanna, L. J., Stocker, S. L., & Clarke, J. A. (2003). Rumination, imagination, and personality: Specters of the past and future in the present. In E. C. Chang & L. J. Sanna (Eds.), *Virtue, vice, and personality: The complexity of behavior* (pp. 105–124). Washington, DC: American Psychological Association.

Sanna, L. J., Turley-Ames, K. J., & Meier, S. (1999). Mood, self-esteem, and simulated alternatives: Thought-provoking affective influences on counterfactual direction. *Journal of Personality and Social Psychology, 76,* 543–558.

Schaller, M., & Cialdini, R. B. (1990). Happiness, sadness, and helping: A motivational integration. In E. T. Higgins & R. M. Sorrentino (Eds.), *Handbook of motivation and cognition: Foundations of social behavior* (Vol. 2, pp. 265–296). New York: Guilford Press.

Schwarz, N. (1998). Accessible content and accessibility experiences: The interplay of declarative and experiential information in judgment. *Personality and Social Psychology Review, 2,* 87–99.

Shepperd, J. A., Findley-Klein, C., Kwavnick, K. D., Walker, D., & Perez, S. (2000). Bracing for loss. *Journal of Personality and Social Psychology, 78,* 620–634.

Shepperd, J. A., Ouellette, J. A., & Fernandez, J. K. (1996). Abandoning unrealistic optimism: Performance estimates and the temporal proximity of self-relevant feedback. *Journal of Personality and Social Psychology, 70,* 844–855.

Strack, F., & Mussweiler, T. (1997). Explaining the enigmatic anchoring effect: Mechanisms of selective accessibility. *Journal of Personality and Social Psychology, 73,* 437–446.

Strack, F., Schwarz, N., & Gschneidinger, E. (1985). Happiness and reminiscing: The role of time perspective, affect, and mode of thinking. *Journal of Personality and Social Psychology, 49,* 1460–1469.

Taylor, S. E., Pham, L. B., Rivkin, I. D., & Armor, D. A. (1998). Harnessing the imagination: Mental simulation, self-regulation, and coping. *American Psychologist, 53,* 429–439.

Taylor, S. E., & Schneider, S. K. (1989). Coping and the simulation of events. *Social Cognition, 7,* 174–194.

Tversky, A., & Kahneman, D. (1973). Availability: A heuristic for judging probability and frequency. *Cognitive Psychology, 5,* 207–232.

Wegener, D. T., & Petty, R. E. (1994). Mood management across affective states: The hedonic contingency hypothesis. *Journal of Personality and Social Psychology, 66,* 1034–1048.

Wilson, T. D., & Gilbert, D. T. (2003). Affective forecasting. In M. P. Zanna (Ed.), *Advances in experimental social psychology* (Vol. 35, pp. 345–411). San Diego, CA: Academic Press.

Wilson, T. D., Wheatley, T., Meyers, J. M., Gilbert, D. T., & Axom, D. (2000). Focalism: A source of durability bias in affective forecasting. *Journal of Personality and Social Psychology, 78,* 821–836.

Wood, J. V., Taylor, S. E., & Lichtman, R. R. (1985). Social comparison in adjustment to breast cancer. *Journal of Personality and Social Psychology, 49,* 1169–1183.

III

PROBLEM-SOLVING
TRAINING AND THERAPY

9

PROBLEM-SOLVING TRAINING FOR CHILDREN AND ADOLESCENTS

MARIANNE FRAUENKNECHT AND DAVID R. BLACK

This chapter focuses on problem-solving training (PST) as the *sine qua non* of behavior change programs for youth. PST teaches children *how* rather than *what* to think, so they can adopt appropriate social solutions on their own to solve idiosyncratic inter- and intrapersonal problems (Pelligrini & Urbain, 1985). At the core of PST is social problem solving (SPS). SPS concepts and skills are transtheoretical and transbehavioral, cutting across divergent treatment approaches and a variety of social problems. SPS may be the single most important social skill that a young person can acquire.

PREVIOUS REVIEWS OF PROBLEM-SOLVING TRAINING RESEARCH WITH CHILDREN AND ADOLESCENTS

The findings of all previous composite reviews of PST research for youth are presented. The impact of PST programs designed to mediate behavioral problems has had moderate success. Urbain and Kendall (1980) found in a review of 14 studies that early PST research was encouraging in spite of the problems associated with methods (i.e., lack of treatment control groups, behavioral observations, and follow-up evaluation). *All* of the studies that measured SPS skill attainment reported increases among treatment groups regardless of length of individual sessions and interventions. The treatments of long duration were the most effective at changing behavior (treatment lengths from 225 minutes to 1,380 minutes). Potential Type III (implementation) errors as well as problems in research design limit the findings.

Pellegrini and Urbain (1985) reviewed primary, secondary, and tertiary PST prevention programs that included two criteria: (a) training in the process of interpersonal problem solving and (b) evaluation of PST on improvements in peer relationships and other related variables (e.g., impulsivity). In total, this review critiqued 19 different programs. Longitudinal studies revealed that interpersonal PST prevented or delayed the development of social adjustment problems among young children. Secondary prevention programs for maladjusted children that demonstrated the greatest improvements in SPS skills also demonstrated the greatest behavioral gains. The authors concluded there was a need for improvement in research methods related to PST because many of the studies lacked attention-control groups, which hampered the ability to determine whether changes were actually a result of treatment.

Tisdelle and St. Lawrence (1986) conducted one of the most thorough reviews of PST research. They reported similar conclusions and methodological problems as Pellegrini and Urbain (1985). Problems elucidated were those related to the following elements: (a) use of instruments with inadequately developed psychometric evaluations, (b) lack of *in vivo* behavioral assessments, (c) no longitudinal follow-up assessments, (d) no social validation of clinical samples with normal samples, (e) lack of examination of the generalization of SPS skills to other problem situations, (f) inability to determine which training strategies produced favorable results, and (g) failure to distinguish the impact of SPS skills from other social competencies used during training procedures. The authors, although supporting the theoretical potential of PST for clinical populations of adolescents, suggested bolstering PST research efforts by attending to these various methodological issues.

Coleman, Wheeler, and Webber (1993) conducted a meta-analysis of nine PST studies published since 1980. The meta-analysis results showed that posttreatment improvements on cognitive SPS measures of knowledge and skills were significant. Studies that especially involved youth with more severe disorders demonstrated significant cognitive gains. However, when evaluating the impact on performance deficits by observing the actual use of SPS skills for behavioral outcomes, fewer than half of the students significantly improved when compared to a control group; none of students with the most severe mental disorders demonstrated the ability to use SPS in actual real-life situations. It is not surprising that those with the most severe disorders did not perform well because SPS is a sophisticated, cognitive strategy that requires concentration that many mental disorders make difficult.

The conclusions of Coleman et al.'s (1993) meta-analysis were consistent with the other reviews previously described, which confirmed the assumption that PST is insufficient by itself to produce social competency, mediate undesirable social behaviors among clinical populations, and generalize to a variety of behaviors and settings. The authors did, however, recommend that, when applied to school settings, the preliminary assessment of students' SPS skills is critical so that individualized training can identify and improve specific repertoire deficits. Once repertoire deficits are enhanced, individualized programs can ascertain and correct performance deficits by assessing the quality of solutions as well as combining the metacognitive strategies of SPS within the context of other situations and relative to the need for other specific social skill amelioration (e.g., assertive communication). The review also emphasized the need for fidelity to the training protocol, which in many studies was a determinant of the program's success or failure. In addition, training that allows for generalization of skills to other situations, people, and settings has become the primary goal of social competence interventions in general (Hansen, Nangle, & Meyer, 1998).

Several key points are abstracted from these reviews as related to "best processes" for program design and implementation. All reviews provide evidence that asymptomatic and symptomatic children and adolescents can learn specific SPS skills. Beyond that, the contention appears to be the lack of consistent and repetitive success of programs to change behavior as well as to enable youth who have improved their skills to generalize the application of SPS to other problematic situations. Both issues may be the result of Type III errors related to program implementation. Professionals who implement PST programs need training and monitoring and to be reminded about the importance of strictly adhering to a pedagogically sound protocol.

Another error related to program design indicated by these reviews suggests children who improve SPS skills may select inappropriate solutions to problems such as aggression (Olexa & Forman, 1984). An effective SPS intervention would guide children to identify *decisional criteria* during the *consequence prediction* step (Frauenknecht & Black, 2003). The consideration of appropriate and *given* decisional criteria (e.g., healthy, legal, and causes "no harm" to self or others) for each of the listed alternatives should positively influence the selection of a solution. Programs that result in increased aggressive behavior should carefully explore the guided approaches used to teach young people *how* to make appropriate decisions.

Another possible program design error is equating decision making and SPS. There are many instances in the adolescent SPS literature where decision-making models are equated with SPS models. This has created confusion and misrepresentation of the scope of SPS theory, programs, and research. Although decision making is one of several specific competencies involved in solving problems, the two constructs are *not* synonymous. Decision-making skills are required during the SPS process when selecting a problem to manage, and consequences of options are evaluated or weighed according to the decisional criteria that are identified as critical to the solution. Decision making also is used when the most salient solution must be selected, which results from predicting and weighing consequences. Although decision-making skills are critical to the SPS process, they are not equivalent and should not be regarded as such in program and research design.

DEVELOPMENT OF BEST PROCESSES FOR SOCIAL PROBLEM-SOLVING PROGRAM DESIGN AND IMPLEMENTATION

The SPS intervention research is summarized next and supports the establishment of "best processes" in programs. Best processes are those practices that have been empirically and repeatedly tested in applied settings and research supports as effective (Black, 2002).

Interpersonal Cognitive Problem Solving or "I Can Problem Solve"

Spivack, Platt, and Shure (1976) discussed the Interpersonal Cognitive Problem Solving or "I Can Problem Solve" (ICPS) curricula for children in preschool, kindergarten, and primary grades. They theorized in the early 1970s that social adjustment and the quality of social relationships depended on one's capability to cope with interpersonal problems, and how well one coped with personal problems depended on a complex combination of cognitive and emotional factors (Shure, 1997). They postulated that if children could learn cognitive ICPS skills that could be generalized to a variety of situations, they could independently apply this process to cope with diverse problems that occur everyday (Pellegrini & Urbain, 1985). Although the simplicity of these assumptions has been challenged (Olexa & Forman, 1984; Tisdelle & St. Lawrence, 1986), some of the earliest and most successful PST programs developed by Spivack and Shure continue to be used (Center for the Study and Prevention of Violence, 2002). Their ICPS program focuses on teaching children prerequisite language and empathy skills in addition to the meta-cognitive SPS processes of alternative-solution thinking, consequential thinking, and means–ends thinking. Also provided are specific training techniques and program assessment.

Prerequisite Skills

Training concepts from Piaget's conservation theory are applied in ICPS, which suggest that the meaning of words and language used by children are requisite and as important to learning cognitive skills as the skills training itself (Shure, 1997). For example, in ICPS training, children are taught word pairs such as "and/or," "same/different," "is/is not," "if/then," and "before/after." Words that describe feelings (glad, sad, mad, fear, calm) are taught and associated with behaviors (e.g., "If he is smiling, then he is happy"). In addition to language skills, ICPS also includes sensitivity training, applied to interpersonal problems that involve another person's feelings or perspectives (e.g., personal actions can hurt others). An additional prerequisite skill also taught to children around the fourth grade is *dynamic orientation,* or the ability to understand another's motive for a behavior so that one can decide how to respond appropriately (Shure, 1997).

Alternative-Solution Thinking

Younger children such as those in preschool and kindergarten can be taught alternative-solution thinking. Young children (e.g., 4- and 5-year-olds) have the ability to think of separate alternative solutions to interpersonal problems. For example, they can comprehend that if their idea is not a good one, they can think of another idea (Shure, 1997). Children are taught to think of as many ways to solve problems as they can using developmentally appropriate teaching strategies such as pictures, storyboards, and puppets, and to recognize the differences and similarities among solutions to a given problem. In fact, Shure (1993) and colleagues have found that "the most powerful ICPS mediator in young children appears to be the ability to conceptualize multiple solutions to interpersonal problems" or the skill of alternative generation (p. 57).

Consequential Thinking

Once the skill of alternative-solution thinking is developed, younger children develop consequential thinking by enhancing their understanding of causality (Shure, 1997). For example, the focus is on teaching children that one person's behavior affects another person's feelings or actions. The comprehension of cause–effect connections allows children to determine what might happen after they implement one of the solutions identified (Shure, 1997). This skill eventually expands to thinking of multiple consequences for the same solution and helps the child determine if a solution for a given problem is good or bad. Training for consequential thinking also involves solution–consequence pairing—in other words, given one solution, children immediately identify a possible consequence that is followed by another solution–consequence pair. This technique teaches children to choose the best solution from a number of solutions based on the most probable consequences. As children get older (8 or 9), they are asked to think of sequenced steps toward an interpersonal goal, a skill called means–ends thinking.

Means–Ends Thinking

Spivack and colleagues (1976) are known for coining the term "means–ends thinking." Shure (1997) described this process as the ability "to plan sequenced steps [means] toward an interpersonal goal [ends], to recognize potential obstacles that could interfere with reaching that goal, and to appreciate that problem solving takes time" (p. 169). Because higher order cognitive processes of means–ends thinking typically do not emerge until middle childhood, it is more effectively introduced at about the fourth grade or beyond (Pellegrini & Urbain, 1985). Storyboards are a technique used to develop means–ends thinking and help children identify the step-by-step processes necessary to solve a problem, starting with identifying the outcome or goal of the selected problem (what *should* be happening as opposed to what currently *is* happening). Children are then instructed to think of means to achieve the goal (alternative-solution thinking), the potential obstacles that would prevent them from achieving the goal (consequential thinking), and how these obstacles could be managed (goal setting). Just as important is the concept of time; for example, children learn that certain times are better for taking action than others to solve a problem and that it may take time to realize their goal and problem resolution.

Training Techniques

Training techniques that Shure (1993) included in ICPS training are *dialoguing* and *distancing*. Dialoguing trains teachers and parents to use the SPS process when real-life problems occur in the classroom or home. In fact, this training demonstrated the greatest improvement in behavior change among children. The following are five principles of effective dialoguing (Shure, 1993, p. 56):

> (a) both the child and the adult must be able to identify the problem, (b) the child's first solution (e.g., hitting) must not be considered the initial problem, (c) the problem identified "must remain relevant to the child and not shifted to suit the adult," (d) the adult must allow the child to solve the problem, or guide the child to the solution, and (e) the emphasis should be on how the child thinks rather than on the child's specific solutions or consequences.

After dialoguing occurs, distancing (adopted from Sigel, 1985) is introduced. Distancing is when an adult poses open-ended questions to the child, which enables the child to consider potential options themselves to a problem they are confronting (Bruene-Butler, Hampson, Elias, Clabby, & Schuyler, 1997).

The most recent review of this program indicated that preschool, kindergarten, and first grade impulsive and inhibited students who were taught ICPS in school had immediate gains as well as behavioral benefits that lasted a full year (Shure, 1993). Children taught ICPS in school by a teacher *and* at home by a parent displayed similar improvement in skills and behaviors. In addition, a dose–response relationship was found, in that children who were trained for two consecutive years in school (i.e., preschool and kindergarten) had superior skills in generating alternative solutions and consequential thinking than children trained only during one year, either in preschool or kindergarten. Similarly, children trained for one year at school and home demonstrated behavioral competence similar to those children trained by their teachers over two years and were able to generalize SPS skills from home to school (Shure, 1993).

Significant improvements in behavior were noted such as decreases in impulsivity and inhibition and increases in cooperation, concern for others in distress, and positive peer relations (Shure, 1997). Children trained in preschool and primary grades exhibited the fewest observed risk behaviors in the fourth grade. Alternative-solution thinking was the most significant skill linked to behavior change, because children who could identify separate alternative solutions were less likely to be impatient, overemotional, aggressive, withdrawn, unpopular, and to display a lack of empathy for others' feelings (Shure, 1997).

Improving Social-Awareness/Social Problem-Solving Project

Elias and colleagues (Elias & Clabby, 1988, 1992; Elias, Gara, Schuyler, Branden-Muller, & Sayette, 1991; Elias & Tobias, 1992) developed a skill-based, systematic, social-competence approach that emphasized self-control, social awareness and group participation, and critical-thinking processes. The school-based curriculum, called Improving Social-Awareness/Social Problem-Solving Project (ISA/SPS) was developed for elementary students and initiated with fourth graders to increase adjustment to middle school (Elias & Clabby, 1988). ISA/SPS skill development is organized into three phases: (a) readiness for decision making, (b) teaching the SPS/decision-making (DM) process, and (c) applying the SPS/DM process to *in vivo* situations (Bruene-Butler et al., 1997).

Readiness for Decision Making

This phase of the ISA/SPS program primarily includes the development of self-control and social awareness skills (Bruene-Butler et al., 1997; Elias & Tobias, 1992). Self-control skills involve the following: (a) controlling emotions and emotional reactions; (b) communicating, especially listening, following directions, being assertive, and communicating nonverbally; (c) focusing on tasks; and (d) staying calm (e.g., deep breathing relaxation). Social awareness skills teach young people peer acceptance and cooperative group participation. Specifically, these skills include the ability to communicate in such ways as sharing ideas and feelings; conversing; expressing appreciation; and asking for, giving of, and receiving help. Social awareness also includes accepting constructive criticism, looking at an issue from another perspective, choosing friends who are caring, and working cooperatively as a team (Elias & Tobias, 1992).

Teaching the Social Problem-Solving/Decision-Making Process

This phase of instruction uses the following eight steps to organize thinking (Bruene-Butler et al., 1997): (a) look for signs of different feelings (self and others); (b) tell yourself what the problem is; (c) decide on your goal; (d) think of as many solutions to the problem as you can; (e) think of what might happen next for each solution; (f) choose the best solution; (g) plan the solution and make a final check; and (h) try it and rethink it. This model is consistent with other SPS models that identify specific steps or components of a logical process used as an organizational system.

Applying the Social Problem-Solving/Decision-Making Process

This phase of the ISA/SPS program provides children with opportunities to apply the self-control and SPS/DM skills to *in vivo* social problems. Application training allows teachers to use *structured spontaneity* to infuse the SPS/DM model into their respective academic discipline using structured lessons (Elias et al., 1991). For example, an SPS lesson in health education might be called "Thinking About What We Hear and See in the Media," while another teacher integrates SPS into a lesson called "Problem Solving and Creative Writing" (Bruene-Butler et al., 1997; Elias & Tobias, 1992). This phase also provides training for teachers in the use of *facilitative questioning* or guided problem solving. This approach, much like dialoguing, uses question-asking skills to coach or prompt children to use a familiar SPS model to solve an *in vivo*, real-time problem, and is most effective when applied to actual social problems that provide teachable moments during class activities.

Program Assessment

The U.S. Department of Education evaluated the ISA/SPS program in 1989 for the National Diffusion Network and revalidated it again in 1995. During both reviews, claims for all three phases of the program were supported (Elias & Tobias, 1992). Students improved in readiness and self-control skills, especially the areas of interpersonal sensitivity and keeping calm during a problematic situation. Students improved in knowledge of SPS/DM skills, especially interpersonal perspective taking, understanding consequences, positive expectancies for problem solving, and means–ends thinking. For the application phase, teachers improved their ability to teach students SPS skills by effectively applying facilitative questioning during class.

More important are claims that learning SPS/DM skills would enable students to engage in prosocial and healthier behaviors. A longitudinal study was conducted that followed students who had previously received the ISA/SPS program during their fourth and fifth grades (Elias et al., 1991). The same students were reevaluated in grades 9 through 11 and compared to students who had not received the ISA/SPS program. Students trained to use SPS/DM skills demonstrated improved levels of prosocial behavior and reduced levels of self-destructive and antisocial behaviors (Elias et al., 1991). Self-report data specifically indicated that students who received the program reported lower rates than controls for alcohol and tobacco use, buying and providing alcohol for another person, vandalism, threatening or hitting others, and attacking others with intent to injure (Elias et al., 1991).

OTHER IMPROVING SOCIAL-AWARENESS/SOCIAL PROBLEM-SOLVING PROJECT PROGRAMS

While the ISA/SPS program has been developed, evaluated, and marketed for upper-elementary students, Elias and Clabby (1992) also have developed curricula for secondary students. At the middle level, SPS skills are infused into the core curriculum (i.e., science, math, language, and geography) as well as other school functions and activities (e.g., art, guidance, and after-school clubs). At the high school level, Clabby (1992) has designed a 32-lesson curriculum called *ASPIRE* that is based on the same SPS model and instructional phases as the elementary program. There is no indication that either of the secondary curricula have been evaluated.

The Coping Power Program

Preventive interventions have been developed for preadolescent children that are aimed at reducing and preventing aggression and other conduct problems such as substance use and delinquency (Crick & Dodge, 1994; Lochman & Dodge, 1994, 1998). The Coping Power Program (Lochman & Wells, 2002a, 2002b) consists of a child component that focuses on training in SPS and social skills and a parent component that focuses on behavioral parenting-skills training. This program has been evaluated in two major outcome studies focusing on aggressive preadolescent children (Lochman & Wells, 2002a, 2002b, 2003). In general, based on evaluations at postintervention and one-year follow-up, this program was found to produce significant preventive effects on delinquency, aggression, and substance use.

Linking the Interest of Families and Teachers Program

A similar preventive program based on the same social–cognitive problem-solving model is the Linking the Interest of Families and Teachers (LIFT) program (Reid, Eddy, Fetrow, & Stoolmiller, 1999), which also includes a child component focusing on SPS and social skills training and a parent component focusing on behavioral parenting skills. In addition, this program also includes a playground behavior-management component. In an outcome study focusing on elementary school children, this program was found to produce significant preventive effects on police arrests and alcohol use during the middle school years (Eddy, Reid, Stoolmiller, & Fetrow, 2003).

Although the results of these outcome studies are promising for the reduction and prevention of aggression and conduct problems in children and adolescents, no definite conclusions are possible concerning the specific effects of PST in these studies because of the multiple components in both intervention programs. Hence, future outcome studies are needed that use a dismantling design to assess and compare the effects of the different components.

COMMON ELEMENTS OF EFFECTIVE PROGRAMS

Based on the previous review and program summaries, a number of potential best-process elements are listed that are common to effective PST programs for children and adolescents. These components are categorized as instructor training, prerequisite skills, and instructional strategies.

Instructor Training

One advantage of integrating PST into school settings is the assumption that most teachers understand and apply instructional theory to learning opportunities and can, therefore, more efficiently and effectively infuse these skills into regular classroom lessons. Programs for youth that exist outside of schools, such as in community clubs and organizations, can be more difficult to implement because of untrained adult volunteers or high staff turnover (Bruene-Butler et al., 1997). All PST programs, regardless of where implemented, should include instructor training. For example, one success story includes the Boys & Girls Clubs who used a series called *Talking With TJ: Conflict Resolution*, a videotaped series of lessons that leaders integrate into group activities and games (Bruene-Butler et al., 1997). Regardless of setting, instructor training and fidelity to the program will greatly diminish, if not eliminate, Type III errors, which influence SPS program effectiveness.

Prerequisite Skills

Several prerequisite skills must be satisfied for a child to be cognitively *ready* to process and use information to effectively solve problems (Gange, 1980). Prerequisite skills basic to PST programs are intellectual readiness, language proficiency, and psychosocial orientations (Spivack et al., 1976).

Intellectual Readiness

Formal operational thinking is a prerequisite intellectual skill that influences SPS abilities by allowing a child to think about his or her thoughts as well as the thoughts of others. Although concrete and formal thought processes are both logical operations, formal operational thinking allows a person to think beyond the current context of a problematic situation to a future, hypothetical, or verbal dilemma that may occur in a variety of contexts (Wadsworth, 1984). This ability enables a young person to engage in introspection, process and organize a number of variables concurrently, use hypotheses in solutions to problems, and develop a comprehension of *causation* (Wadsworth, 1984).

Children who are not yet at the formal operational stage of thinking may be able to follow a step-by-step procedure, but will find applying the framework to *in vivo* problems difficult, if not frustrating (Wadsworth, 1984). Therefore, children must be *guided* through the SPS process as it relates to a specific and present problem. They also need to be directed to identify the appropriate *decisional criteria*, important to predicting consequences and making decisions. This may, in fact, be one reason that some studies with youth in this period of developmental cognitive transition (e.g., fourth and fifth graders) reported mixed results or limited translation to positive behavioral outcomes. The application of PST with aggressive children has especially reported increases in observed aggressive behavior and increases in identification of aggressive solutions among trained children (Olexa & Forman, 1984). Amish, Gesten, Smith, Clark, and Stark (1988) also found that children between 7 and 12 years old diagnosed with severe behavioral disorders trained to problem solve significantly improved in generating more solutions, but the solutions were more antisocial than those generated by the control group. As noted previously, when children inappropriately select aggressive strategies to solve conflicts, specific guidance is required regarding decisional criteria (i.e., can do "no harm" to self or others) for weighing options conducive to healthy problem resolution and appropriate social goals.

Language Proficiencies

Verbal competency also is required to effectively solve problems. Necessary interpersonal and personal language skills include the ability to listen to and converse with others, to articulate one's feelings to oneself and others, and use the language of problem solving (Spivack et al., 1976). As Spivack and Shure's ICPS program demonstrates, the younger the child is, the more important it is to include training in language skills that prepare him or her to think of alternatives, consequences, solutions, and means to an end.

Psychosocial Orientations

Closely linked to communication skills are the emotional and social competencies that must develop to effectively solve interpersonal problems. Youth must be affectively *oriented* to problem solve; in other words, they must value the process and believe that the time and effort expended will produce desirable outcomes (Frauenknecht & Black, 2003). The concept of problem orientation is considered to be the motivational component of SPS and reflects the self-efficacy of the person in terms of a cognitive set (has confidence in intellectual capacities), an emotional set (identifies positive affect about the process), and a behavioral set (attempts to solve a problem rather than avoid the situation). Developing a positive problem orientation evolves from success at SPS and will likewise positively influence a child's sense of confidence to continue to apply the process and act independently without adult guidance (Frauenknecht & Black, 2003; Gange, 1980).

Young people must develop the emotional skills required to solve social problems that include awareness, identification, and management of feelings (Elardo & Caldwell, 1979). In addition, expanding social knowledge and skills such as the acknowledgment of social cues; identification of social goals; recognition of social rules, norms, and conventions; appreciation of other social perspectives; and sensitivity to others' problems will enable a young person to succeed in the resolution of interpersonal problems (Gange, 1980; Pelligrini & Urbain, 1985; Spivack et al., 1976). As noted in the ISA/SPS program by Elias and colleagues, the preliminary development of other skills in combination with SPS competencies may, in fact, be required because these other skills serve as prerequisites to more effective SPS applications, such as assertiveness skills if the solution requires this form of communication (Christoff, Scott, Kelley, Schlundt, & Kelly, 1985; Pelligrini &

Urbain, 1985). Therefore, program failure may be a result of not receiving prerequisite skill training or insufficient training in SPS.

Developmentally Appropriate Instructional Strategies

PST programs, like any other educational, behavior-changing endeavor, must comprise developmentally appropriate lessons. Selecting instructional strategies that are developmentally appropriate for the maturity level of the child are critical to success. The use of puppets, storyboards, videotapes, role-play scenarios, discussions, and cooperative group projects are examples of strategies that will, when applied appropriately and to relevant social issues, stimulate thought and conversation central to problem situations to which participants can relate (Spivack et al., 1976). When teaching SPS skills, the instructor must effectively help younger children identify desirable goals and outcomes and guide the process by demonstrating skills while translating cognitive strategies into behaviors (Spivack et al., 1976). Children must repeatedly practice SPS in simulations of *in vivo* interpersonal events among their peers while being supervised in a safe environment (Spivack et al., 1976). It also is the responsibility of facilitators to help younger children clearly define criteria for selecting healthy options such as choosing nonaggressive solutions to conflict (Pellegrini & Urbain, 1985).

NEW FEATURES IN PROBLEM-SOLVING TRAINING AND MEASUREMENT

PST is being applied in new environments with different populations facing complex performance problems. A new PST program has been developed and evaluated called *POWER*, which integrates SPS and the transtheoretical model of stress to help young athletes more effectively cope with excessive stress (Brylinsky & Frauenknecht, 1997). The PST program focuses on specific problem identification, which was lack of time for all school and sport activities. Options for this problem were generated according to the rules for brainstorming and then weighed according to the list of decisional criteria established to predict consequences. After the best option was selected, athletes enacted a plan using a five-part behavioral objective. Finally, once the solution was applied, athletes reflected and recycled to determine if the solution worked and, if not, which step in the SPS process needed to be revisited. Findings indicated that this sample of young athletes was able and willing to use systematic SPS strategies, and group SPS scores were higher than other groups of comparable age. These athletes also reported a belief in the SPS process and a willingness to approach rather than avoid problems.

There are new SPS instruments available with developed norms and psychometric data. One example is called the Social Problem-Solving Inventory for Adolescents (SPSI–A; Frauenknecht & Black, 2003). The SPSI–A, developed according to the Black and Frauenknecht model of SPS (Frauenknecht & Black, 2003), is a structured personality test used to assess covert and overt self-reported SPS beliefs and behaviors, which occur either in a social or personal context (Frauenknecht & Black, 1995). There are three scales and nine subscales. There is a long (64 items) and short (30 items) version of the test, which can be administered individually and in groups. Electronic scoring is available.

CONCLUSION

This chapter provides a critical review of social problem solving (SPS) theory, research, and training as applied to children and adolescents. Four reviews of SPS research over the past two decades indicated the ability of both children and adolescents to develop SPS skills. These reviews also hold promise for the ability of SPS programs to effect behavioral change, although this outcome has been inconsistent. In addition, two innovative school-based PST programs are presented, including their core elements and best processes for program design and implementation. Both programs identified the importance of requisite skill development for children before PST, especially comprehension and use of language, intellectual readiness, social awareness, and psychosocial orientations to problem solve. These SPS programs emphasized the use of pedagogically sound instructional strategies that are theory-based, contextually applied, and developmentally appropriate. The critical element of program success, however, appeared to be planning and implementing strategies that systematically allow students to apply SPS in planned, simulated situations using modeling and role playing as well as during spontaneous and *in vivo* problematic situations.

In addition, if the ultimate goal is to teach SPS skills so that they can be generalized to other contexts and settings, programs must include instructions that teach this process. This is accomplished by providing graduated experiences within a safe classroom environment that use a variety of contexts and eventually increase exposure to *in vivo* SPS experiences within the confines of the school environment. These types of lessons need to be evaluated to ascertain if SPS skills are generalizable.

The reviews also stressed best processes for SPS instructor training. Instructors must be trained systematically and carefully. They must maintain program fidelity by implementing SPS lessons as designed; deviation from planned instruction may jeopardize the impact and outcomes of the program. On the other hand, instructor training also must include the strategies of dialoguing, distancing, and facilitative questioning. These strategies allow for infusion of SPS into the school venue as well as capitalizing on spontaneous opportunities to lead students through the SPS process when teachable moments arise. Both situations increase students' independent application and generalization of the SPS process to life.

Type III errors must be reduced to avoid false conclusions that SPS is ineffective. Six ways were identified to reduce these errors: (a) train instructors and observe and evaluate their skills before program implementation; (b) inform instructors that they must take responsibility and disallow student solutions that are unethical or are behavioral and socially inappropriate, destructive, or deleterious to self or others; (c) test children for stages of intellectual development to select a SPS program and content curriculum that are age or developmentally appropriate; (d) teach generalizability of skills; (e) use well-designed or evaluated SPS programs; and (f) develop a pedagogically sound content-specific SPS curriculum.

To avoid research errors (Type I and II errors), (a) use a validated, model-based measure of SPS appropriate for children and adolescents; (b) assess at pretreatment individual and group problem-solving orientation; (c) assess SPS skill development during training and *in vivo* and incorporate a variety of behavioral indexes; and (d) evaluate acquisition of program content information. A research priority is to conduct longitudinal studies that address behavioral translation of SPS skills to *in vivo* situations. Also, it is important to ascertain the following: (a) whether all adolescent populations respond in the same way to the same type of SPS training or if there are gender, racial, functional, and cultural differences; (b) whether all SPS models are equally effective or if some provide greater specificity or simplicity for certain groups of young people; and (c) whether there are unintended or unexpected negative consequences that can evolve from SPS training and, if so, how these can be eliminated.

In conclusion, SPS is a process that holds promise for addressing critical issues facing the youth of America. SPS offers potential because it is a skill that teaches youth *how* rather than *what* to think and can be used in a variety of situations with diverse problems if training is appropriately conducted. SPS, however, is at a critical point of evolution and utilization. It is doubtful that it will reach maturation or wide-spread infusion unless the issues addressed earlier are viewed as viable and critical. Future success depends not only on whether the process is effective but also on the fidelity of adhering to the highest standards of training, implementation, and evaluation. New innovations, applications, and measurement devices will help generate enthusiasm and excitement about the virtues and benefits of SPS for youth.

REFERENCES

Amish, P., Gesten, E., Smith, J., Clark, H., & Stark, C. (1988). Social problem-solving training for severely emotionally and behaviorally disturbed children. *Behavioral Disorders, 13,* 175–186.

Black, R. (2002). A strategic plan for winning the war in public health. *American Journal of Health Education, 33,* 265–275.

Bruene-Butler, L., Hampson, J., Elias, M., Clabby, J., & Schuyler, T. (1997). The Improving Social Awareness–Social Problem Solving Project. In G. Albee & T. Gullotta (Eds.), *Primary prevention works* (pp. 239–267). Thousand Oaks, CA: Sage.

Brylinsky, J., & Frauenknecht, M. (1997). *The problem with adolescent tennis players: Social problem solving for effectively managing stress.* Key Biscayne, FL: U.S. Tennis Association.

Center for the Study and Prevention of Violence. (2002). *Blueprints for violence prevention: I Can Problem Solve.* Retrieved March 1, 2001, from http://www.Colorado.EDU/cspv/ blueprints/promise/ICPS.htm

Christoff, K., Scott, W., Kelley, M., Schlundt, D., & Kelly, J. (1985). Social skills and social problem-solving training for shy young adolescents. *Behavior Therapy, 16,* 468–477.

Clabby, J. (1992). *ASPIRE: Adolescent problem-solving interventions with relaxation exercises.* Unpublished manuscript, University of Medicine and Dentistry of New Jersey, Community Mental Health Center at Piscataway.

Crick, N. R., & Dodge, K. A. (1994). A review and reformulation of social information-processing mechanisms in children's social adjustment. *Psychological Bulletin, 115,* 74–101.

Coleman, M., Wheeler, L., & Webber, J. (1993). Research on interpersonal problem-solving training: A review. *Remedial and Special Education, 14,* 25–37.

Eddy, J. M., Reid, J. B., Stoolmiller, M., & Fetrow, R. A. (2003). Outcomes during middle school for an elementary school-based preventive intervention for conduct problems: Follow-up results from a randomized trial. *Behavior Therapy, 34,* 535–552.

Elardo, P., & Caldwell, B. (1979). The effects of an experimental social development program on children in the middle childhood period. *Psychology in Schools, 16,* 93–100.

Elias, M., & Clabby, J. (1988). Teaching social decision making. *Educational Leadership, 45,* 52–55.

Elias, M., & Clabby, J. (1992). *Building social problem-solving skills: Guidelines from a school-based program.* San Francisco: Jossey-Bass.

Elias, M., Gara, M., Schuyler, T., Branden-Muller, L., & Sayette, M. (1991). The promotion of social competence: Longitudinal study of a preventive school-based program. *American Journal of Orthospychiatry, 61,* 409–417.

Elias, M., & Tobias, S. (1992). *Building social problem-solving skills*. San Francisco: Jossey-Bass.

Frauenknecht, M., & Black, D. R. (1995). The Social Problem-Solving Inventory for Adolescents (SPSI–A): Development and preliminary psychometric evaluation. *Journal of Personality Assessment, 64*, 522–539.

Frauenknecht, M., & Black, D. R. (2003). *The Social Problem-Solving Inventory for Adolescents (SPSI–A): A manual for application, interpretation, and psychometric evaluation*. Morgantown, WV: PNG Press.

Gange, R. M. (1980). Learnable aspects of problem solving. *Educational Psychologist, 15*, 84–92.

Hansen, D., Nangle, D., & Meyer, K. (1998). Enhancing the effectiveness of social skills interventions with adolescents. *Education and Treatment of Children, 21*, 489–513.

Lochman, J. E., & Dodge, K. A. (1994). Social cognitive processes of severely violent, moderately aggressive, and nonaggressive boys. *Journal of Consulting and Clinical Psychology, 62*, 366–374.

Lochman, J. E., & Dodge, K. A. (1998). Distorted perceptions in dyadic interactions of aggressive and nonaggressive boys: Effects of prior expectations, context, and boys' age. *Development and Psychopathology, 10*, 495–512.

Lochman, J. E., & Wells, K. D. (2002a). Contextual social–cognitive mediators and child outcome: A test of the theoretical model in the Coping Power Program. *Development and Psychopathology, 14*, 971–993.

Lochman, J. E., & Wells, K. D. (2002b). The Coping Power Program at the middle school transition: Universal and indicated prevention effects. *Psychology of Addictive Behaviors, 16*, S40–S54.

Lochman, J. E., & Wells, K. D. (2003). Effectiveness of the Coping Power Program and of classroom intervention with aggressive children: Outcomes at a 1-year follow-up. *Behavior Therapy, 34*, 493–515.

Olexa, D., & Forman, S. (1984). Effects of social problem-solving training on classroom behavior of urban disadvantaged students. *Journal of School Psychology, 22*, 165–175.

Pelligrini, D., & Urbain, E. (1985). An evaluation of interpersonal cognitive problem-solving training with children. *Journal of Child Psychology and Psychiatry, 26*, 17–41.

Reid, J. B., Eddy, J. M., Fetrow, R. A., & Stoolmiller, M. (1999). Description and immediate impacts of a preventative intervention for conduct problems. *American Journal of Community Psychology, 24*, 483–517.

Shure, M. (1993). I Can Problem Solve (ICPS): Interpersonal cognitive problem solving for young children. *Early Child Development and Care, 96*, 49–64.

Shure, M. (1997). Interpersonal cognitive problem solving: Primary prevention of early high-risk behaviors in the preschool and primary years. In G. Albee & T. Gullotta (Eds.), *Primary prevention works* (pp. 167–188). Thousand Oaks, CA: Sage.

Sigel, I. (Ed.). (1985). *Parental belief systems: The psychological consequences for children*. Hillsdale, NJ: Erlbaum.

Spivack, G., Platt, J., & Shure, M. (1976). *The problem-solving approach to adjustment*. San Francisco: Jossey-Bass.

Tisdelle, D., & St. Lawrence, J. (1986). Interpersonal problem-solving competency: Review and critique of the literature. *Clinical Psychology Review*, 6, 337–356.

Urbain, E., & Kendall, P. (1980). Review of social–cognitive problem solving with children. *Psychological Bulletin*, 88, 105–143.

Wadsworth, B. (1984). *Piaget's theory of cognitive and affective development* (3rd ed.). New York: Longman.

10

PROBLEM-SOLVING THERAPY FOR ADULTS

ARTHUR M. NEZU, THOMAS J. D'ZURILLA,
MARNI L. ZWICK, AND CHRISTINE MAGUTH NEZU

This chapter focuses on problem-solving therapy (PST) approaches for adults that are based on the prescriptive model originally developed by D'Zurilla and Goldfried (1971; see also chap. 1, this book) and later revised by D'Zurilla, Nezu, and their colleagues (e.g., D'Zurilla & Nezu, 1999; Nezu & D'Zurilla, 1989; Nezu, Nezu, & Perri, 1989). We begin with a description of the relational/problem-solving model of stress that represents the conceptual framework underlying this treatment approach, followed by a brief overview of the evidence supporting its efficacy. For detailed descriptions of PST therapy guidelines, the reader is referred elsewhere (D'Zurilla & Nezu, 1999, 2001; Nezu et al., 1989; Nezu, Nezu, Friedman, Faddis, & Houts, 1998),

A RELATIONAL/PROBLEM-SOLVING MODEL OF STRESS

D'Zurilla and Nezu (1999; D'Zurilla, 1990; Nezu & D'Zurilla, 1989; Nezu et al., 1989) developed a PST approach that is based on the assumption that much of what is viewed as "psychopathology" can be understood in terms of ineffective or maladaptive coping behavior and its negative personal–social consequences, such as anxiety, depression, anger, interpersonal conflicts, physical symptoms, and the creation of new problems (D'Zurilla & Goldfried, 1971; D'Zurilla & Nezu, 1982). As such, the importance of PST is conceptualized within a relational/problem-solving model of stress whereby social problem solving (SPS) is given a central role as a general coping strategy that can increase adaptive functioning while reducing and preventing the negative effects of daily stress on personal–social functioning and well-being (D'Zurilla, 1990; D'Zurilla & Nezu, 1999; Nezu, 2004; Nezu & D'Zurilla, 1989). This model integrates Richard Lazarus's relational model of stress (Lazarus, 1999; Lazarus & Folkman, 1984) with the SPS model presented in chapter 1.

Lazarus defined "stress" as a particular type of person–environment relationship in which demands are appraised by the person as taxing or exceeding coping resources and endangering well-being (Lazarus & Folkman, 1984). Comparing this relational definition of stress to the definition of a "problem" in SPS theory, it is clear that a problematic situation is also a stress situation if it is at all difficult and significant for well-being. According to Lazarus's model, a person in a stress situation significantly influences both the quality and intensity of stress responses through two major processes: (a) cognitive appraisal and (b) coping.

Cognitive appraisal is the process by which a person evaluates the meaning or personal significance of a specific stress situation. Two important kinds of cognitive appraisals are primary appraisal and secondary appraisal. *Primary appraisal* refers to a person's evaluation of the relevance of the situation for physical, social, or psychological well-being. *Secondary appraisal* involves the person's evaluation of his or her coping options and resources. The term *coping* refers to the various cognitive and behavioral activities by which the person attempts to manage stressful demands, as well as the emotions that such stress generates. Two major types of coping include problem-focused coping and emotion-focused coping. *Problem-focused coping* is directed at changing the stressful situation for the better. *Emotion-focused coping*, on the other hand, is aimed at managing the emotions that are generated by the situation. In general, problem-focused coping predominates when stressful conditions are appraised as changeable or controllable, whereas emotion-focused coping is more common when a situation is appraised as unchangeable or uncontrollable (see Lazarus, 1999). Although neither strategy is universally effective, problem-focused coping is often considered to be the more useful and adaptive form of coping. In the Lazarus model, problem solving is defined as a form of problem-focused coping, which means that problem-solving goals are equated with mastery goals, or control of the environment. In this view, problem solving is futile and maladaptive when stressful conditions are unchangeable.

Our relational/problem-solving model of stress retains the basic assumptions and essential features of Lazarus's model but are cast within a general problem-solving framework that gives SPS an expanded and more important role as a general coping strategy. Within this model, stress is viewed as a function of the reciprocal relations among three major variables: (a) stressful life events, (b) emotional stress responses, and (c) problem-solving coping.

Stressful life events are life experiences that present a person with strong demands for personal, social, or biological readjustment (Bloom, 1985). Two important types of stressful life events are major negative events and daily problems. A *major negative event* is a broad life experience, such as a major negative life change, which often demands sweeping readjustments in a person's life (e.g., divorce, death of a loved one, job loss, major illness or injury). A *daily problem* is a more narrow and specific life experience characterized by a perceived discrepancy between adaptive demands and coping response availability. In the stress literature, these specific stressful events are also called "daily hassles" (Kanner, Coyne, Schaefer, & Lazarus, 1981). Although daily problems or hassles are less dramatic than major negative events, research suggests that an accumulation of these stressors over time may have a greater impact on psychological and physical well-being than the number of major negative events (Kanner et al., 1981; Nezu & Ronan, 1985).

The concept of *emotional stress* refers to the immediate emotional responses of a person to a stressful life event, as modified or transformed by appraisal and coping processes (Lazarus, 1999). Although emotional stress responses are often negative (e.g., anxiety, anger, depression), they can also be positive in nature (e.g., hope, relief, exhilaration). Negative emotions are likely to predominate when the person (a) appraises a problem as harmful or threatening to well-being, (b) doubts his or her ability to cope with the situation effectively, or (c) makes ineffective or maladaptive coping responses. On the other hand, positive emotions may emerge and compete with negative emotionality when the person (a) appraises the problem as a challenge or opportunity for benefit, (b) believes that he or she is capable of coping with the situation effectively, and (c) engages in coping responses that are effective in reducing harmful or threatening conditions or the negative emotions that are generated by them.

The most important concept in the relational/problem-solving model is *problem-solving coping,* which integrates all cognitive appraisal and coping activities within a general SPS framework. A person who applies the problem-solving coping strategy perceives a stress situation as a problem-to-be-solved, believes that he or she can solve it successfully, generates alternative "solutions" or coping responses, chooses the "best" solution, implements it, and then carefully observes and evaluates the outcome. In contrast with Lazarus's view of problem solving as a form of problem-focused coping, our model conceives of problem solving to be a broader, more versatile coping strategy in that problem-solving goals are not limited to mastery goals. The goals may include problem-focused goals, emotion-focused goals, or both, depending on the nature of the particular problematic situation and how it is defined and appraised (i.e., controllable or uncontrollable).

In addition to providing a theoretical rationale for PST, this model of stress also provides a useful cognitive–behavioral framework for assessing clinical problems. During assessment, the problem-solving therapist identifies and pinpoints major negative life events, current daily problems, emotional stress responses, problem-orientation deficits, problem-solving skills deficits, and solution implementation deficits. Based on this assessment, PST is then applied to improve problem orientation and problem-solving skills, which is expected to increase adaptive situational coping, general competence, and psychological–physical wellness that, in turn, is expected to reduce, moderate, or prevent the negative effects of stress on psychological and physical well-being.

During the past two decades, a number of empirical studies have provided support for the major assumptions of the relational/problem-solving model (D'Zurilla & Nezu, 1999; Nezu, 2004). These studies have examined the associations between SPS and a wide range of adaptational outcomes, including adaptive and maladaptive coping, behavioral competence (e.g. social performance, academic performance, caregiving effectiveness), positive psychological well-being (e.g., positive affectivity, self-esteem, life satisfaction), psychological distress and symptomatology (e.g., depression, anxiety, suicidal ideation), and health-related behaviors, symptoms, and adjustment. Participants have included high school students, college students, middle-aged adults, elderly adults, depressed college students, emotionally disturbed adolescents, suicidal adolescents, clinically depressed adults, suicidal adults, agoraphobic patients, alcoholics, drug addicts, psychiatric patients, abusive and neglectful mothers, pregnant women, cancer patients, physically disabled individuals, and caregivers of people with serious illness and disabilities. Among the various research findings, the strongest support for this model is provided by studies showing that problem solving moderates or mediates the negative effects of stressful life events on emotions (e.g., Folkman & Lazarus, 1988; Kant, D'Zurilla, & Maydeu-Olivares, 1997;

Nezu, 1986c; Nezu, Nezu, Saraydarian, Kalmar, & Ronan, 1986; Nezu & Ronan, 1985, 1988).

EFFICACY OF PROBLEM-SOLVING THERAPY

To present a more objective appraisal of the PST outcome literature, we attempted to review for this chapter only those investigations that met a minimal set of methodological standards. In particular, such studies had to (a) evaluate the efficacy of PST as a single or "stand alone" intervention (i.e., PST was not one part of a larger treatment package) for adults, (b) include at least one comparison between PST and another experimental condition (i.e., alternative treatment condition, attention-placebo, wait-list control, or no-treatment control), (c) use random assignment of participants to the differing conditions, and (d) be based to some degree on the models delineated by D'Zurilla, Nezu, and their colleagues (e.g., D'Zurilla & Nezu, 1999; Nezu et al., 1989, 1998).

The appendix lists outcome investigations that met these criteria. These studies cut across various traditional mental health problems (e.g., depression, phobia, schizophrenia), experienced by various medical patient populations (e.g., cancer, arthritis, obesity), and treatment settings (e.g., primary care, inpatient, outpatient). Overall, as can be seen by a perusal of the general results of these studies, although not across the board, PST appears to be an efficacious clinical intervention, as briefly highlighted next.

Anxiety-Related Disorders

PST has not been evaluated frequently for the treatment of anxiety disorders, although substantial research has identified a negative correlation between anxiety and effective problem solving (e.g., Bond, Lyle, Tappe, Seehafer, & D'Zurilla, 2002; Nezu, 1985, 1986c; Nezu & Carnevale, 1987). Of the two studies identified that applied PST for the treatment of agoraphobia, one found PST to be equal to a graded exposure intervention (Jannoun, Munby, Catalan, & Gelder, 1980), whereas the second found such an approach to be superior to PST. PST was found to be equally effective compared with rational–emotive therapy, cognitive therapy, and self-instructional training regarding the treatment of social phobia (DiGiuseppe, Simon, McGowan, & Gardner, 1990). D'Zurilla and Maschka (1988) found PST to be more effective than a supportive communication training program regarding "highly stressed" community residents, whereas mixed results were obtained by Mendonca and Siess (1976) regarding anxiety related to vocational indecision.

Depression

Substantial research has documented a significant relationship between depressive symptoms and ineffective problem solving (e.g., Gotlib & Asarnow, 1979; Marx, Williams, & Claridge, 1992; Nezu, 1985, 1986a, 1987). As such, it is not surprising that PST has been most frequently evaluated as a potentially effective intervention for the treatment of depression. With regard to major depressive disorder, three studies provide significant support for the efficacy of PST with regard to adult (Nezu, 1986b; Nezu & Perri, 1989) and older adult (Arean et al., 1993) samples. Although not using formal diagnostic procedures, Hussian and Lawrence (1981) found PST to be more effective than a social reinforcement protocol for the treatment of highly depressed (mean BDI score of 35.64) institutionalized elderly patients.

Of particular significance are the results of one of these studies (Nezu & Perri, 1989), in which the importance of training in the problem-orientation component was especially underscored. More specifically, adults reliably diagnosed with major depressive disorder were randomly assigned to one of three conditions: (a) PST (10 group sessions that focused on the entire training model); (b) "abbreviated" PST (APST; 10 group sessions in which training in problem orientation was *excluded* as a means to evaluate the unique contribution such training made to the positive treatment effects found in previous research, e.g., Nezu, 1986b); and (c) a waiting-list control (WLC). Results of this dismantling study indicated that whereas APST patients were significantly less depressed at posttreatment than WLC individuals, individuals receiving the entire PST training model were significantly less depressed than members of *both* the APST and WLC conditions. In addition, these findings were maintained at a six-month follow-up assessment. In essence, such results strongly suggest that PST should include training in both problem orientation *and* rational problem solving when treating depression.

With regard to treating minor depressive disorder or dysthymia, PST has not fared as well compared with its treatment of major depression. In their multisite study, for example, Barrett et al. (2001) found PST to be equally effective as antidepressant medication (i.e., paroxetine), as well as a drug placebo condition, regarding reduction in actual depressive symptoms among patients seen in a primary care setting. However, both PST and drug treatment were found to be significantly more effective than the placebo condition in terms of remission rates. In a related study that used the same design but focused on older adults, Williams et al. (2000) found PST to be less effective than the antidepressant medication but more effective than the drug placebo. However, the effects of PST were found to be subject to site differences and had a slower onset.

One possible reason why PST in these two studies that addressed minor depression were not as effective compared with the effects on major depression involves the difference in training models. The designers of the PST approach for patients in primary care (entitled PST–PC, with the "PC" representing a primary care population) did not include a treatment focus on problem-orientation variables (see Barrett et al., 1999) as the D'Zurilla and Nezu models would advocate. As such, a sizable treatment impact is potentially missing. For example, as noted previously, results from the Nezu and Perri (1989) dismantling study provide strong empirical support for the importance of including problem orientation in an overall PST intervention. Given this context, it is possible that had these investigators included the entire PST model as delineated in, for example, the Nezu et al. (1989) treatment manual for depression, the efficacy of their problem-solving intervention may have been more robust. A study by Lynch, Tamburrino, and Nagel (1997) that found PST, provided over the telephone, to be effective for patients with minor depression in a family practice, did base their therapy protocol on the Nezu et al. (1989) PST treatment manual, and as such, provides additional support for this argument.

Suicidal Ideation/Behavior

Four studies were identified that evaluated PST as a treatment for reducing suicidal ideation and behaviors. In general, PST was found to be more effective than alternative treatments or control conditions in three studies (Lerner & Clum, 1990; McLeavey, Daly, Ludgate, & Murray, 1994; Salkovskis, Atha, & Storer, 1990) in reducing targeted behaviors, and the fourth (i.e., Patsiokas & Clum, 1985) investigation found it to be superior to an attention-placebo with regard to hopelessness but not concerning suicidal intent. In addition, of particular importance are the findings that such positive treatment effects were maintained three to six months post-treatment.

Emotional Problems

Two of the three studies in this category focused on primary care patients suffering from various emotional disorders, whereas the third applied PST as the treatment for college students scoring high on a measure of anger. In both primary care studies, PST appeared to be more effective than standard medical care, but in one of them (Mynors-Wallis, Davies, Gray, Barbour, & Gath, 1997), this was only with regard to lowered disability and sick days taken rather than concerning the emotional symptoms themselves. With regard to the treatment of anger, PST was found equal to two other treatment approaches (i.e., stress inoculation and social skills training), whereas all three were superior to an attention-placebo condition (Moon & Eisler, 1983).

Substance Abuse

Two of the identified investigations in this category focused on adult alcoholic inpatients. The Intagliatia (1978) study indicated that adding PST to a standard care protocol led to superior results compared with standard care alone The second alcohol treatment project found PST to be more effective than an attention-placebo and a no-treatment control condition (Chaney, O'Leary, & Marlatt, 1978). Note that in this study, the positive effects of PST were maintained at one-year posttreatment. Karol and Richards (1978) also found that adding PST to a standard behavioral treatment program to reduce cigarette smoking during a maintenance phase led to superior effects compared with the behavioral treatment alone. Such results were maintained eight months posttreatment. On the other hand, PST was not found to be more effective than a standard day treatment program for the treatment of individuals with substance abuse problems and concomitant psychiatric difficulties (Carey, Carey, & Meisler, 1990).

Adults With Mental Retardation

Given the seeming meta-cognitive nature of many of the constructs inherent in PST (e.g., consequential reasoning, subjective probability estimation), one might question whether this approach, which on the surface appears to require at least average intelligence, would be effective for individuals with limited cognitive abilities. This question was directly addressed in a study conducted with adults with mental retardation (C. M. Nezu, Nezu, & Arean, 1991). Using a counter-balanced design, adults with dual diagnoses (i.e., mental retardation and mental illness) were randomly assigned to one of three conditions: (a) PST–assertiveness; (b) assertiveness–PST; and (c) a WLC. Members of the first condition received five weekly group sessions of PST, followed by five weekly group sessions of behavioral assertiveness training. Participants in the second condition received the same treatment protocols, but in the reverse order. Overall, results strongly support the efficacy of the PST component for decreasing self-reported psychiatric symptoms, as well as facilitating (clinician-rated) adaptive behavior. By adapting what might initially be considered a complex treatment strategy for a population of mentally retarded adults, it was found that PST was equally effective regardless of one's basic intellectual functioning. Similar findings regarding the efficacy of PST for persons with mental retardation are provided by Benson, Rice, and Miranti (1986) regarding anger management; by Castles and Glass (1986) regarding improved social competence; and by Loumidis and Hill (1997) regarding decreasing maladaptive behavior in the community.

Schizophrenia and Psychiatric Inpatients

A similar concern might be voiced regarding the relevance of PST for individuals experiencing severe mental illness, such as schizophrenia. However, among the five studies that met inclusion criteria for this category, four found PST to be superior to various attention-placebo control conditions. Only in one was an alternative treatment (i.e., coping skills training) found to be more effective than PST (Bradshaw, 1993). However, this difference disappeared at a six-month posttreatment assessment point. In the last study, PST was equal to a group therapy protocol, but a significant treatment by gender interaction was identified, where men improved more with PST and women improved more with the interactive group therapy paradigm (Coché, Cooper, & Petermann, 1984).

Medical Patient Populations

Although the initial application of PST was geared toward more traditional mental health problems, such as depression and anxiety, it more recently has been evaluated as an important psychosocial treatment approach to enhance the quality of life of various medical patient populations, most notably cancer patients and their families (Nezu, Nezu, Felgoise, & Zwick, 2003). Two of the five investigations focusing on such populations applied PST as a means of decreasing psychological distress and improving the overall quality of life for adult cancer patients themselves (Allen et al., 2002; Nezu, Nezu, Felgoise, McClure, & Houts, 2003), whereas Sahler et al. (2002) used PST to help mothers of children newly diagnosed with cancer. In all three instances, PST was found to be particularly effective in reducing overall psychological distress, although in comparison to standard medical care, the PST protocol in the Allen et al. (2002) study was only effective for patients with "good problem-solving skills" at baseline.

It should be noted that in the Nezu et al. (2003) investigation, the positive effects of PST were maintained at six-month and one-year follow-up assessment points. Moreover, because these investigators incorporated an additional treatment condition that involved providing PST to both the cancer patient and his or her significant other, their study was able to find that such spousal involvement did lead to enhanced treatment effects. More specifically, patients receiving PST along with a significant other were found, at the six-month follow-up, to have experienced continued and significant improvement compared to individuals receiving PST by themselves.

In the other two outcome studies, PST was used as a means to enhance the likelihood that women would seek a breast self-exam after being notified that they were a first-degree relative of someone newly diagnosed with breast cancer (Audrain et al., 1999; Schwartz et al., 1998). In both cases, PST was found to be more effective than general health counseling, but in the Schwartz et al. investigation, this finding held true for only those women who actually reported practicing the problem-solving skills.

Another health-related problem that has been the target of problem-solving interventions is obesity. In the three randomized studies listed in the appendix, PST was found to be an effective means to enhance weight loss. Rather than being the primary clinical strategy applied to promote weight loss, however, PST in these cases helped patients to better adhere to a standard behavioral weight loss protocol. More specifically, Perri et al. (2001) hypothesized that PST would be an effective means by which to foster improved adherence to a behavioral weight loss intervention by helping participants to overcome various barriers to adherence, such as scheduling difficulties, completing homework assignments, or the interference of psychological distress. More specifically, after completing 20 weekly group sessions of standard behavioral treatment for obesity, 80 women were randomly assigned to one of three conditions: (a) no further contact (behavior therapy [BT] only); (b) relapse-prevention training; and (c) PST. At the end of 17 months, no differences in overall weight loss were observed between relapse prevention and BT-only or between relapse prevention and PST. However, PST participants had significantly greater long-term weight reductions than BT-only participants, and a significantly larger percentage of PST participants achieved "clinically significant" losses of 10% or more in body weight than did BT-only members (approximately 35% versus 6%).

In summary, when conducting a somewhat conservative review of the outcome literature regarding the efficacy of PST (i.e., only choosing studies that met a minimal set of criteria regarding methodological soundness), it appears that the evidence overwhelmingly underscores the positive impact that this intervention has across a multitude of adult populations and psychological disorders. However, whereas many answers are provided by such a review, additional questions arise as well. To that end, we offer the following set of recommendations concerning future directions.

CONCLUSION

In looking to the future, we believe three major goals should be pursued by the discipline: (a) to evaluate the potential applicability and efficacy of

PST to new patient populations and for new intervention goals, including more "positive psychology" themes (e.g., increasing hope and optimism, Chang & D'Zurilla, 1996; Snyder et al., 2000); (b) to devise and evaluate new methods of *implementing* PST as a means of increasing patient accessibility, such as telephone counseling (e.g., Allen et al., 2002; Lynch et al., 1997); and (c) to improve the methodological rigor of the research studies evaluating the previously stated two points (e.g., include a measure of problem solving to determine if improvements in problem solving are significantly correlated with improvements in patient functioning and include an assessment of therapist adherence and competence to ensure that what the investigators believe is being conducted is actually being implemented; Nezu, 2004).

APPENDIX 10.1: TREATMENT-CONTROL COMPARISONS OF PROBLEM-SOLVING THERAPY

Reference and participants	Treatment conditions	General results
Agoraphobia		
Cullington, Butler, Hibbert, & Gelder (1984): outpatient agoraphobics	PST vs. graded exposure (GE)	GE > PST
Jannoun et al. (1980): outpatient agoraphobics	PST vs. graded exposure (GE)	PST = GE
Anger		
Moon & Eisler (1983); undergraduates with high anger scores	PST vs. stress inoculation (SI) vs. social skills training (SST) vs. AT	PST = SI = SST > AT
Cancer		
Allen et al. (2002): breast cancer patients beginning first course of chemotherapy	PST vs. standard medical care (SMC) (PST delivered over the phone for four of six sessions)	PST > SMC but only for patients with "good" problem-solving skills at baseline
Audrain et al. (1999): relatives of newly diagnosed breast cancer patients	PST vs. general health counseling (GHC; both single-session protocols)	PST > GHC regarding breast self-exam adherence
Nezu, Nezu, Felgoise, McClure, & Houts (2003): clinically distressed cancer patients	PST vs. PST with a significant other (PST/SO) vs. WLC	PST = PST/SO > WLC; PST/SO > PST at six months and one year
Sahler et al. (2002): mothers of children newly diagnosed with cancer	PST vs. standard care (SC)	PST > SC
Schwartz et al. (1998): distressed women with first-degree relative recently diagnosed with breast cancer	PST vs. general health counseling (GHC; both single session protocols)	PST = GHC; when PST participants divided into those who practiced skills vs. those who did not, "PST-practitioners" > "nonpractitioners" = GHC
Depression		
Arean et al., (1993): depressed elderly	PST vs. reminiscence therapy (RT) vs. WLC	PST > RT > WLC; maintained at three months

Reference and participants	Treatment conditions	General results
Depression *Continued*		
Barrett et al. (2001): primary care patients with minor depression/ dysthymia (multisite study)	PST vs. paroxetine vs. drug placebo	PST = paroxetine = placebo regarding reduction in depressive symptoms; PST = Paroxetine > placebo regarding remission
Hussian & Lawrence (1981): geriatric patients in nursing home	PST vs. social reinforcement (SR) vs. WLC	PST > SR > WLC; maintained at two weeks
Mynors-Wallis et al. (1995): depressed primary care patients	PST vs. amitriptyline (AMT) vs. drug placebo	PST = AMT > placebo; maintained at three months
Lynch et al. (1997): patients in family practice with minor depression	PST vs. control (?) (PST provided over the phone)	PST > control
Nezu (1986b): depressed outpatients	PST vs. problem-focused therapy (PFT) vs. WLC	PST > PFT > WLC; maintained at six months
Nezu & Perri (1989): depressed outpatients	PST vs. APST ("abbreviated" i.e., without training in problem orientation) vs. WLC	PST > APST > WLC; maintained at six months
Teri, Logsdon, Uomoto, & McCurry (1997): depressed Alzheimer's patients + their caregivers	PST vs. increasing pleasant events (PE) vs. typical care control (TCC) vs. WLC	PST = PE > TCC = WLC; maintained at six months
Williams et al. (2000): minor depression/ dysthymia in older adults (60+) (multisite study)	PST vs. paroxetine vs. drug placebo	Paroxetine > PST > placebo (effects of PST subject to site differences)
Mentally retarded adults		
Benson et al. (1986): anger management	PST vs. relaxation training (RT) vs. self-instruction training (SIT) vs. combined	PST = RT = SIT = combined
Castles & Glass (1986): social competence in mild/ moderate retarded adults	PST vs. social skills training (SST) vs. PST + SST vs. control	PST led to improvements in problem solving; SST led to improvements in social skills; combined training led to improvement on a measure of responsibility; little generalization

Reference and participants	Treatment conditions	General results
Mentally retarded adults *Continued*		
Loumidis & Hill (1997): maladaptive behavior in hospital and community residents	PST vs. matched no treatment control (NTC)	PST > WLC, but only with regard to the community residents
C. M. Nezu et al. (1991): mentally retarded adults with concomitant Axis I and/or II diagnoses	PST vs. assertiveness training (AT) vs. WLC	PST = AT > WLC; maintained at three months
Obesity		
Black & Scherba (1983): obese adults	Behavioral contracting to practice PST vs. behavioral contracting to practice weight control skills (control)	PST > control
Perri et al. (1987): obese adults	Peer-led PST vs. therapist-led PST as maintenance strategies vs. no maintenance strategy control	Therapist-led > peer-led = control
Perri et al. (2001): obese adults	PST vs. relapse prevention training (RPT; as maintenance strategies) vs. no maintenance control	PST > RPT > control regarding clinically significant weight loss
Primary care patients		
Catalan, Gath, Bond, Day, & Hall (1991): emotional disorders	PST vs. control (general practitioner providing his/her choice of treatment, including psychosocial or drugs)	PST > control; maintained at sixteen weeks
Mynors-Wallis et al. (1997): emotional disorders	PST provided by nurses vs. standard medical care (SMC)	PST > SMC, but only concerning fewer disability and sick days; no difference regarding symptoms
Psychiatric inpatients		
Bedell, Archer, & Marlowe (1980): psychiatric inpatients	PST vs. AP (recreation)	PST > AT on measures of problem solving
Bradshaw (1993): schizophrenic patients in day treatment program	PST vs. coping skills training (CST)	CST > PST; at six months, differences disappeared

Reference and participants	Treatment conditions	General results
Psychiatric inpatients *Continued*		
Coché & Douglas (1977): psychiatric inpatients	PST vs. AP (reading comedies) vs. NTC	PST > AP = NTC; however no differences regarding improvements on problem-solving measure
Coché et al. (1984): psychiatric inpatients	Group PST vs. group therapy (GT)	PST = GT; interaction effect between gender and treatment
Coché & Flick (1975): psychiatric inpatients	PST vs. AP (reading plays) vs. NTC	PST > AP = NTC on measures of problem solving
Medalia, Revheim, & Casey (2001): inpatient adults with schizophrenia	PST vs. NTC vs. computer-based remediation of memory deficits (Com)	PST > NTC = Com on measures of impersonal problem solving
Social phobia		
DiGiuseppe et al. (1990): social anxiety	PST vs. rational–emotive therapy (RET) vs. cognitive therapy (CT) vs. self-instruction training (SIT) vs. WLC	PST = RET = CT = SIT > WLC
Stress management		
D'Zurilla & Maschka (1988): highly stressed community residents	PST vs. supportive communication training (SCT)	PST > SCT; maintained at six months
Mendonca & Siess (1976): vocational indecision anxiety	PST vs. anxiety management training (AMT) vs. PST + AMT vs. discussion control (DC) vs. NTC	Mixed results—on some measures combined condition fared better (e.g., generating alternatives), whereas for others, PST > AMT and control groups (e.g., information gathering); no differences among conditions regarding anxiety reduction
Substance abuse		
Carey et al. (1990): substance abusers with concomitant psychiatric diagnosis	PST vs. standard day treatment program	PST = control
Chaney et al. (1978): VA male inpatient alcoholics	PST vs. placebo control (PC) vs. NTC	PST > PC = NTC; maintained at one year

Reference and participants	Treatment conditions	General results
Substance abuse *Continued*		
Intagliatia (1978): VA male inpatient alcoholics	PST + standard VA program (VA) vs. VA alone	PST > VA regarding problem solving; no measures of drinking behavior included
Karol & Richards (1978): PST as maintenance strategy for behavioral treatment of cigarette smoking	Behavioral treatment (BT) vs. BT + PST vs. WLC	BT + PST = BT > WLC at posttreatment; PST + BT > BT = WLC at eight months
Suicidal ideation/behavior		
Lerner & Clum (1990): suicidal ideators	PST vs. supportive therapy (ST)	PST > ST; maintained at three months
McLeavey et al., (1994): self-poisoners	PST vs. crisis intervention (CI)	PST > CI; maintained at six months
Patsiokas & Clum (1985): suicide attempters in inpatient setting	PST vs. cognitive restructuring (CR) vs. nondirective control (NC)	PST > NC regarding hopelessness; all participants experienced reduction in suicide intent
Salkovskis, Atha, & Storer (1990): hospitalized suicide repeaters	PST vs. standard care (SC)	PST > SC; maintained at six months

Note. AP = attention-placebo; NTC = No treatment control; WLC = waiting-list control.

REFERENCES

Allen, S. M., Shah, A. C., Nezu, A. M., Nezu, C. M., Ciambrone, D., Hogan, J., et al. (2002). A problem-solving approach to stress reduction among younger women with breast carcinoma: A randomized controlled trial. *Cancer, 94,* 3089–3100.

Arean, P. A., Perri, M. G., Nezu, A. M., Schein, R. L., Christopher, F., & Joseph, T. X. (1993). Comparative effectiveness of social problem-solving therapy and reminiscence therapy as treatments for depression in older adults. *Journal of Consulting and Clinical Psychology, 61,* 1003–1010.

Audrain, J., Rimer, B., Cella, D., Stefanek, M., Garber, J., Pennanen, M., et al. (1999). The impact of a brief coping skills intervention on adherence to breast self-examination among first-degree relatives of newly diagnosed breast cancer patients. *Psycho-Oncology, 8,* 220–229.

Barrett, J. E., Williams, J. W., Oxman, T. E., Frank, E., Katon, W., Sullivan, M., et al. (2001). Treatment of dysthymia and minor depression in primary care: A randomized trial in patients aged 18 to 59 years. *Journal of Family Practice, 50,* 405–412,

Barrett, J. E., Williams, J. W., Oxman, T. E., Katon, W., Frank, E., Hegel, M. T., et al. (1999). The treatment effectiveness project: A comparison of the effectiveness of paroxetine, problem-solving therapy, and placebo in the treatment of minor depression and dysthymia in primary care patients: Background and research plan. *General Hospital Psychiatry, 21,* 260–273.

Bedell, J. R., Archer, R. P., & Marlowe, H. A., Jr. (1980). A description and evaluation of a problem solving skills training program. In D. Upper & S. M. Ross (Eds.), *Behavioral group therapy: An annual review* (pp. 92–121). Champaign, IL: Research Press.

Benson, B. A., Rice, C. J., & Miranti, S. V. (1986). Effects of anger management training with mentally retarded adults in group treatment. *Journal of Consulting and Clinical Psychology, 54,* 728–729.

Black, D. R., & Scherba, D. S. (1983). Contracting to problem solve versus contracting to practice behavioral weight loss skills. *Behavior Therapy, 14,* 100–109.

Bloom, B. L. (1985). *Stressful life event theory and research: Implications for primary prevention* (DHHS Publication No. [AMD] 85-1385). Rockville, MD: National Institute of Mental Health.

Bond, D. S., Lyle, R. M. Tappe, M. K., Seehafer, R. S. & D'Zurilla, T. J. (2002). Moderate aerobic exercise, T'ai Chi, and social problem-solving ability in relation to psychological stress. *International Journal of Stress Management, 9,* 329–343.

Bradshaw, W. H. (1993). Coping-skills training versus a problem-solving approach with schizophrenic patients. *Hospital and Community Psychiatry, 44,* 1102–1104.

Carey, M. P., Carey, K. B., & Meisler, A. W. (1990). Training mentally ill chemical abusers in social problem solving. *Behavior Therapy, 21,* 511–518.

Castles, E. E., & Glass, C. R. (1986). Training in social and interpersonal problem-solving skills for mildly and moderately mentally retarded adults. *American Journal of Mental Deficiency, 91*, 35–42.

Catalan, J., Gath, D. H., Bond, A., Day, A., & Hall, L. (1991). Evaluation of a brief psychological treatment for emotional disorders in primary care. *Psychological Medicine, 21*, 1013–1018.

Chang, E. C., & D'Zurilla, T. J. (1996). Relations between problem orientation and optimism, pessimism, and trait affectivity: A construct validation study. *Behaviour Research and Therapy, 34*, 185–195.

Chaney, E. F., O'Leary, M. R., & Marlatt, G. A. (1978). Skill training with alcoholics. *Journal of Consulting and Clinical Psychology, 46*, 1092–1104.

Coché, E., Cooper, J. B., & Petermann, K. J. (1984). Differential outcomes of cognitive and interactional group therapies. *Small Group Behavior, 15*, 497–509.

Coché, E., & Douglas, A. A. (1977). Therapeutic effects of problem-solving training and play-reading groups. *Journal of Clinical Psychology, 33*, 820–827.

Coché, E., & Flick, A. (1975). Problem solving training groups for hospitalized psychiatric patients. *Journal of Psychology, 91*, 19–29.

Cullington, A., Butler, G., Hibbert, G., & Gelder, M. (1984). Problem solving: Not a treatment for agoraphobia. *Behavior Therapy, 15*, 280–286.

DiGiuseppe, R., Simon, K. S., McGowan, L., & Gardner, F. (1990). A comparative outcome study of four cognitive therapies in the treatment of social anxiety. *Journal of Rational-Emotive and Cognitive–Behavior Therapy, 8*, 129–146.

D'Zurilla, T. J. (1990). Problem-solving training for effective stress management and prevention. *Journal of Cognitive Psychotherapy: An International Quarterly, 4*, 327–355.

D'Zurilla, T. J., & Goldfried, M. R. (1971). Problem solving and behavior modification. *Journal of Abnormal Psychology, 78*, 107–126.

D'Zurilla, T. J., & Maschka, G. (1988, Nov.). *Outcome of a problem-solving approach to stress management: I. Comparison with social support.* Paper presented to the Association for Advancement of Behavior Therapy, New York.

D'Zurilla, T. J., & Nezu, A. M. (1982). Social problem solving in adults. In P. C. Kendall (Ed.), *Advances in cognitive–behavioral research and therapy* (Vol. 1, pp. 202–274). New York: Academic Press.

D'Zurilla, T. J., & Nezu, A. M. (1999). *Problem-solving therapy: A social competence approach to clinical intervention* (2nd ed.). New York: Springer.

D'Zurilla, T. J., & Nezu, A. M. (2001). Problem-solving therapies. In K. S. Dobson (Ed.), *The handbook of cognitive–behavioral therapies* (2nd ed., pp. 211–245). New York: Guilford Press.

Folkman, S., & Lazarus, R. S. (1988). Coping as a mediator of emotion. *Journal of Personality and Social Psychology, 54*, 466–475.

Gotlib, I. H., & Asarnow, R. F. (1979). Interpersonal and impersonal problem-solving skills in mildly and clinically depressed university students. *Journal of Consulting and Clinical Psychology, 47,* 86–95.

Hussian, R. A., & Lawrence, P. S. (1981). Social reinforcement of activity and problem-solving training in the treatment of depressed institutionalized elderly patients. *Cognitive Therapy and Research, 5,* 57–69.

Intagliatia, J. C. (1978). Increasing the interpersonal problem solving skills of an alcoholic population. *Journal of Consulting and Clinical Psychology, 46,* 489–498.

Jannoun, L., Munby, M., Catalan, J., & Gelder, M. (1980). A home-based treatment program for agoraphobia: Replication and controlled evaluation. *Behavior Therapy, 11,* 294–305.

Kanner, A. D., Coyne, J. C., Schaefer, C., & Lazarus, R. S. (1981). Comparison of two modes of stress measurement: Daily hassles and uplifts versus major life events. *Journal of Behavioral Medicine, 4,* 1–39.

Kant, G. L., D'Zurilla, T. J., & Maydeu-Olivares, A. (1997). Social problem solving as a mediator of stress-related depression and anxiety in middle-aged and elderly community residents. *Cognitive Therapy and Research, 21,* 73–96.

Karol, R. L., & Richards, C. S. (1978, Nov.). *Making treatment effects last: An investigation of maintenance strategies for smoking reduction.* Paper presented to the Association for Advancement of Behavior Therapy, Chicago.

Lazarus, R. S. (1999). *Stress and emotion: A new synthesis.* New York: Springer.

Lazarus, R. S., & Folkman, S. (1984). *Stress, appraisal, and coping.* New York: Springer.

Lerner, M. S., & Clum, G. A. (1990). Treatment of suicide ideators: A problem-solving approach. *Behavior Therapy, 21,* 403–411.

Loumidis, K. S., & Hill, A. (1997). Training social problem-solving skill to reduce maladaptive behaviours in intellectual disability groups: The influence of individual difference factors. *Journal of Applied Research in Intellectual Disabilities, 10,* 217–237.

Lynch, D. J., Tamburrino, M. B., & Nagel, R. (1997). Telephone counseling for patients with minor depression: Preliminary findings in a family practice setting. *Journal of Family Practice, 44,* 293–298.

Marx, E. M., Williams, J. M. G., & Claridge, G. C. (1992). Depression and social problem solving. *Journal of Abnormal Psychology, 101,* 78–86.

McLeavey, B. C., Daly, R. J., Ludgate, J. W., & Murray, C. M. (1994). Interpersonal problem-solving skills training in the treatment of self-poisoning patients. *Suicide and Life-Threatening Behavior, 24,* 382–394.

Medalia, A., Revheim, N., & Casey, M. (2001). The remediation of problem-solving skills in schizophrenia. *Schizophrenia Bulletin, 27,* 259–267.

Mendonca, J. D., & Siess, T. F. (1976). Counseling for indecisiveness: Problem solving and anxiety in management training. *Journal of Counseling Psychology, 23,* 330–347.

Moon, J. R., & Eisler, R. M. (1983). Anger control: An experimental comparison of three behavioral treatments. *Behavior Therapy, 14,* 493–505.

Mynors-Wallis, L., Davies, I., Gray, A., Barbour, F., & Gath, D. (1997). A randomized controlled trial and cost analysis of problem-solving treatment for emotional disorders given by community nurses in primary care. *British Journal of Psychiatry, 170,* 113–119.

Mynors-Wallis, L. M., Gath, D. H., Lloyd-Thomas, A. R., & Tomlinson, D. (1995). Randomised controlled trial comparing problem solving treatment with amitriptyline and placebo for major depression in primary care. *British Medical Journal, 310,* 441–445.

Nezu, A. M. (1985). Differences in psychological distress between effective and ineffective problem solvers. *Journal of Counseling Psychology, 32,* 135–138.

Nezu, A. M. (1986a). Cognitive appraisal of problem-solving effectiveness: Relation to depression and depressive symptoms. *Journal of Clinical Psychology, 42,* 42–48.

Nezu, A. M. (1986b). Efficacy of a social problem-solving therapy approach for unipolar depression. *Journal of Consulting and Clinical Psychology, 54,* 196–202.

Nezu, A. M. (1986c). Negative life stress and anxiety: Problem solving as a moderator variable. *Psychological Reports, 58,* 279–283.

Nezu, A. M. (1987). A problem-solving formulation of depression: A literature review and proposal of a pluralistic model. *Clinical Psychology Review, 7,* 122–144.

Nezu, A. M. (2004). Problem solving and behavior therapy revisited. *Behavior Therapy, 35,* 1–33.

Nezu, A. M., & Carnevale, G. J. (1987). Interpersonal problem solving and coping reactions of Vietnam veterans with posttraumatic stress disorder. *Journal of Abnormal Psychology, 96,* 155–157.

Nezu, A. M., & D'Zurilla, T. J. (1989). Social problem solving and negative affective states. In P. C. Kendall & D. Watson (Eds.), *Anxiety and depression: Distinctive and overlapping features* (pp. 285–315). New York: Academic Press.

Nezu, A. M., Nezu, C. M., Felgoise, S. H., McClure, K. S., & Houts, P. S. (2003). Project Genesis: Assessing the efficacy of problem-solving therapy for distressed adult cancer patients. *Journal of Consulting and Clinical Psychology, 71,* 1036–1048.

Nezu, A. M., Nezu, C. M., Felgoise, S. H., & Zwick, M. L. (2003). Psychosocial oncology. In A. M. Nezu, C. M. Nezu, & P. A. Geller (Eds.), *Health psychology* (pp. 267–292). New York: Wiley.

Nezu, A. M., Nezu, C. M., Friedman, S. H., Faddis, S., & Houts, P. S. (1998). *Helping cancer patients cope: A problem-solving approach.* Washington, DC: American Psychological Association.

Nezu, A. M., Nezu, C. M., & Perri, M. G. (1989). *Problem-solving therapy for depression: Theory, research, and clinical guidelines.* New York: Wiley.

Nezu, A. M., Nezu, C. M., Saraydarian, L., Kalmar, K., & Ronan, G. F. (1986). Social problem solving as a moderator variable between negative life stress and depressive symptoms. *Cognitive Therapy and Research, 10,* 489–498.

Nezu, A. M., & Perri, M. G. (1989). Problem-solving therapy for unipolar depression: An initial dismantling investigation. *Journal of Consulting and Clinical Psychology, 57,* 408–413.

Nezu, A. M., & Ronan, G. F. (1985). Life stress, current problems, problem solving, and depressive symptomatology: An integrative model. *Journal of Consulting and Clinical Psychology, 53,* 693–697.

Nezu, A. M., & Ronan, G. F. (1988). Stressful life events, problem solving, and depressive symptoms among university students: A prospective analysis. *Journal of Counseling Psychology, 35,* 134–138.

Nezu, C. M., Nezu, A. M., & Arean, P. A. (1991). Assertiveness and problem-solving therapy for mild mentally retarded persons with dual diagnoses. *Research in Developmental Disabilities, 12,* 371–386.

Patsiokas, A. T., & Clum, G. A. (1985). Effects of psychotherapeutic strategies in the treatment of suicide attempters. *Psychotherapy: Theory, Research, Practice, Training, 22,* 281–290.

Perri, M. G., McAdoo, W. G., McAllister, D. A., Lauer, J. B., Jordan, R. C., Yancey, D. Z., et al. (1987). Effects of peer support and therapist contact on long-term weight loss. *Journal of Consulting and Clinical Psychology, 55,* 615–617.

Perri, M. G., Nezu, A. M., McKelvey, W. F., Schein, R. L., Renjilian, D. A., & Viegener, B. J. (2001). Relapse prevention training and problem-solving therapy in the long-term management of obesity. *Journal of Consulting and Clinical Psychology, 69,* 722–726.

Sahler, O. J. Z., Varni, J. W., Fairclough, D. L., Butler, R. W., Noll, R. B., Dolgin, M. J., et al. (2002). Problem-solving skills training for mothers of children with newly diagnosed cancer: A randomized trial. *Developmental and Behavioral Pediatrics, 23,* 77–86.

Salkovskis, P. M., Atha, C., & Storer, D. (1990). Cognitive–behavioural problem solving in the treatment of patients who repeatedly attempt suicide: A controlled trial. *British Journal of Psychiatry, 157,* 871–876.

Schwartz, M. D., Lerman, C., Audrain, J., Cella, D., Rimer, B., Stefanek, M., et al. (1998). The impact of a brief problem-solving training intervention for relatives of recently diagnosed breast cancer patients. *Annals of Behavioral Medicine, 20,* 7–12.

Synder, C. R., Ilardi, S. S., Cheavens, J., Michael, S. T., Yamhure, L., & Sympson, S. (2000). The role of hope in cognitive–behavioral therapies. *Cognitive Therapy and Research, 24,* 747–762.

Teri, L., Logsdon, R. G., Uomoto, J., & McCurry, S. M. (1997). Behavioral treatment of depression in dementia patients: A controlled clinical trial. *Journals of Gerontology Series B—Psychological Sciences and Social Sciences, 52,* 159–166.

Williams, J. W., Barrett, J., Oxman, T., Frank, E., Katon, W., Sullivan, M., et al. (2000). Treatment of dysthymia and minor depression in primary care: A randomized controlled trial in older adults. *Journal of the American Medical Association, 284,* 1519–1526.

11

PROBLEM-SOLVING TRAINING FOR COUPLES

JAMES V. CORDOVA AND SHILAGH A. MIRGAIN

There are few areas in life that require skillful social problem solving as consistently as marriage. Differences between partners and the resulting friction are part of the natural fabric of marriage, and how successfully partners cope with those inevitable relationship problems determines how healthy their marriage will be. Marital therapy was among the first to adopt the social problem-solving model as a basis for treatment (e.g., Jacobson & Margolin, 1979).

The evolution of behavioral couple interventions has followed from its roots in social problem solving to include emphases on both acceptance and motivation to change. The goal of this chapter is to present the evolution of couple interventions in the service of expanding the social problem-solving model to include an emphasis on acceptance and motivation to change.

RELATIONSHIP DISTRESS

Ninety percent of adults will marry at least once (Norton & Moorman, 1987) and almost all marriages begin with happy partners. Despite the initial promise, it has been estimated that 20% of all couples are experiencing significant relationship distress (Beach, Arias, & O'Leary, 1987) and approximately half of all first marriages end in divorce (see Sayers & Cordova, 2001).

Relationship distress is associated with a number of other problems, including risk of depression (Whisman, 2001), substance abuse (Maisto, O'Farrell, Connors, McKay, & Pelcovits, 1988), domestic violence (Holtzworth-Munroe, Smutzler, Bates, & Sandin, 1997), diminished immune system functioning (Newton, Kiecolt-Glaser, Glaser, & Malarkey, 1995), and poorer adherence to medical treatment (Schmaling & Sher, 1997). In addition, marital distress is associated with child difficulties such as diminished mental health, increased problem behavior, and poorer school performance (e.g., Amato, 2001).

Destructive communication and ineffective conflict are among the biggest contributors to marital distress (e.g., Gottman, 1994). Distressed partners tend to ignore relationship problems, have difficulty generating viable solutions, and physically withdraw in response to conflict (Christensen & Shenk, 1991). Dissatisfied partners are less likely to engage in active listening and more likely to criticize and blame each other (Weiss & Heyman, 1997). Thus, it appears that poor social problem solving plays a substantial role in marital deterioration. Given the amount of suffering resulting from relationship deterioration, developing effective treatments for couple distress is essential to the health and welfare of the population as a whole. It is toward this end that the social problem-solving model was first applied as a treatment for marital deterioration.

THE SOCIAL PROBLEM-SOLVING MODEL

D'Zurilla and Goldfried (1971) first defined social problem-solving as the process by which an individual attempts to identify, discover, or invent effective coping responses to everyday problems. They proposed a model consisting of two components: (a) problem orientation and (b) problem-solving skills.

A problem orientation is the response set brought to a problem based on past experience (D'Zurilla & Sheedy, 1992). It comprises the specific ways in which a person perceives and appraises a new problem. It involves motivation to address a problem, as well as a person's general awareness of problems, assessment of problem-solving competence, and effectiveness expectations (Reinecke, DuBois, & Schultz, 2001). A person's problem orientation affects the quality of problem solving by influencing when problem solving begins, the amount of time and effort expended, the emotions generated, and the efficiency of the solution.

Partners develop their unique relationship problem orientations over their lifetimes, from early childhood experiences with family and peers through later adult experiences with romantic partners. These histories shape how well prepared a person is to identify and respond to relationship issues. For example, there is evidence that individuals with anxious–ambivalent attachment styles (compared to those with more secure styles) may be hyperattuned to fluctuations in relationship quality, leaving them uniquely vulnerable to depressive symptoms when relationship quality declines (Scott & Cordova, 2002).

A set of four skills makes up the second component of the social problem-solving model. The first skill is problem definition and formulation, or the ability to obtain relevant, factual information about a problem, clarify the nature of the problem, and delineate a set of realistic goals. The second skill involves the ability to identify, discover, or create a range of solutions. The third skill is decision making, which involves comparing and choosing the best solution for the situation. The fourth skill is solution implementation and verification, or evaluating the actual outcome of the solution. Training in these four skills was incorporated into behavioral couple therapy as the principal means of improving failing marriages.

BEHAVIORAL MARITAL THERAPY

Social learning theorists proposed that marital discord results from poor communication and problem-solving skills, leading to decreases in positive interactions and increases in aversive interactions (Jacobson & Margolin, 1979). Behavioral Marital Therapy (BMT) was grounded on the principle that improving partners' problem-solving skills would improve relationship quality. BMT consists of three strategies: (a) increasing partners' exchange of positive behaviors, (b) increasing consistent and effective communication, and (c) teaching effective problem solving.

The first BMT strategy, Behavior Exchange (BE), is designed to increase the number of positive interactions between partners. BE consists of two steps. First, partners identify things they could do to increase the other's relationship satisfaction but that do not require significant personal change. Next, each partner is assigned to do at least one thing from the list during the week and to observe the effect on the other partner. When BE works, the increased level of positivity provides a quick boost to partners' marital satisfaction.

Although BE provides a quick boost, communication and problem-solving training are the primary methods for improving relationship quality (Cordova & Jacobson, 1997). Communication training (CT) involves teaching principles of effective communication. The first principle is the inherent difficulty of effective communication. Although in day-to-day conversation we generally understand each other well enough to get by, that understanding is usually less than completely accurate. What we hear of what others say to us is clouded by our preconceptions, lack of attention, and focus on our own thoughts. This clouding is usually not terribly disruptive; however, the more important or emotionally challenging the conversation, the greater the likelihood that it will result in destructive misunderstandings.

The next principle involves sharing thoughts and feelings during a conversation. Partners are taught to avoid mind reading, criticizing, and blaming because doing so often results in defensiveness and polarization. Partners are also taught to take turns talking, to avoid interrupting, and to keep each turn short so the other partner can hear and remember the message. Finally, partners are taught to paraphrase as a means of double-checking their initial understanding of what the other person said. Paraphrasing consists of (a) privately acknowledging that one's initial understanding of what the partner said may be wrong, (b) sharing one's initial understanding and, (c) asking if what one heard is what the partner meant to convey. Paraphrasing also allows the *speaker* to hear what the other partner is hearing and to clarify the message before misunderstandings derail effective communication.

Problem-solving training (PST) teaches couples concrete strategies for addressing relationship problems. PST closely follows D'Zurilla and Goldfried's (1971) steps for effective problem solving. The first step involves distinguishing between two phases of problem solving: (a) problem definition and (b) problem solution. This is an important distinction because problem solving can become bogged down if the problem is poorly understood. In addition, jumping back and forth between defining and attempting to solve a problem can easily derail partners. Partners begin the definition phase by expressing appreciation, understanding, and positive regard for each other. Because partners bring a history of hurt and anger to discussion of the problem, an initial demonstration of affection lays the foundation for improved collaboration. Couples next identify the specific circumstances and behaviors that define the problem. Thus, instead of the husband saying that the problem is that the wife does not care about him, he is guided to the specific statement that he feels ignored when his wife spends her evening talking on the phone with friends. The therapist also asks the partners to express their feelings about the problem. This allows each partner to develop a deeper understanding of the other's experience.

Following definition, couples begin the problem-solution phase. Brainstorming involves generating as many solutions as possible while refraining from evaluating their viability. Partners are instructed to be creative, offering both genuine and outlandish suggestions. The goal is to increase the probability that partners will discover the best available solution rather than settling for the first solution that comes to mind. After generating a list of solutions, partners review each item and remove the ones that are impossible, silly, or inadequate.

Next, partners review the remaining items, discuss the pros and cons of each, and work together to make a decision about each item. The couple is asked to find solutions that do not impose too heavy a burden on either partner. Changes to items are explored until some compromise is worked out or the item is eliminated.

Next partners write a change agreement that details their solution. Partners anticipate obstacles that might interfere with implementation, and plans are made for dealing with those obstacles. Verification occurs over the following sessions. At the beginning of each session, partners review how the agreement is working and collaborate on any necessary changes.

More empirical research has been conducted on BMT than on any other approach to couple therapy, and the results have been promising. Studies show that 72% of couples improve during treatment (58% scoring in the maritally satisfied range), and most couples maintain gains through six months (Jacobson, 1984). However, continued follow-up revealed that approximately 30% of recovered couples relapsed after two years (Jacobson, Schmaling, & Holtzworth-Munroe, 1987). Overall 50% of all couples treated with BMT achieve lasting benefits.

Social problem solving with couples, as originally implemented, required a lot of active collaboration between partners for the treatment to be successful. Partners had to collaborate to (a) increase positive exchanges; (b) learn, practice, and adhere to the CT guidelines; and (c) negotiate solutions to emotionally volatile problems. This expectation of collaboration is viable for many couples; however, for many others, anger, polarization, and problem embeddedness precluded partners' ability to work with each other to practice new skills. Research found that the couples least likely to benefit from BMT were older, more distressed, more emotionally disengaged, and more polarized in their disagreements (e.g., Jacobson, Follette, & Pagel, 1986), all characteristics likely to undermine partners' capacity for collaboration.

In addition, BMT also required partners to adhere to a well-defined rule structure. One difficulty with this is that during emotionally challenging interactions, partners find it difficult to follow rules. Some researchers have commented on the emotional gymnastics required to use rational skills in emotionally challenging contexts (Gottman, Coan, Carrere, & Swanson, 1998).

Another difficulty with teaching rules is that the initial contingencies for following them are imposed by the teacher, who praises or corrects partners' adherence. Reinforcement does not stem naturally from the transaction between the individual and the out-of-session environment. Rules are only beneficial in the long run if the behavior they elicit eventually comes under the direct control of naturally occurring contingencies. Thus, partners may follow the rules of CT and PST in the presence of the therapist, but unless they make direct contact with the benefits of following those rules in their real-world relationship, they are unlikely to continue doing so outside of therapy. Research suggests that couples are unlikely to continue using BMT techniques after therapy, even if those couples remain maritally satisfied. Instructing couples to begin their discussion with a positive statement is an example of rule-governed behavior. The therapist reinforces the couple for compliance with the rule in the hope that natural contingencies will maintain the behavior. However, because the behavior is "following a rule," rather than genuinely praising or reassuring the partner, it feels forced and not genuine. In turn, a positive response from the partner is improbable and the behavior is unlikely to continue for lack of reinforcement. The implication is that the skills may never come to be controlled by naturally occurring contingencies. Therefore, they may not generalize outside therapy and they may be susceptible to quick extinction once therapy is over.

Thus, although a 50% success rate for BMT was laudable, there were empirical and theoretical reasons to suspect that the approach could be improved by attending to the underlying causes of noncollaboration and developing techniques using natural contingencies

INTEGRATIVE COUPLES THERAPY

Advances in couples' therapy in the 1990s consisted of integrating an approach to coping with problems that emphasized acceptance. Promoting acceptance can facilitate intimacy and reestablish effective problem solving. D'Zurilla's model anticipates this evolution toward addressing emotional climate. D'Zurilla (1990) stated that problem solving is conceived as a broad strategy whose goals are not limited to problem-focused goals but may include emotion-focused goals, depending on the nature of the problem and how it is defined and appraised. D'Zurilla (1990) defined a problem-focused goal as one that is aimed at managing situational demands and an emotion-focused goal as one that is aimed at managing emotions generated by the problem. He stated that when the problem is appraised as unchangeable or uncontrollable, an emotion-focused goal would be emphasized. On the other hand, if the situation were appraised as changeable or controllable, then a problem-focused goal would be appropriate, although an emotion-focused goal might be included to cope with emotional stress.

Christensen and Jacobson (e.g., 1998) developed Integrative Couples Therapy (ICT) emphasizing a similar distinction between controllable versus uncontrollable situations. The wise application of acceptance came to be seen as an adaptive repertoire for coping with relationship problems that do not lend themselves to negotiated change. When partners find themselves stuck struggling to change the unchangeable, bitterness, resentment, anger, and polarization can begin to define the relationship's emotional climate. In fact, it is impossible to assess for true problem-solving deficits before the emotional climate is healthy. If the emotional climate is clouded by anger and bitterness, even partners with excellent problem-solving abilities may not use those abilities to help their relationship. A couple's problems are not always solvable through negotiated change because two individuals will naturally have differences such as spending habits or intimacy needs. Techniques for promoting acceptance were developed to help partners cope more gracefully with the unchangeable aspects of their relationship while preserving the best parts of the relationship as a whole. Promoting acceptance is intended to help partners escape unwinnable battles, freeing up the time and energy spent fighting for relationship-healthy practices. Acceptance strategies foster intimacy and compassionate understanding, thus fostering the type of emotional climate in which partners genuinely want to behave lovingly and are willing to negotiate with each other toward instrumental change.

ICT begins by assessing each partner's experience of the problems that have led them to seek treatment. One goal of assessment is to determine the emphasis to place on change versus acceptance. Assessing partners' problem orientations allows the therapist to determine whether partners are defining solvable problems in unsolvable ways or whether they are defining unsolvable differences as solvable problems. A partner's likes and dislikes—whether she is a morning person or evening person; whether he is exuberant or neurotic, shy or gregarious, a spender or a saver, neat or messy—are unlikely to be bargained away. Although unchangeable differences can be a source of significant friction in a relationship, ICT proposes that gracefully accepting such differences is the key to long-term adaptive coping. Alternatively, framing such natural differences as problems that can be solved is often the root of chronic, corrosive conflict. The assessment phase consists of a conjoint interview followed by individual interviews with each spouse and a final conjoint feedback session. In the conjoint session, the therapist asks each partner what has brought him or her into therapy. It is often the case that partners' views of their problems differ in important ways. As partners describe their issues, the therapist models active listening and judicious paraphrasing. Paraphrasing provides a means for the therapist to understand each person's perspective and it communicates acceptance and validation of each partner. When done well, those initial sessions build rapport with each individual partner and helps partners to gain a deeper and more compassionate understanding of each other. Because they are not talking to each other but are instead listening to the other partner talk to the therapist, it is often easier for partners to hear each other without the filtering of self-defensiveness. Next, the therapist describes the framework of therapy, explaining that assessment consists of the conjoint interview, the two individual interviews, and a final feedback session. Partners are told that they will decide whether to continue with therapy at the feedback session. Letting partners know early that they will be asked to decide whether to continue therapy helps them to recognize that engaging in therapy remains their choice and that they are free to choose otherwise at any time.

The individual sessions explore each partner's unique take on relationship issues without fear of hurting the other partner. It also allows the therapist to safely assess for domestic violence, secret affairs, and private thoughts of divorce. Finally, it allows the therapist to assess for individual issues such as depression, substance use, and individual stressors.

Six areas are assessed during the initial phase. The first is the couple's level of relationship distress. The more severe and chronic the distress, the more likely the therapist will begin by fostering acceptance. The second area assessed is relationship commitment. The less committed partners are, the more the therapist will focus initially on uncovering the couple's strengths and the positive aspects of the relationship.

Third, the therapist assesses the major issues in the relationship. Issues that are unlikely to change, such as those centered around private experiences (e.g., different desires for physical affection) are likely targets for acceptance, whereas issues concerning more instrumental behaviors (e.g., household tasks) are likely targets for problem-solving training.

The next area addressed is how the couple is currently dealing with their problems. Identifying the couple's patterns forms the basis for much of the following acceptance work, because it is often not the issues themselves but how the couple deals with these issues that determines their current level of distress. The final area assessed is the couple's strengths, because it is their strengths that motivate them to work on the relationship.

Following assessment, the therapist designs a treatment plan that is presented at the feedback session. Depending on the particular needs of the couple, the therapist will propose a combination of acceptance and change strategies. The goal of feedback is to move the couple toward a shared understanding of their difficulties and increase their compassion for each other. The therapist also begins constructing a theme that captures the main problematic pattern in the relationship. The theme reframes problems as arising out of understandable reactions to fundamental differences. The theme is formulated in a way that diminishes partners' blaming of each other, instead moving the blame onto the theme. The theme is described as a pattern that emerges naturally out of understandable differences between partners. Thus, rather than tell the story of the couple's problems in terms of individuals in conflict injuring and being injured by each other, the therapist constructs a story about a union that, like any individual, has weaknesses that are blameless and that can be compensated for.

After feedback, the therapist begins the intervention stage. Intervention involves three general strategies for promoting acceptance: (a) empathic joining around the problem, (b) unified detachment from the conflict, and (c) tolerance building. The goal of empathic joining is to increase partners' compassionate understanding and to promote greater intimacy. The technique involves facilitating discovery of the soft emotions associated with partners' biggest area of conflict. Partners are encouraged to describe their experience of hurt, vulnerability, sadness, fear, and love. Soft emotions such as these tend to elicit empathy, compassion, and closeness. Hard emotions, such as hostility, naturally elicit defensiveness and counterattack. When soft emotions are emphasized over blame and recrimination, then each partner is better able to see the other's distress without the distorting cloud of accusation and is less likely to view the other as an enemy to be condemned but as a fellow sufferer who deserves compassion. For example, when one partner is angry because her partner neglects her, the therapist might lead her to reveal any feelings of loneliness and fear underlying the anger. By associating her anger with underlying feelings of loneliness and fear, the therapist hopes to make that anger more understandable and thus more acceptable. This process also occasionally results in partners spontaneously changing behavior (e.g., providing more attention), such that emotional acceptance and behavior change are both achieved. Thus change and acceptance are not mutually exclusive terms. Acceptance itself is positive change and in addition can help partners achieve negotiated changes previously unavailable to them.

Unified detachment reframes partners' problem as an "it" versus something that each partner does maliciously. The problem is reframed such that it is no longer "that thing my partner did to me" but becomes instead "that thing that happens to us sometimes." The therapist helps the couple describe their typical negative interactions to help them see the underlying pattern. As the couple begins to discern the pattern, it becomes the source of their shared pain and something that the partners can cope with together. For example, it is simply neither partner's fault that they have different needs for closeness. Although that difference may be a friction point, the partners will never solve it by pushing for change. At the same time, that friction point does not have to be corrosive. Partners can learn to acknowledge their different needs without judgment. Partners are then in a better position to give up the unwinnable struggle to change each other in fundamental ways and to instead use that energy to cope with their mutual difficulty as partners (Cordova & Jacobson, 1997).

Another way to facilitate acceptance is to increase tolerance for partner behavior. Tolerance is a point on the continuum from aversion to attraction (Cordova, 2001). When therapy starts, partners perceive the complained about situation as wholly aversive and struggle to avoid, escape, or destroy it. The difficulty with this strategy is that more often than not it means avoiding, escaping, or destroying the relationship as a whole. If one's partner is a tad neurotic, one cannot simply avoid or destroy that single aspect of his or her character. One can either tolerate and embrace it as part of the complex and lovable whole, or one can complain, attack, reject, belittle, and generally fight to diminish that person in the service of pursuing an imaginary partner that is "better" than the real one.

Acceptance strategies are designed to change the stimulus function of the unchangeable things that partners struggle against such that they are no longer wholly aversive but instead take on some of the positive qualities of the person and relationship as a whole (Cordova, 2001). When these strategies work exceptionally well, those things that were wholly aversive become attractive and embraceable. For example, as a person comes to associate exercise with its benefits, then, despite its initially aversive qualities, that person will come to embrace the feelings of strenuous exercise that were initially wholly aversive. Although this type of outcome is rare in couples therapy, it is the ideal toward which ICT therapists strive.

Further back on the continuum lays tolerance. Tolerance is not enthusiastic embracing. It results from a mix of attractive and aversive elements such that the original source of aversion no longer sets off the same destructive relationship patterns. Although the target situation is still experienced as less than pleasant, there are enough positive things about it to make it tolerable (the person is not actively trying to destroy it). For example, partners may never be thrilled that their needs for intimacy do not match, but a more compassionate understanding of that mismatch may make it easier to tolerate and less likely to corrode the foundation of the relationship.

Emotional acceptance through tolerance building is promoted in several ways. For example, positive reemphasis is a strategy for increasing tolerance by uncovering the positive features of the partner's negative behavior. This strategy commonly frames the spouse's negative behavior as part of an otherwise attractive characteristic. For example, it may be that the constant need to have friends around that is currently driving the spouse crazy is an aspect of the gregariousness that he initially found compelling.

Highlighting complementary differences is another strategy for increasing tolerance. The point is that some differences create a well-rounded relationship, and without them the couple might experience more distress. For example, if one partner is a spender and the other is a saver, then the therapist can frame this difference as complementary in that if both were savers, they would never enjoy the fruits of their work and if both were spenders they would have little saving to rely on for the future.

Preparing the couple for backsliding is another tolerance strategy. It is inevitable that couples will both make progress and backslide. Therefore, it is important that the therapist prepare the couple for the inevitability of slip-ups so that they do not misinterpret a lapse as utter defeat. This is especially important during the initial stage of therapy when a couple may believe that the changes they have made are impervious to relapse. Preparing partners builds tolerance for slip-ups and allows them to remain positive about the health of their relationship throughout the ups and downs of relating.

The implications of acceptance for the theory of social problem solving derive from the increased emphasis on the limits of framing all problems as solvable through instrumental change. Although D'Zurilla and colleagues did not limit social problem-solving theory to the pursuit of instrumental change over acceptance, the spirit of the times resulted in the bulk of the emphasis being on instrumental, manipulate the environment, change. This is, of course, a warranted emphasis in that most of the problems that we are confronted with are of the type that can be solved in the same way that puzzles are solved and machines are repaired. However, currently there is an appreciation that applying this one way of pursuing solutions to all perceived problems often results in more harm than good. Trying to solve the problem of unpleasant thoughts and feelings or trying to solve the problem of naturally occurring individual differences in the same way that one solves the problem of waking up on time for work is not simply foolhardy but actually dangerous. The theoretical lesson of ICT is that struggling to change the unchangeable in a relationship often destroys the very thing that the person is trying to save. Similarly, recent advances in thinking about the etiology of depression, anxiety, and substance abuse suggest that the struggle to solve the problem of unpleasant thoughts and feelings or simply the struggle to solve all discrepancies between what is and what should be is at the heart of a great deal of psychopathology (Hayes, 1994; Marlatt, 1994; Teasdale et al., 2002).

MOTIVATIONAL INTERVIEWING WITH COUPLES AND SOCIAL PROBLEM SOLVING

The first component of social problem solving is a person's problem orientation, including when he or she recognizes a problem exists and whether he or she is motivated to change. Both BMT and ICT assume that partners have recognized the existence of problems in their relationship and that they are motivated to seek treatment and pursue change. However, it is likely that there exists in the population of couples a subset that are experiencing relationship-threatening problems but that do not yet recognize those problems or are ambivalent about what, if anything, to do about them. Although these at-risk couples may have perfectly adequate social problem-solving skills, those skills will remain unused if the partners do not recognize the problems or are ambivalent about change. Whereas couples seeking therapy and premarital education are motivated to pursue these interventions either by their distress or by their desire to start their married lives on the right foot, at-risk couples in established marriage are motivated by neither. These couples may be suspicious of therapy or may not think of it as a viable or desirable option for economic, time, or social reasons.

To reach these couples and to facilitate their natural problem-solving abilities, Cordova and his colleagues (Cordova, Warren, & Gee, 2001) designed an intervention called the Marriage Checkup (MC) to apply the techniques of motivational interviewing to couples that are at-risk of marital deterioration but that are not actively working to solve those problems. The MC is an assessment and feedback intervention using Miller and Rollnick's (1991) motivational interviewing (MI) strategies and Jacobson and Christensen's (1998) acceptance promotion strategies. The MC is intended to fill the niche between the inoculations against marital distress provided by prevention programs (e.g., PREP; Freedman, Low, Markman, & Stanley, 2002) and the intensive treatment of severe distress provided by couples therapy.

The MC facilitates the motivational component of partners' problem orientation to elicit effective problem solving. Specifically, the MC facilitates couples' progress through the stages of change. Prochaska and DiClemente (1984) argued that people that achieve successful change pass through five distinct stages. The first is a precontemplative stage, in which partners suffering from problems do not recognize these areas as problematic or subject to change. The second is a contemplation stage in which partners recognize problems but are ambivalent about what to do. The third is a determination stage in which partners are determined to address their problems but may not know what to do. The fourth is an action stage, in which partners are taking specific steps to address their problems. At this stage, efforts to change may or may not be effective. The fifth stage is a maintenance stage, in which partners work to maintain positive changes. The sixth stage can be either a stage in which the problems are resolved or a stage in which the problems recur and the couple returns to one of the former stages.

MI moves people through the stages of change by helping them identify problems that interfere with important personal goals and values and to channel any motivation to change in productive directions. To attract couples that may be ambivalent about seeking help, the MC offers community couples an opportunity to receive a thorough relationship health checkup followed by tailored feedback about the results. The service is advertised as informational only and it is made clear that partners are free to do with that information whatever they wish. This allows partners to remain ambivalent and still participate in the checkup.

As part of the checkup, partners complete a battery of questionnaires covering all areas of their relationship from satisfaction, stability, commitment to housework, decision-making, sex, and children. In addition, partners are interviewed about the early history of their relationship, because studies have found that how partners describe their early history is predictive of their future relationship health (Buehlman, Gottman, & Katz, 1992). Next, partners' problem-solving skills are assessed by asking them to identify two of the most pressing problems in their relationship and then asking them to spend 15 minutes trying to work toward some resolution of each problem. These 15-minute interactions are videotaped and analyzed for the presence of any behavior patterns that have been associated with relationship deterioration. The assessment session ends with an interview in which the therapist works to facilitate improved understanding between the partners using the techniques of ICT for highlighting softer emotions, promoting unified detachment, and developing improved tolerance.

Two weeks later, couples return for their feedback. Partners are given the results of the questionnaire battery, as well as feedback concerning how they talk about their early history and how they work with each other to solve problems. The results are presented simply as data for the partners to consider. Motivation is facilitated by juxtaposing problematic behavior with partners' valuing of the health of their relationship. The assumption is that when partners learn that certain behaviors such as criticism and withdrawal are predictive of relationship deterioration, they will be motivated by their desire to have a healthy marriage to work toward changing those destructive behaviors. In addition, the feedback provides the couple with ways of reframing any unchangeable differences so that those differences are less likely to wear away at the foundation of their relationship. The therapist also attempts to facilitate improved intimacy by highlighting each partner's vulnerability in relation to the other and by underscoring the role of vulnerability in sustaining and deepening intimacy (Cordova & Scott, 2001). Finally, to the degree that partners are motivated to pursue change, they are offered a number of alternative strategies for pursuing that change, including therapy.

The implication of the MC for social problem-solving theory is in its emphasis on eliciting partners' motivation to identify and work toward solving relationship problems. In addition, it assumes that most people have adequate problem-solving skills and will be able to effectively address their own problems given the proper motivation. MI contributes to the evolution of social problem solving by providing an effective means of actively eliciting the motivation necessary for effectively coping with day-to-day relationship problems.

CONCLUSION

Social problem-solving theory has provided a framework for understanding the essential role of effective problem-solving skills in interpersonal settings. It contributed directly to early behavioral interventions for marital distress and continues to provide an important perspective on recent developments in the field of couple intervention. Recent developments have added to problem-solving skills training an emphasis on acceptance as an essential problem-solving tool, as well as tools for promoting the motivation necessary to begin the processes of effective coping.

REFERENCES

Amato, P. R. (2001). Children of divorce in the 1990s: An update of the Amato and Keith (1991) meta-analysis. *Journal of Family Psychology, 15,* 355–370.

Beach, S. R. H., Arias, I., & O'Leary, K. D. (1987). The relationship of marital satisfaction and social support to depressive symptomatology. *Journal of Psychopathology and Behavioral Assessment, 8,* 305–316.

Buehlman, K. T., Gottman, J. M., & Katz, L. F. (1992). How a couple views their past predicts their future: Predicting divorce from an oral history interview. *Journal of Family Psychology, 5,* 295–318.

Christensen, A., & Jacobson, N. S. (1998). *Acceptance and change in couple therapy: A therapist's guide to transforming relationships.* New York: Norton.

Christensen, A., & Shenk, J. L. (1991). Communication, conflict, and psychological distance in non-distressed, clinic, and divorcing couples. *Journal of Consulting and Clinical Psychology, 59,* 458–463.

Cordova, J. V. (2001). Acceptance in behavior therapy: Understanding the process of change. *Behavior Analyst, 24,* 213–226.

Cordova, J. V., & Jacobson, N. S. (1997). Acceptance in couple therapy and its implications for the treatment of depression. In R. J. Sternberg & M. Hojjat (Eds.), *Satisfaction in close relationships* (pp. 307–334). New York: Guilford Press.

Cordova, J. V., & Scott, R. L. (2001). Intimacy: A behavioral interpretation. *Behavior Analyst, 24,* 75–86.

Cordova, J. V. Warren, L. Z., & Gee, C. B. (2001). Motivational interviewing as an intervention for at-risk couples. *Journal of Marital and Family Therapy, 27,* 315–326.

D'Zurilla, T. J. (1990). Problem-solving training for effective stress management and prevention. *Journal of Cognitive Psychotherapy, 4,* 327–354.

D'Zurilla, T. J., & Goldfried, M. R. (1971). Problem solving and behavior modification. *Journal of Abnormal Psychology, 78,* 107–126.

D'Zurilla, T. J., & Sheedy, C. F. (1992). The relation between social problem-solving ability and subsequent level of academic competence in college students. *Cognitive Therapy and Research, 16,* 589–599.

Freedman, C. M., Low, S. M., Markman, H. J., & Stanley, S. M. (2002). Equipping couples with the tools to cope with predictable and unpredictable crisis events: The PREP program. *International Journal of Emergency Mental Health, 4,* 49–56.

Gottman, J. M. (1994). *What predicts divorce? The relationship between marital processes and marital outcomes.* Hillsdale, NJ: Erlbaum.

Gottman, J. M., Coan, J., Carrere, S. & Swanson, C. (1998). Predicting marital happiness and stability from newlywed interactions. *Journal of Marriage and the Family, 60,* 5–22.

Hayes, S. C. (1994). Content, context, and the types of psychological acceptance. In S. C. Hayes, N. S. Jacobson, V. M. Follette, & M. J. Dougher (Eds.), *Acceptance and change: Content and context in psychotherapy* (pp. 13–32). Reno, NV: Context Press.

Holtzworth-Munroe, A., Smutzler, N., Bates, L., & Sandin, E. (1997). Husband violence: Basic facts and clinical implications. In W. K. Halford & H. J. Markman (Eds.), *Clinical handbook of marriage and couples interventions* (pp. 129–151). New York: John Wiley & Sons.

Jacobson, N. S. (1984). A component analysis of behavioral marital therapy: The relative effectiveness of behavioral exchange and problem solving training. *Journal of Consulting and Clinical Psychology, 42,* 295–305.

Jacobson, N. S., & Christensen, A. (1998). *Acceptance and change in couple therapy: A therapist's guide to transforming relationships.* New York: W. W. Norton.

Jacobson, N. S., Follette, W. C. & Pagel, M. (1986). Predicting who will benefit from behavioral marital therapy. *Journal of Consulting and Clinical Psychology, 54,* 518–522.

Jacobson, N. S., & Margolin, G. (1979). *Marital therapy: Strategies based on social learning and behavior exchange principles.* New York: Brunner/Mazel.

Jacobson, N. S., Schmaling, K. B., & Holtzworth-Munroe, A. (1987). Component analysis of behavioral marital therapy: 2-year follow-up and prediction of relapse. *Journal of Marital and Family Therapy, 13,* 187–195.

Maisto, S. A., O'Farrell, T. J., Connors, G. J., McKay, J. R., & Pelcovits, M. (1988). Alcoholics' attributions of factors affecting their relapse to drinking and reasons for terminating relapse episodes. *Addictive Behaviors, 13,* 79–82.

Marlatt, G. A. (1994). Addiction and acceptance. In S. C. Hayes, N. S. Jacobson, V. M. Follette, & M. J. Dougher (Eds.), *Acceptance and change: Content and context in psychotherapy* (pp. 175–197). Reno, NV: Context Press.

Miller, W. R., & Rollnick, S. (1991). *Motivational interviewing: Preparing people to change addictive behavior.* New York: Guilford Press.

Newton, T. L., Kiecolt-Glaser, J. K., Glaser, R., & Malarkey, W. B. (1995). Conflict and withdrawal during marital interaction: The roles of hostility and defensiveness. *Personality and Social Psychology Bulletin, 21*, 512–524.

Norton, A. J., & Moorman, J. E. (1987). Current trends in marriage and divorce among American women. *Journal of Marriage and the Family, 49*, 3–14.

Prochaska, J. O., DiClemente, C. C. (1984). *The transtheoretical approach: Crossing the traditional boundaries of therapy*. Malabar, FL: Krieger.

Reinecke, M. A., DuBois, D. L., & Schultz, T. M. (2001). Social problem solving, mood, and suicidality among inpatient adolescents. *Cognitive Therapy and Research, 25*, 743–756.

Sayers, S. L., & Cordova, J. V. (2001). Rates of marital success and failure. *Couple Research and Therapy, 7*, 4–7.

Schmaling, K. B., & Sher, T. G. (1997). Physical health and relationships. In W. K. Halford & H. J. Markman (Eds.), *Clinical handbook of marriage and couples interventions* (pp. 323–336). New York: John Wiley & Sons.

Scott, R. L., & Cordova, J. V. (2002). The influence of adult attachment styles on the association between marital adjustment and depressive symptoms. *Journal of Family Psychology, 16*, 199–208.

Teasdale, J. D., Moore, R. G., Hayhurst, H., Pope, M., Williams, S., & Segal, Z. V. (2002). Metacognitive awareness and prevention of relapse in depression: Empirical evidence. *Journal of Consulting and Clinical Psychology, 70*, 275–287.

Weiss, R. L., & Heyman, R. E. (1997). A clinical–research overview of couples interactions. In W. K. Halford & H. J. Markman (Eds.), *Clinical handbook of marriage and couples intervention* (pp. 13–42). New York: John Wiley & Sons.

Whisman, M. A. (2001). The association between depression and marital dissatisfaction. In S. R. H. Beach (Ed.), *Marital and family processes in depression* (pp. 3–24). Washington, DC: American Psychological Association.

12

PROBLEM-SOLVING TRAINING FOR FAMILIES

SAM VUCHINICH

Families are often closely involved with the psychological problems of individuals. A family member may be a primary cause of the problem or an essential ally in implementing a solution. The range of family connections with psychological disorder is broad. Because of these linkages, training in social problem solving often includes family members of those in therapy or prevention programs. Families may have a secondary, supportive role in training or be a central focus of training. There has been a steady expansion of the use of family training in problem solving over the past 20 years because it has been associated with success in treatment and prevention in a wide variety of applications (e.g., Braswell & Bloomquist, 1991; Cooke, McNally, Mulligan, Harrison, & Newman, 2001; Falloon, 1988a, 1988b; Russ & Ollendick, 1999; Shure & Spivak, 1978; Spoth, Redmond, & Shin, 2000).

This chapter reviews work on social problem solving with families in terms of its theoretical basis, research on its effectiveness, and practical issues that arise in training. The chapter explains how the involvement of families can improve the success of programs that use training in social problem solving from a social competence perspective (D'Zurilla & Nezu, 1999). The participation of families from this perspective differs from other treatment approaches that use problem-solving components, such as parent training based on social learning theory (Forgatch & Patterson, 1989), social skills training (Barkley, Edwards, Laneri, Fletcher, & Metevia, 2001), or various types of family therapy (Falloon, 1988a; Haley, 1987). This chapter focuses on cognitive–behavioral aspects of family involvement in problem-solving therapy. It considers the involvement of two or more family members, but not marital couple relationships that are addressed in chapter 11 (this volume).

Efforts to improve treatment success have led to the integration of family members in various forms of cognitive–behavioral therapy that include problem-solving components. This is especially prevalent in therapy and prevention programs for child and adolescent clients (Hibbs & Jensen, 1996; Lewinsohn, Clarke, Rohde, Hops, & Seeley, 1996; Spoth et al., 2000; Stark, Swearer, Kurowski, Sommer, & Bowen, 1996). Family members are not only useful in the therapy itself but are especially relevant to the generalization and maintenance of treatment gains (Braswell, 1991). By training family members in problem solving, the therapist has the opportunity to improve the client's adaptation by changing both the client and the client's social environment.

LOGISTICS OF TRAINING FAMILIES IN PROBLEM SOLVING

Family training can be done with individuals, in families, in groups with several families involved, or with a combination of these formats. Training is often done in groups, usually with separate group sessions for family members and clients (Braswell & Bloomquist, 1991; D'Zurilla & Nezu, 1999; Spoth et al., 2000). Separate group sessions are especially relevant with child or adolescent clients because training materials and methods are quite different for children and adults. Group training is cost-effective compared with individual or single-family sessions and has some advantages in terms of educational and therapeutic techniques available. For example, a group of parents who all have a child with the same disorder usually have many similar experiences and stories (e.g., Braswell, 1991). Skillful trainers can integrate such commonalities to help motivate parents to learn problem solving and use exercises that are especially relevant for the parents in the group. Training includes coaching, modeling, shaping, rehearsal, and performance feedback (D'Zurilla & Nezu, 1999).

Training of a single family as a group provides some special benefits worth noting. This allows the details of the client's disorder, the family member characteristics and other family features to be taken into account. In this context the trainer can identify both the strengths and weaknesses a given family has in terms of problem solving. Thus feedback, homework, and recommendations on how to improve can be more focused. Ideally some training of the family with the client would take place in all programs. Such training of individual families is often done as a component in combination with group sessions, or it is done as part of family therapy, where all sessions include only the family.

Some cautions are in order for any kind of group sessions with certain types of clients. Training in problem solving is usually approached as a straightforward learning process. But communication and emotional processes that are not part of the training can occur simply as a result of clients or parents having something in common. This can have undesirable consequences. For example, training sessions with antisocial adolescents may promote more antisocial behavior if the adolescents reinforce antisocial attitudes and behaviors among others in their peer group (Dishion, McCord, & Poulin, 1999).

FOUR APPROACHES TO FAMILY TRAINING IN SOCIAL PROBLEM SOLVING

Families of clients are typically involved in social problem-solving therapy in one of four ways: (a) education, (b) facilitation, (c) conflict management, and (d) family system change.

These four categories are not mutually exclusive but represent the primary clinical approaches to family training in social problem solving. They differ in how much training families receive and the role of the family in the treatment process.

Education

Education about the problem-solving procedures provides general support for therapy in the home. With education the basic problem-solving process is explained in the context of the client's disorder. The elements of social problem solving are reviewed and families are told what to expect as the client tries to implement the procedures. This is usually done in conjunction with family education about the nature of the client's disorder. With this technique the family members can develop an understanding of the therapeutic approach and be supportive of the client's efforts at problem solving, even though they are not using the problem-solving procedures themselves.

This education can be implemented with a wide variety of methods. These include pamphlets, videotapes with examples of clients using problem-solving techniques, role playing, didactic group education sessions with members of several families, and sessions with only one family present. Use of multiple methods is desirable. This education is often short-term, with the use of one or two sessions supplemented with other materials being a common strategy. In the context of prevention, educational components can range from one session to several weekly meetings that may involve telephone contacts or Internet-based materials.

Some education of family members about a client's disorder and the form of treatment is standard practice in most clinical settings. This provides a ready opportunity to inform families about problem-solving training. Family members who have frequent contact with the client should be provided with this information. The following example shows how basic education of family members is used to support problem-solving therapy.

> A 72-year-old male sought treatment for severe anxiety and social phobia that developed after a fall left him with hearing loss. Although a hearing aid corrected his auditory functioning to near normal levels, he became fearful and avoided any social interaction with anyone except his wife. His social network deteriorated. After several sessions the therapist chose to use problem-solving therapy to help the client define social situations in different ways and generate alternative solutions to fear-inducing situations related to his hearing problem. His wife attended a two-hour introductory workshop on problem-solving techniques, viewed two half-hour videotapes of examples, and was given a 10-page pamphlet. This allowed her to support and encourage his implementation of the therapy.

Facilitation

Explicit family training can facilitate the client's implementation of problem-solving procedures. With this technique family members are taught to use the problem-solving process to help the client apply it. The goal is to intensify training and help generalize the client's use of the process from the clinical session to the home environment (Shure, 1996; Shure & Spivack, 1978). When members of the family are able to apply social problem-solving procedures they can help the client determine when they should be used. They can help with the details of defining problems, generating solutions, decision making, and so on. They can prompt the client to use problem-solving procedures and reinforce the client when they are used. In addition, relatives can serve as models of how to use problem solving. Furthermore, this can all occur in the home environment as the problems emerge (e.g., Braswell & Bloomquist, 1991; Kazdin, 1996; Lewinsohn et al., 1996; Stark et al., 1996).

In this approach family members are essentially asked to help teach the client social problem solving. This is most frequently applied with the parents of child or adolescent clients. The primary focus is still with change in the identified client. Family members are not identified as clients or as a key part of the client's problem.

This approach involves detailed problem-solving training for members of the family who have frequent contact and a close relationship with the client. The training for families usually coincides with the step-by-step training for clients. For this technique to be effective the family needs to be competent at the elements of problem solving. Thus the typical four- to eight-week training period (D'Zurilla & Nezu, 1999) is advisable for family members, depending on the diagnosis and population. The following case is typical of this application.

> A 6-year-old male was referred for treatment of conduct disorder after eight months of persistent aggression, culminating in him intentionally breaking a schoolmate's arm with a baseball bat. One component of the therapy was problem-solving training that had an initial emphasis on changing the way he defined problematic situations and generated alternative solutions. For four weeks his parents received, separate from their son, weekly training in problem solving, viewed a half-hour training video each week, and had written homework. They learned to anticipate problematic situations and prompt their son to be clear about how he was defining the situation. They could be especially helpful in encouraging alternate solutions and evaluating them. Persistent application of this approach with a few conjoint sessions ultimately led to treatment success.

Conflict Management

Families training in problem solving can improve family conflict management. In this technique family members are trained in problem solving with the explicit goal of changing the way they manage conflicts. Family members are expected to do more than just assist the trainer in teaching the client to use problem-solving procedures. They are expected to change the way they deal with family conflicts. This is an important clinical distinction because family members are often reluctant to change the ways they deal with problems. The acknowledgment that they need to change their approach to dealing with problems implies that they have been somehow deficient in an important aspect of their family life. The basic training in problem solving is the same as that applied when family members are enlisted as assistants in the training process. Those procedures were described earlier.

Better conflict management in the family environment is beneficial as a component of treatment for a wide variety of psychological disorders (e.g., Hibbs & Jensen, 1996). One of the most well-researched applications is for training of family members of schizophrenic individuals (Falloon, 1988b). Difficulties in conflict management in families with schizophrenic individuals are well-known, with particular reference to the pattern of expressed emotion (Falloon, 1988b). Similar benefits have been found for treatments of other disorders, where improvements in family conflict management are a part of the therapy or prevention (e.g., Forgatch & Patterson, 1989; Hibbs & Jensen, 1996; Robin & Foster, 1989; Russ & Ollendick, 1999)

In general terms, families that have members with a psychological disorder often have difficulties with managing conflict. The person with the disorder may be a source for conflicts, as is the case with conduct disorder or oppositional-defiant disorder. With other disorders family members often disagree about how to deal with the problem one of them is having. In other situations families may be in denial and avoid any conflict whatsoever, which short-circuits effective problem solving. In all these situations social problem-solving procedures have been useful in regulating family conflicts and promoting better adaptations between the client and the environment. The amount of training needed depends on several factors, including the disorder, its severity, family characteristics, and social competence of the family.

Used in this manner, problem-solving training for families is often applied as a component in broader prevention or treatment plans that may include drug and various types of individual therapy. Here the problem-solving procedures are typically given the limited function of improving family conflict management, which in turn facilitates the success of the other treatment modalities. An example follows.

> A 17-year-old female was referred for treatment of posttraumatic stress disorder. At age 14 she had been in an auto accident in which two of her best friends were killed. Her symptoms of irritability, loss of sleep after nightmares, and poor concentration led to escalating problems at home and school. Increasingly she fought with her parents and ran away from home twice. The therapist chose to use, as one treatment component, problem-solving training to reduce the tense emotional climate at home. The parents and daughter received six weeks of conjoint training in problem-solving techniques, along with videotapes and homework. The father–daughter dyad emerged as the source of much of the negative emotion, as the most conflictual problem areas had to do with his expectations for her to "get over" the accident and her feelings that he did not care about what the accident did to her. Structured family discussions were done at home for four weeks. Family conflict at home was reduced and contributed to the progress of therapy.

Family System Change

Families training in problem solving can promote family system change. The three approaches to family training described earlier represent increasing levels of involvement of family members and change in the family environment. The fourth approach involves the highest level of family involvement and the greatest change in the family environment. The promotion of family system change entails using problem-solving procedures to facilitate basic changes in relationships, family interaction patterns beyond conflict management, family beliefs, or structures (Haley, 1987; Robin & Foster, 1989). These are features of a family that are shared by family members and are thus distinct from the cognitions, feelings, and behaviors of the individuals. The family systems approach ultimately seeks broader changes for family members than just their conflict management behavior referred to in the third approach. Thus this fourth type of application brings about an integration of social problem-solving techniques with family systems techniques (Braswell, 1991; Robin & Foster, 1989).

The family systems approach is indicated when some aspect of family dynamics or structure serves to promote or maintain primary features of the client's disorder. In such cases eliminating the family maintenance pattern may be necessary before the client can successfully apply social problem-solving procedures to reduce symptoms. In the prevention context, this family system approach is indicated when certain family interaction patterns are known to promote the development of specific disorders or negative outcomes (Falloon, 1988b; Hawkins, Catalano, & Miller, 1992; Spoth et al., 2000; Webster-Stratton, 1998). The prevention rationale is that if the family patterns are changed before the client's disorder emerges, then the disorder will have been prevented.

The following case gives a simple example of how change in an element of a family system, a family relationship, helped treat depression.

> A 45-year-old supermarket cashier entered therapy because of two suicide attempts, persistent suicidal ideation, and other symptoms of depression associated with his feelings that he is a failure in life. His financially successful father moved into the same town at about the time his depression symptoms began. The father's belief that his son is a failure permeated interactions between them and forestalled the father from granting any acceptance or emotional support to the son. At all family events the father found some way of expressing his disappointment in his son's accomplishments in life. The son's depressive cognitions and behaviors directly correspond with unpleasant interactions with the father and family events. Treatment of the son's depression could have proceeded without any involvement of the father. That would have entailed, for example, the son finding better ways of coping with situations when he feels inferior, especially those situations involving his father. However it was determined that the father's disparaging behavior toward him was a contributing factor to the son's depression. The father participated in problem-solving training separately from the son and began by considering his son's inadequacies as the basic problem in the situation. However he also acknowledged that he was troubled by the

distant relationship they had as well as his negative attitudes toward the son. The therapist got him to define these as problems to be solved. Part of the solution was eliminating the disparaging behaviors toward the son. Once that occurred, the relationship with the son improved. Subsequently the son's efforts to solve his problems of negative feelings about himself and self-destructive behavior were more successful and the depressive symptoms were steadily reduced. This example involved no conjoint sessions with the father and son. However, such sessions could be used to promote the same treatment goal.

This approach to training family members in problem solving can involve elements of family therapy. One example of this is the Robin and Foster model for treating adolescent conduct disorder (Robin & Foster, 1989). These authors supplement problem-solving therapy with elements of structural and functional family therapy. Their logic is that problem-solving training provides a primary treatment approach to adolescent conduct disorder. But that disorder can have some unique features that require special attention. These include weak parental coalitions, cross-generational coalitions, triangulation, and adolescent behavior preventing any healthy marital conflict (Robin & Foster, 1989; Vuchinich, Wood, & Angelelli, 1996). Their treatment includes specific procedures drawn from family therapy for dealing with these issues. Training in problem solving can work well in conjunction with several types of family therapy (Braswell, 1991; Haley, 1987; Russ & Ollendick, 1999; Vuchinich, 1999).

ENGAGEMENT AND RETENTION OF FAMILY MEMBERS IN PROBLEM-SOLVING TRAINING

Getting family members to participate in problem-solving training can present challenges (e.g., Spoth & Redmond, 1994). Such training requires the family's investment of time and effort over a period of at least several weeks, and often includes requests for changes of behavior for an indefinite period. Ideally, family members would be concerned with their relative's problem and be willing to participate to help alleviate the problem. Indeed this occurs frequently. But family members may not see why they should participate in prevention programs or therapy if they themselves do not have a disorder. The common family expectation is that the identified client has the psychological problem and the therapy will focus on this person alone. In the prevention arena, family members are often confused about why they need to do anything because nothing bad has happened yet. The various difficulties that can be encountered in gaining a client's own compliance to attend sessions and follow treatment regimens are expanded when compliance is sought from the client's family. A variety of techniques have been used to achieve this family compliance and avoid resistance (Patterson & Forgatch, 1985). These issues have long been basic elements in the practice of family therapy (Braswell, 1991; Haley, 1987; Mikesell, Lusterman, & McDaniel, 1995; Russ & Ollendick, 1999).

Perhaps the most important general recommendation is to anticipate the need for motivational tactics that will be effective for family members of the population involved in treatment or prevention. A wide variety of methods have been used. It is important for the training to include written material, motivational videotapes, live testimonials, portions of group sessions dedicated to motivation, or individual counseling of family members on the importance of their involvement. Attractive materials and props can be integrated into the training and homework (Braswell, 1991; Braswell & Bloomguist; 1991; Forgath & Patterson, 1989). Some programs with multiple family group sessions include a meal, or other "fun activity" time, as part of the training program to create positive associations that promote retention. In the realm of prevention programs, providing transportation for families and other inducements that make family participation easier and more enjoyable will promote retention. This may be essential in some populations. The research on family-focused training is discovering what is takes to elicit family involvement in training (e.g., Hawkins et al., 1992; Spoth & Redmond, 1994; Spoth et al., 2000).

Certain procedures can increase the likelihood of success with family problem-solving techniques. First is *screening families* to make sure they are appropriate candidates for problem-solving therapy involving multiple family members. This can be done as part of basic assessment procedures (Braswell, 1991). Part of the screening determines whether family members have a sufficient level of cognitive, affective, and social functioning to make problem-solving training a feasible option. Ideally screening would also determine whether deficits in problem solving are associated with the symptoms presented (D'Zurilla & Nezu, 1999). In addition the screening should also consider aspects of anger management, conflict regulation styles, and family power structures that could disrupt training. Selected aspects of individual histories and questionnaires may be useful for this information. A family intake interview is also a useful part of the screening (Robin & Foster, 1989), as the most serious disruptive family patterns would typically emerge in such sessions.

Second, it is useful to have a *written statement of expectations* of families that addresses logistical issues such as rules about appointments as well as therapeutic issues such as demeanor during sessions and a commitment to doing homework from the sessions. Especially pertinent are rules about how many family members need to be present to hold a session and written products of homework activities. This document can be formulated as a contract signed by family members. This should be given to clients with an explanation of the reasons for all the main areas covered. Such a document can be referred to during training to help maintain compliance with the treatment program.

Third is *establishing a collaborative relationship with key family members* early in the training process. This is related to concepts of "joining" with a family or therapeutic alliance. In family training it is especially valuable for the trainer to foster the sense that "we" are working on solving the problems together. Clients are more willing to participate in the procedures and cooperate with guidance when they feel the trainer is "on their side" or "on the same team." However the trainer must be sure to define his or her role so that he or she is still able to guide and control the therapeutic process. It is usually helpful to overtly acknowledge the appropriate power of parents in the family context and show respect for that from the outset. But within the therapy sessions the trainer may need to assert rights of expert authority if challenges emerge.

EMPIRICAL EVIDENCE ON EFFECTS OF PROBLEM-SOLVING TRAINING WITH FAMILIES

Numerous studies have empirically examined the efficacy of prevention and treatment programs that include training in family problem solving as a component. Some of the earliest compelling evidence came from Falloon's randomized trials for a family-based program to prevent morbidity in schizophrenia (Falloon, 1988b). After two years, only 33% of the patients in the family-based group showed continuing symptoms of schizophrenia. But 83% of the patients in the comparison group that received the typical individual therapy showed such symptoms. Both groups received the same drug therapy during the two years.

An important benefit of family problem-solving training is its ability to make change that can be maintained over time. An example of this is a randomized trial of a family-based program to reduce aggressive and hostile behavior with a brief intervention for families with an adolescent in the seventh grade (Spoth et al., 2000). After four years the treatment group showed reductions in aggressive and destructive behavior ranging from 32 to 77%. Similar long-term effects have been found in studies of problem-solving training for children and parents in the preschool and primary school years (Shure, 1997).

Kazdin's work has shown that problem-solving training involving families can be especially useful in treating conduct disorder and oppositional disorder in children 7 to 13 years of age (Kazdin, 1996). Clinically significant reductions in symptoms were found at posttreatment and at one-year follow-up. Similar benefits were found with a parenting program to prevent conduct disorder in high-risk children (ages 5 to 6 years) enrolled in Head Start programs (Webster-Stratton, 1998). Benefits were maintained in a one-year follow-up. Such results have also been found in a randomized trial with teenagers diagnosed with attention deficit hyperactivity disorder as well as oppositional defiant disorder (Barkley et al., 2001). These are only a few examples of the many evaluations of programs that include problem-solving training involving families.

CONCLUSION

Over the past fifty years there has been a steady increase in the integration of family members into psychological treatment and prevention programs (e.g., Mikesell et al., 1995; Russ & Ollendick, 1999; Vuchinich, 1999). The primary reason for this is that family members represent a valuable resource for promoting the health of individuals. The fields of medicine, psychotherapy, and prevention science are discovering how to use that resource. In the area of social problem solving, the realization of that potential has begun. Training families in problem solving has already become a ubiquitous component in a wide variety of treatment and prevention programs, as reviewed in this chapter. The widespread success of these programs will undoubtedly motivate expansion of these techniques into other areas in the future.

Although the success of family training has been apparent, there has been great variation in the specific ways that it has been implemented. In one sense this variation is an asset because it means that problem-solving training has a robust flexibility that allows it to provide benefits in many treatment and prevention contexts. But this variation also makes it difficult to draw systematic conclusions about what form of family training works best in what context. The available research indicates that programs with a family training component are effective. But there is little research yet that compares the relative effectiveness of different types of family training. Several variables are of practical relevance, such as how many training sessions are used, whether group training is used, what training techniques are used, how many family members are trained, and so on. Research on such comparisons has started (e.g., Barkley et al., 2001; Spoth et al., 2000; Webster-Stratton, 1998) and will shape future applications of problem-solving training with families.

A related issue for future comparative research is the identification of the unique contribution of family training components in treatment and prevention. Are programs with family training components more effective than those without them? There is not yet sufficient rigorous empirical research available to answer this question. Involving families in programs means added complications and costs in the delivery of services. Research verifying therapeutic benefits of family training will be needed to justify the additional expense compared with individual training. Such research can also quantify the therapeutic contribution of family training components. That will make it possible to determine what form of family training works best with other treatment components. With these kinds of questions still unanswered, research on family problem-solving training is still in its infancy. But it is already clear that family training in problem solving has found a permanent niche in a broad range of treatment and prevention programs. On-going research will more clearly specify the extent of its contribution to treatment and prevention success. Ultimately that work has the potential to improve these beneficial effects.

REFERENCES

Barkley, R. A., Edwards, G., Laneri, M., Fletcher, K., & Metevia, L. (2001). The efficacy of problem-solving communication training alone, behavior management training alone, and their combination for parent–adolescent conflict in teenagers with ADHD and ODD. *Journal of Consulting and Clinical Psychology, 69*, 926–941.

Braswell, L. (1991). Involving parents in cognitive–behavioral therapy with children and adolescents. In P. C. Kendall (Ed.), *Child and adolescent therapy: Cognitive–behavioral procedures* (pp. 316–352). New York: Guilford Press.

Braswell, L., & Bloomquist, M. L. (1991). *Cognitive–behavioral therapy with ADHD children: Child, family and school interventions.* New York: Guilford Press.

Cooke, D. D., McNally, L., Mulligan, K. T., Harrison, M. J., & Newman, S. P. (2001). Psychosocial interventions for caregivers of people with dementia: A systematic review. *Aging and Mental Health, 5*, 120–135.

Dishion, T. J., McCord, J., & Poulin, F. (1999). When interventions harm: Peer groups and problem behavior. *American Psychologist, 54*, 755–764.

D'Zurilla, T. J., & Nezu, A. M. (1999). *Problem solving therapy: A social competence approach to clinical intervention* (2nd ed.). New York: Springer.

Falloon, I. R. H. (1988a). *Handbook of behavioral family therapy* New York: Guilford Press.

Falloon, I. R. H. (1988b). Prevention of morbidity in schizophrenia. In I. R. H. Falloon (Ed.), *Handbook of behavioral family therapy* (pp. 316–349). New York: Guilford Press.

Forgatch, M. S., & Patterson, G. R. (1989). *Parents and adolescents living together Part 2: Family problem solving.* Eugene, OR: Castalia.

Haley, J. (1987). *Problem-solving therapy* (2nd ed.). San Francisco: Jossey-Bass.

Hawkins, J. D., Catalano, R. F., & Miller, Y. (1992). Risk and protective factors for alcohol and other drug problems in adolescence and early adulthood:

Implications for substance abuse prevention. *Psychological Bulletin, 112,* 64–105.

Hibbs, E. D., & Jensen, P. S. (1996). *Psychosocial treatments for child and adolescent disorders: Empirically based strategies for clinical practice.* Washington, DC: American Psychological Association.

Kazdin, A. G. (1996). Problem solving and parent management in treating aggressive antisocial behavior. In E. D. Hibbs & P. S. Jensen (Eds.), *Psychosocial treatments for child and adolescent disorders: Empirically based strategies for clinical practice* (pp. 377–408). Washington, DC: American Psychological Association.

Lewinsohn, P. M., Clarke, G. N., Rohde, P., Hops, H., & Seeley, J. R. (1996). A course in coping: Cognitive–behavioral approach to the treatment of adolescent depression. In E. D. Hibbs & P. S. Jensen (Eds.), *Psychosocial treatments for child and adolescent disorders: Empirically based strategies for clinical practice* (pp. 207–238). Washington, DC: American Psychological Association.

Mikesell, R., Lusterman, D., & McDaniel, S. H. (1995). *Integrating family therapy: Handbook of family psychology and systems theory.* Washington, DC: American Psychological Association.

Patterson, G. R., & Forgatch, M. S. (1985). Therapist behavior as a determinant for client noncompliance: A paradox for behavior modification. *Journal of Consulting and Clinical Psychology, 53,* 53–70.

Robin, A. L., & Foster, S. L. (1989). *Negotiating parent–adolescent conflict: A behavioral–family systems approach.* New York: Guilford Press.

Russ, S. W., & Ollendick, T. (1999). *Handbook of psychotherapies with children and families.* New York: Plenum Press.

Shure, M. B. (1996). *Raising a thinking child: Help your child to resolve everyday conflicts and get along with others.* New York: Pocketbooks.

Shure, M. B. (1997). Interpersonal cognitive problem solving: Primary prevention of early high risk behaviors in the preschool and primary years. In G. W. Albee & T. P. Gulkotta (Eds.), *Primary prevention works* (pp. 167–188). Thousand Oaks, CA: Sage.

Shure, M. B., & Spivak, G. (1978). *Problem solving techniques in child rearing.* San Francisco: Jossey-Bass.

Spoth, R. L., & Redmond, C. (1994). Effective recruitment of parents into family focused prevention research: A comparison of two strategies. *Psychology and Health, 9,* 353–370.

Spoth, R. L., Redmond, C., & Shin, C. (2000). Reducing adolescent's aggressive and hostile behaviors: Randomized trial effects of a brief family intervention 4 years past baseline. *Archives of Pediatric and Adolescent Medicine, 154,* 1248–1257.

Stark, K. D., Swearer, S., Kurowski, C., Sommer, D., & Bowen, B. (1996). Targeting the family: A holistic approach to treating child and adolescent depressive disorders. In E. D. Hibbs & P. S. Jensen (Eds.), *Psychosocial treatments for child and adolescent disorders: Empirically based strategies for clinical practice* (pp. 207–238). Washington, DC: American Psychological Association.

Vuchinich, S. (1999). *Problem solving in families: Research and practice*. Thousand Oaks, CA: Sage.

Vuchinich, S., Wood, B., & Angelelli, J. (1996). Coalitions and family problem solving in the psychosocial treatment of adolescents. In E. D. Hibbs & P. S. Jensen (Eds.), *Psychosocial treatments for child and adolescent disorders: Empirically based strategies for clinical practice* (pp. 497–518). Washington DC: American Psychological Association.

Webster-Stratton, C. (1998). Preventing conduct problems in Head Start children: Strengthening parenting competencies. *Journal of Consulting and Clinical Psychology, 66,* 715–730.

13

PROBLEM-SOLVING THERAPY FOR CAREGIVERS

CHRISTINE MAGUTH NEZU, ANDREW D. PALMATIER,
AND ARTHUR M. NEZU

In addition to the effects on patients themselves, the experience of chronic illness and its treatment can change the lives of significant people in the patient's life, especially the primary caregiver. For example, with regard to chronic medical illnesses such as cancer, stroke, or AIDS, shifts in health care economics, especially during the end of the 20th century and into the 21st century, have increased the degree to which the care, recovery, or end-of-life concerns of such patients takes place in the home. Thus, there is a potentially greater impact on the roles and responsibilities of family members (Houts, Nezu, Nezu, & Bucher, 1996). With regard to chronic mental impairment, such as dementia or developmental disabilities, early hospital discharges and greater reliance on family and community care have increased demands on individuals who may have little preparation for such significant caregiving responsibilities.

This shift in caretaking has also increased professionals' attention to the vital roles, participation, and impact of the experience that chronic illness has on families and caregivers as they are required to become an extension of the health care or case management team (Houts et al., 1996). This chapter focuses on the role that problem-solving therapy or training (PST) has played in helping to meet the various psychological, emotional, and social needs of caregivers of individuals suffering from a variety of chronic medical or psychological problems. We begin with an overview of the deleterious effects of the caregiving role. Next, we provide a conceptual model that describes the relevance of PST for caregivers, followed by a brief review of the treatment outcome literature.

THE STRESS OF CAREGIVING

The potential demands and subsequent burden of physical illness on caregivers is significant. For example, in a study by Barg et al. (1998), 61% of a sample of 750 caregivers of people with cancer reported that caregiving was the center of their activities. In addition, 58% of this sample indicated that to provide care, they were required to give up many other activities. For the majority of caregivers (62%), their responsibilities to the patient warranted 24-hour-per-day availability, whereas 42% of the sample provided 6 to 40 hours of care per week. With regard to other chronic disorders, caregivers often face lifelong responsibilities, which may be further compounded by the social stigmatization that accompanies certain chronic problems (e.g., dementia). Because caregivers are laypersons who usually have not had professional training in preparation for caring for an individual with a chronic illness, such demands and responsibilities can lead to significant distress. For example, in the Barg et al. (1998) sample, 89% of the caregivers reported feeling "stressed" by their responsibilities. In addition, those caregivers who experienced more stress also reported significantly lowered self-esteem, less family support, more negative impact on their schedules, more negative impact on their physical health, and more caregiving demands than nonstressed caregivers. Anxiety, posttraumatic stress disorder, eating disorders, sleep disturbances, and depression have all been found to be a consequence of the caregiving role (Kristjanson & Aschercraft, 1994). In addition, this set of responsibilities has been shown to have negative biological (e.g., immunologic, cardiovascular, metabolic) consequences (Vitaliano, 1997). For example, 62% of a sample of 465 caregivers reported declines in health resulting from their caregiving experiences (Barg et al., 1998).

PST can then serve two purposes: to (a) enhance caregiving skills and (b) minimize the stressful nature of the caregiving role. In other words, successfully solving problems can increase one's sense of mastery or control, which, in turn, contributes to positive mental health.

A PROBLEM-SOLVING CONCEPTUAL FRAMEWORK FOR CAREGIVING STRESS

As a general description, problem solving is the process by which people both understand and react to problems in living by altering the problematic nature of the situation itself, the person's reactions to the situation, or both (D'Zurilla & Nezu, 1999; Nezu, Nezu, Freidman, Faddis, & Houts, 1998). This definition is important because it points to the dual focus of problem solving—the focus on the problem itself, as well as on the person who is coping with the problem. Moreover, these dual goals interact reciprocally such that (a) success in solving a problem can improve one's cognitive and emotional reactions to the problem, and (b) such reactions (e.g., expectations of competency or success, positive affect) can increase the likelihood of additional successful problem-solving attempts. This process can be observed in caregivers who learn to solve day-to-day responsibilities more effectively. As they experience success as caregivers, they increasingly expect success, which can give both the caregiver and the patient confidence in future management of the illness. This confidence can also increase caregiver motivation and satisfaction (Houts et al., 1996). This interaction between objective personal decision skills and subjective emotional response to the problem is captured in our definition of a problem, which is not a characteristic of the environment or person alone but usually reflects an interaction of both. Similarly, a solution is defined as a coping response geared to alter the nature of the problem situation itself, one's negative response to it, or both (Nezu et al., 1998).

According to the D'Zurilla and Nezu (1999) social problem-solving model (see also chap. 1, this volume), outcomes are determined by two interdependent processes: (a) problem orientation and (b) problem-solving style. *Problem orientation* represents the motivational component of the overall process, involving the operation of a set of cognitive schemas, emotional reactions, and motivational tendencies regarding problems in living. In caregiving for people with mental and physical chronic illnesses, orientation refers to how the caregiver views such a role along with his or her expectations for fulfilling that role successfully. A caregiver's role often involves a mixed and complicated orientation, including the experience of burden, challenge, expectations of failure, or sense of competency.

Problem-solving style refers to the general tendencies with which people approach their management of life problems. Research has indicated that there are two maladaptive styles that characterize a wide range of mood and behavior disorders (D'Zurilla & Nezu, 1999). First, an *impulsive-careless style* is marked by impulsive, hurried, and careless attempts at problem resolution. Second, an *avoidant style* is characterized by procrastination, denial, passivity, and dependency. Each of these problem-solving styles can negatively affect the other component skill areas of the problem-solving process. For example, an impulsive and careless response style is likely to result in a person's tendency to "rush to judgment" concerning the way an individual recognizes or appraises a problem. This may not produce the most effective response in the long run and thus lead to more problems. As an example, one caregiver, distressed on observing his partner's sense of loss following a stroke, became angry with the health care team and insisted on a prescription of antidepressant medication for the patient. The caregiver in this instance had difficulty tolerating his partner's sadness and wanted instant relief from his own distress, rather than exploring his partner's sense of loss and working toward acceptance of new limitations or creative solutions to personal goals. In this case, the patient still needed to adjust to her illness, became angry at her partner for what appeared to her as impatience with her pain, experienced untoward side effects of the additional medication, and experienced more problems communicating with the health care team.

This definition of problem solving further emphasizes the importance of a third problem-solving style—a positive one—in which the behavior is directed toward changing the nature of the situation so that it is no longer problematic. Identifying such effective and appropriate solutions or coping efforts is achieved through four specific problem-solving tasks that make up this *rational problem-solving style*. These problem-solving tasks include (a) problem definition and formulation, (b) generation of alternatives, (c) decision making, and (d) solution implementation and verification. These four skills represent goal-directed tasks that enable a person to solve a particular problem successfully and can be defined as the rational, planful, systematic, and skillful application of various effective problem-solving principles and techniques. Each task makes a distinct contribution toward the discovery of an adaptive solution or coping response in a problem-solving situation. The following is a discussion of how each of these processes is relevant to the caregiving process.

Problem Orientation

A positive orientation includes perspectives that (a) problems in living are predictable and inevitable; (b) problem solving can be an effective way of coping with them; and (c) one's problem-solving efforts, given time and effort, will be successful (D'Zurilla & Nezu, 1999). As such, a positive problem orientation is extremely important for caregivers who need to recognize and address their caregiving problems in a realistic and optimistic manner. A positive problem orientation can help them to learn to be more aware of problems when they occur, recognize their own emotional cues as an aide to identifying problems, and learn to restructure their cognitive misattributions or overgeneralized tendencies to respond to these new and difficult circumstances. in addition, they must be able to communicate this optimism to the people for whom they are caring.

Problem Definition and Formulation

Individuals who are skillful in the way they define and formulate problems know how to (a) seek all available information and facts about a problem; (b) describe those facts in clear and unambiguous terms; (c) differentiate relevant from irrelevant information; (d) discriminate objective facts from unverified assumptions; and (e) set specific, realistic problem-solving goals. These tasks are extremely important skills for caregivers, because they may have little previous knowledge about the physical and mental health problems that the patient is experiencing and may need guidance from health professionals in formulating and defining problems. Therefore, obtaining expert information and guidance can be emphasized as an important part of the problem-solving process as applied to caregivers. Often family members are required to implement instructions regarding home care or medications from health professionals. However, obstacles that interfere with this work (e.g., lack of resources, lack of patient cooperation, skills deficits, and emotional reactions to required tasks) are problems in their own right, and it is in these circumstances that skills in problem definition and formulation become especially important. For caregivers, prescriptive training in problem-definition skills can directly target such obstacles and help caregivers to make effective decisions in spite of these obstacles.

Generation of Alternative Solutions

Caregivers who possess strong skills in terms of generating alternative solutions are able to maximize the likelihood that the most effective solution will be discovered. To accomplish this, the caregiver must be able to step back from the problem and view it from other perspectives to generate new and creative options. Brainstorming techniques are critical. As with problem definition and formulation, the help of informed and expert information from others can be sought and incorporated into this brainstorming activity. For example, suppose an individual was caring for a person who was recovering from cardiac surgery. In this case, the individual appeared depressed and nonadherent with his rehabilitation plan. Seeking expert information, the caregiver may be able to define the problem as the patient's depression and learn of research that associates depression in cardiac patients with poor outcome. When generating alternatives, the caregiver could ask health professionals for ideas and seek information through the Internet or by talking with other people who have experienced similar problems as a way of using multiple sources from which to generate alternatives. The caregiver would then be more likely to complete a comprehensive list of possible solutions from which to make future informed caregiving choices. These might include increasing the patient's level of pleasant activities and experiences, increasing social support, sharing concerns with the patient, obtaining a referral to a psychologist, joining a group therapy focused on improving mood, obtaining a referral for possible antidepressant medication, giving the patient more opportunity to express his feelings, and so forth. It is important to note that useful suggestions can be gleaned from various sources, but there are times when the caregiver is the primary source of creative options, one of which is generating specific solutions that include dealing with unique obstacles that may exist in any individual circumstance.

Decision Making

Within the context of PST, training individuals to make effective decisions involves teaching them to proceed through a systematic weighing of the costs and benefits of each solution they generate. This includes an evaluation of the likelihood that a given solution will be effective in the specific, relevant circumstance and how consistent the solution is with regard to both caregivers' and patients' desired consequences. This is an important skill for caregivers because they are often faced with opinions or solutions that work effectively for others but are not good for them and the person for whom they are caring. Possessing the skills to systematically evaluate alternative solutions within the context of what works for their situation, within a particular case and context, can provide confidence to follow one's own ideas and avoid being influenced by others.

Solution Implementation and Verification

Caring for someone with chronic illness is a learning process. Many times individuals are facing situations and obstacles with which they have previously not had to cope. Therefore, the use of rational problem-solving skills provides them with an opportunity to actually implement decisions arrived at through this cognitive–behavioral process, monitor outcome, and then personally review the match of desired versus actual outcome of problem-solving efforts. When the outcome is successful or effective, it is important for caregivers to be aware of the success and to reinforce themselves in light of it. This leads to confidence in future problem-solving efforts. When the outcome is less than optimal, it is important to examine the problem-solving process and review where skills could be improved.

In summary, each component of the problem-solving process can provide a unique, additive benefit to the coping-skills repertoire of caregivers for people with physical and mental illnesses.

PROBLEM-SOLVING PROGRAMS FOR CAREGIVERS

In this section we briefly review the literature regarding caregiving stress and possible links to problem-solving ability for a range of common chronic illness areas.

Problem-Solving Training for Cancer Caregivers

As noted earlier in the study by Barg et al. (1998), the negative effects of caregiving for a person with cancer can be substantial. For example, in a study by Kelly et al. (1999), 67% of a sample of caregivers of spouses with various cancer diagnoses reported "high to very high" illness-related distress levels. In addition to the impact on their psychological and physical health, cancer caregivers have also reported that many of their needs as caregivers continue to go unmet (Houts, Yasko, Kahn, Schelzel, & Marconi, 1986). For example, Hinds (1985) found that 53% of a sample of family caregivers of cancer patients identified several areas of unresolved psychosocial needs.

Given these issues, several problem-solving interventions have been developed for caregivers of people with cancer (Nezu, Nezu, Felgoise, & Zwick, 2003). For example, using a randomized design, Toseland, Blanchard, and McCallion (1995) evaluated a protocol including six individual counseling sessions that included both support and training in problem-solving and coping skills. Caregivers in a control group received standard medical care. Initial overall results comparing the intervention to "usual treatment" showed no differences on a wide range of measures. However, post-hoc analyses evaluating the interaction of distressed and moderately burdened caregivers by condition showed favorable outcomes for patients in the treatment condition. Specifically, distressed caregivers who participated in the intervention reported significant improvements in their physical, role, and social functioning. In addition, burdened caregivers significantly improved their ability to cope with pressing problems.

Houts et al. (1996) described a problem-solving approach to family caregiver education called the Prepared Family Caregiver Course, which was adapted from the D'Zurilla and Nezu (1982) PST model. The course is taught over three two-hour group sessions and includes prepared instructional videotapes to guide interactive practice exercises and an instructor's manual. Caregivers are provided with information about a series of medical (e.g., fatigue, hair loss) and psychosocial (e.g., depression, loneliness) problems, and are trained to (a) better define the problem; (b) know when to obtain professional help; (c) learn to deal with, as well as prevent, a problem; (d) identify obstacles when they arise and to plan to overcome them; and (e) effectively implement a problem-solving plan and adjust it if the initial attempts are not successful. The *Home Care Guide for Cancer* (Houts, Nezu, Nezu, Bucher, & Lipton, 1994), an informational resource consistent with this model, is a key element of this training.

Results from a program evaluation study of this educational approach, which included a sample of 41 caregivers, indicated that 78% of these participants reported an improvement in their feelings of burden and stress (Houts et al., 1996). In addition, 48% and 58%, respectively, reported using their plans for tiredness and depression in their caregiving. Additional program evaluation investigations of the Prepared Family Caregiver Course revealed a high level of satisfaction with and interest in using the course information. Obviously, well-controlled studies are necessary before making definitive conclusions about the potential efficacy of such an approach. However, preliminary results are promising.

Problem-solving-based interventions may hold particular promise for improving negative mood among parental caregivers of children who are diagnosed with cancer. In a study conducted by Sahler and colleagues (2002), 92 mothers of children with cancer were randomly assigned to receive PST or standard psychosocial care. After an eight-week intervention, mothers in the problem-solving group had significantly enhanced their problem-solving skills and significantly decreased negative affectivity, compared to a control group. Additional analyses revealed that changes in problem solving accounted for 40% of the variance in mood change.

Problem-Solving Training for Caregivers of Persons With Dementia

Family members often take the responsibility for much of the care and support for individuals who are diagnosed with dementia (Cummings, Long, Peterson-Hazan, & Harrison, 1998). Such demands can lead to a variety of difficulties, such as health problems, psychosocial difficulties, and financial problems (Adkins, 1999). For example, several studies have reported a significant prevalence of psychosocial distress symptoms, such as depression and anxiety, that these caregivers experience (Coppel, Burton, Becker, & Fiore, 1985; Haley et al., 1995).

Problem-solving coping strategies have been shown to be associated with better outcomes related to depression, health problems, and life satisfaction among caregivers of people with dementia (Haley, Levine, Brown, & Bartolucci, 1987). In a study that examined the use of caregiver problem solving to treat depression in dementia patients, the authors found that both patients and caregivers benefited from the treatment (Teri, Logsdon,

Uomoto, & McCurry, 1997). Problem-solving training, combined with expression of negative emotion, has also been shown to be more helpful then problem solving alone in reducing psychiatric symptoms and with regard to improving the relationship between the caregiver and patient (Schmidt, Bonjean, Widem, Schefft, & Steele, 1988).

The PST model developed by D'Zurilla and Nezu (1982, 1999) was the basis of several investigations of caregivers of individuals with dementia. Lovett and Gallagher (1988) provided preliminary data regarding the first 111 family member caregivers who participated in a psychoeducational program designed to teach specific skills for coping more effectively with caregiving. Based on previous research showing PST to be effective in decreasing depression (Nezu, 1986), it was one of two treatment conditions that was compared to a wait-list control. The second intervention involved teaching caregivers to increase the frequency of their positive activities based on research demonstrating a similar effect regarding depressive affect (Lewinsohn, Munoz, Youngren, & Zeiss, 1986). Both programs were found to lead to increased morale and decreased depression.

Zarit, Anthony, and Boutselis (1987) reported that two intervention groups that included social problem-solving training components demonstrated improvements in caregiver burden and psychiatric symptoms, but these results were not significantly greater than the outcomes for caregivers in a wait-list group. However, a reanalysis of this study revealed that both intervention groups were more effective than the wait-list group in reducing caregiver distress in each of the areas studied (Whitlatch, Zarit, & von Eye, 1991).

In a more recent study (Roberts et al., 1999), caregivers of individuals with dementia that were trained in problem-solving skills did not significantly improve on measures of distress, psychosocial adjustment to the patient's illness, or caregiver burden during the six-month and one-year follow-up periods. However, the majority of caregivers (i.e., 92%) rated the counseling program as helpful. In addition, a smaller subset of caregivers that revealed greater deficits in many logical analysis problem-solving skills at baseline measurement, but who went through the problem-solving counseling, did report less psychological distress and greater psychosocial adjustment at the one-year follow-up period. These mixed results may suggest that PST can be especially useful for individuals who reveal greater problem-solving deficits and high distress levels at baseline.

Problem-Solving for Caregivers of Persons With Developmental Disabilities

It is well-documented that families of individuals with a mental disability, such as mental retardation, experience chronic stressful problems (Orr,

Cameron, & Day, 1991). With a national trend toward deinstitutionaliza-
tion, and social goals of maintaining such individuals in the community,
the majority of management decisions and responsibilities have rested on
family or community caregivers. Families have difficulty coping with this
experience for several reasons, including a lost sense of control, loss of
positive expectations of the future, and negative emotional consequences
such as symptoms of burnout (Holyroyd, 1974). Burnout, in particular, has
been observed in caregivers of individuals with developmental disabilities
because they must face both the emotional tasks of accepting small gains
and successes, as well as heavy caregiving demands of their situation. In
response to such demands, parents of disabled children have been found to
be depressed, have lowered self-esteem, and experience a chronic sense
of dissatisfaction (Cummings, Bayles, & Rie, 1966; Nezu, Nezu, & Gill-
Weiss, 1992).

Results from a longitudinal study focusing on mothers of adults diagnosed with mental retardation found that those who reported greater use of
problem-focused coping strategies appeared to buffer the impact of caregiving
stress on their emotional well-being (Seltzer, Greenberg, & Krauss, 1995).
Other research has highlighted the importance of problem-solving ability
in both seeking social support and mobilizing help with caregiving responsibilities (Hayden & Heller, 1997). Although such studies support the idea
that problem-solving interventions may be helpful to caregivers, and possibly
serve to reduce symptoms of burnout in this population, no systematic studies
have evaluated the effectiveness of a problem-solving-based intervention.
The lifelong care of people with developmental disabilities implies a plethora
of day-to-day problems and an ongoing need for effective decision-making
that can have impact on the lives of individuals with developmental disabilities even after their caregivers are deceased. These may include decisions
concerning group home placement, access to health and mental health
resources, and access to adaptive educational opportunities. As such, studies
of problem-solving-based interventions, in which caregivers are provided
with tools to manage these challenges, should be developed (C. M. Nezu
et al., 1992).

Problem-Solving Training for Caregivers of Spinal Cord Injuries

Caregivers of patients with a spinal cord injury (SCI) may be
expected to assist the SCI patient with a variety of activities over the
course of a lifetime, such as daily functions (e.g., bathing, dressing) and
vocational activities. Researchers have found that social support, provided
as part of the caregiver role, is important for the psychosocial well-being
(e.g., patients report less depressive behavior, less psychosocial impairment)
of the SCI patient (Elliott, Herrick, Witty, Godshall, & Spruell, 1992a;

Elliott, Herrick, Witty, Godshall, & Spruell, 1992b). In addition, Shewchuk, Richards, and Elliott (1998) found that caregivers of SCI patients, during the first year after onset of injury, tend to experience problems related to their own social support that affect their physical and mental health. Moreover, if the caregiver's overall heath is compromised, then this may affect both the short- and long-term well-being of the SCI patient (Elliott & Shewchuk, 1998, 2001; Elliott, Shewchuk, & Richards, 1999). As such, researchers have started to apply heath care models (e.g., caregiver social support groups, problem-solving skills training) to better understand the association between caregiver coping and the SCI patient's overall health.

With specific regard to the application of a problem-solving model to caregivers of individuals with SCI, caregivers who reported having a negative problem-solving orientation were reported to experience more depression, anxiety, and health complaints during the first year following the patient's injury (Elliott, Shewchuk, & Richards, 2001). Caregiver problem-solving style has also been found to be related to the psychological and physical well-being of the SCI patient. Specifically, Elliott et al. (1999) found that impulsive and careless problem-solving styles in caregivers were associated with patients who had lower acceptance of their disability at discharge from the rehabilitation hospital and more pressure sores at their first annual medical evaluation. Subsequent to these studies, Elliott and his colleagues have developed programs that teach social problem-solving skills as a way to positively assist the caregiver–patient relationship. Kurylo, Elliott, and Shewchuk (2001), for example, recently described Project FOCUS, which is similar to projects that assist other populations such as cancer patients and uses the five-component problem-solving model (Nezu et al., 1998). One of the more unique features of this project involves the use of a sorting task to help caregivers identify problems that are specifically relevant to their caregiving situation and to figure out which of these problems require more immediate attention.

Problem-Solving Training for Caregivers of Stroke Victims

Although cerebrovascular accidents (strokes) are most common in elderly individuals, they can affect adults of all age groups. Individuals who experience a stroke may have life-long deficits such as aphasia, dementia, and other cognitive problems, psychological problems (e.g., depression), and hemiplegia (Grant & Davis, 1997). Family caregivers assume much of the responsibility for assisting these individuals, and research indicates that psychological distress (i.e., depression) on the caregiver's part may affect the patient's well-being (i.e., increased depression) and rehabilitation progress (Han & Haley, 1999).

PST has been suggested as an appropriate intervention for treating such factors as depression and health problems in caregivers of stroke patients (Grant, Elliott, Giger, & Bartolucci, 2001). However, only a few studies have been conducted with this population. In one study, providing caregivers with education and PST, the combination was demonstrated to be more effective for family functioning, caregiver knowledge, and patient adjustment then using education alone or routine care after a one-year poststroke event (Evans, Matlock, Bishop, Stranahan, & Pederson, 1988). Grant and her colleagues have adapted PST as the major component of a telephone counseling protocol for caregivers (Grant, 1999). This program has been found to lead to more positive problem-solving skills, more caregiver preparedness, and a reduction in depression. In addition, in a similar study, this protocol was shown to decrease depression, promote positive problem-solving skills and more caregiver preparedness and also improve vitality, social functioning, mental health, and role limitations related to emotional problems (Grant, Elliott, Weaver, Bartolucci, & Giger, in press).

CONCLUSION

In addition to the patients themselves, chronic illness can have a profound impact on caregivers. Because of recent changes in health care delivery and economics, there has been a significant shift in caregiving responsibility from the professional health care team to family caregivers. This shift increases the potential demands and responsibilities for such individuals. As such, caregivers experience an increased vulnerability to both psychological and medical difficulties. In response to these problems, researchers have begun to develop and evaluate problem-solving-based interventions geared to improve the caregiving skills of such individuals, as well as decrease their burden and improve their quality of life. Because such research is in its nascent stage, increased attempts to develop effective programs are particularly needed to improve the quality of life of people with chronic illness and their families. Although a substantial body of research exists examining problems facing caregivers and the negative impact of such stress, we need to know more about what types of treatment approaches are effective for improving quality of life. Medical disorders that require much caregiving responsibilities from family and friends, such as HIV/AIDS and cardiovascular disease, represent fertile areas for new program development and research with regard to the role that PST might play.

REFERENCES

Adkins, V. K. (1999). Treatment of depressive disorders of spousal caregivers of persons with Alzheimer's disease: A review. *American Journal of Alzheimer's Disease, 14,* 289–293.

Barg, F. K., Pasacreta, J. V., Nuamah, I. F., Robinson, K. D., Angeletti, K., Yasko, J. M., et al. (1998). A description of a psychoeducational intervention for family caregivers of cancer patients. *Journal of Family Nursing, 4,* 394–414.

Coppel, D. B., Burton, D., Becker, J., & Fiore, J. (1985). Relationships of cognitions associated with coping reactions to depression in spousal caregivers of Alzheimer's disease patients. *Cognitive Therapy and Research, 9,* 253–266.

Cummings, S. T., Bayles, H. C., & Rie, H. E. (1966). Effects of the child's deficiency on the mother: A study of mothers of mentally retarded, chronically ill, and neurotic children. *American Journal of Orthopsychiatry, 36,* 595–608.

Cummings, S. M., Long, J. K., Peterson-Hazan, S., & Harrison, J. (1998). The efficacy of a group treatment model in helping spouses meet the emotional and practical challenges of early stage caregiving. *Clinical Gerontologist, 20,* 29–45.

D'Zurilla, T. J., & Nezu, A. M. (1982). Social problem solving in adults. In P. C. Kendall (Ed.), *Advances in cognitive–behavioral research and therapy* (Vol. 1). New York: Academic Press.

D'Zurilla, T. J., & Nezu, A. M. (1999). *Problem-solving therapy: A social competence approach to clinical intervention* (2nd ed.). New York: Springer.

Elliott, T., Herrick, S., Witty, T., Godshall, F., & Spruell, M. (1992a). Social relationships and psychosocial impairment of persons with spinal cord injury. *Psychology and Health, 7,* 55–67.

Elliott, T., Herrick, S., Witty, T., Godshall, F., & Spruell, M. (1992b). Social support and depression following spinal cord injury. *Rehabilitation Psychology, 37,* 37–48.

Elliott, T., & Shewchuk, R. (1998). Recognizing the family caregiver: Integral and formal members of the rehabilitation process. *Journal of Vocational Rehabilitation, 10,* 123–132.

Elliott, T., & Shewchuk, R. (2001). Problem-solving therapy for family caregivers of persons with severe physical disabilities. In C. Radnitz (Ed.), *Cognitive–behavioral interventions for persons with disabilities* (pp. 309–327). New York: Aronson.

Elliott, T., Shewchuk, R., & Richards, J. S. (1999). Caregiver social problem-solving abilities and family member adjustment to recent-onset physical disability. *Rehabilitation Psychology, 44,* 104–123.

Elliott, T., Shewchuk, R., & Richards, J. S. (2001). Family caregiver social problem-solving abilities and adjustment during the initial year of the caregiving role. *Journal of Counseling Psychology, 48,* 223–232.

Evans, R. L., Matlock, A.-L., Bishop, D. S., Stranahan, S., & Pederson, C. (1988). Family intervention after stroke: Does counseling or education help? *Stroke, 19,* 1243–1248.

Grant, J. S. (1999). Social problem-solving partnerships with family caregivers. *Rehabilitation Nursing, 24,* 254–260.

Grant, J. S., & Davis, L. L. (1997). Living with loss: The stroke family caregiver. *Journal of Family Nursing, 3,* 36–56.

Grant, J. S., Elliott, T., Giger, J. N., & Bartolucci, A. A. (2001). Social problem-solving abilities, social support, and adjustment among family caregivers of individuals with a stroke. *Rehabilitation Psychology, 46,* 44–57.

Grant, J. S., Elliott, T., Weaver, M., Bartolucci, A. A., & Giger, J. N. (in press). A telephone intervention with family caregivers of stroke survivors after rehabilitation. *Stroke.*

Haley, W. E., Brown, L., & Levine, E. G. (1987). Experimental evaluation of the effectiveness of group interventions for dementia caregivers. *Gerontologist, 27,* 376–382.

Haley, W. E., Levine, E. G., Brown, S. L., & Bartolucci A. A. (1987). Stress, appraisal, coping, and social support as predictors of adaptational outcome among dementia caregivers. *Psychology and Aging, 2,* 323–330.

Haley, W. E., West, C. A. C. Wadley, V. G. Ford, G. R. White, F. A. Barrett, J. J., et al. (1995). Psychological, social, and health impact of caregiving: A comparison of black and white dementia family caregivers and non-caregivers. *Psychology and Aging, 10,* 540–552.

Han, B., & Haley, W. E. (1999). Family caregiving for patients with stroke: Review and analysis. *Stroke, 30,* 1478–1485.

Hayden., M. F., & Heller, T. (1997). Support, problem-solving/coping ability, and personal burden of younger and older caregivers of adults with mental retardation. *Mental Retardation, 35,* 364–372.

Hinds, C. (1985). The needs of families who care for patients with cancer at home: Are we meeting them? *Journal of Advanced Nursing, 10,* 575–581.

Holyroyd, J. (1974). The questionnaire on resources and stress: An instrument to measure family response to a handicapped member. *Journal of Community Psychology, 2,* 92–94.

Houts, P. S., Nezu, A. M., Nezu, C. M., & Bucher, J. A. (1996). A problem-solving model of family caregiving for cancer patients. *Patient Education and Counseling, 27,* 63–73.

Houts, P. S., Nezu, A. M., Nezu, C. M., Bucher, J. A., & Lipton, A. (Eds.). (1994). *Homecare guide for cancer.* Philadelphia: American College of Physicians.

Houts, P. S., Yasko, J., Kahn, S. B., Schelzel, G., & Marconi, K. (1986). Unmet psychological, social and economic needs of persons with cancer in Pennsylvania. *Cancer, 58,* 2355–2361.

Kelly, B., Edwards, P., Synott, R., Neil, C., Baillie, R., & Battistutta, D. (1999). Predictors of bereavement outcome for family caregivers of cancer patients. *Psycho-oncology, 8,* 237–249.

Kristjanson, L. J., & Aschercraft, T. (1994). The family's cancer journey: A literature review. *Cancer Nursing, 17,* 1–17.

Kurylo, M., Elliott, T., & Shewchuk, R. (2001). FOCUS on the family caregiver: A problem-solving training intervention. *Journal of Counseling and Development, 79,* 275–281.

Lewinsohn, P. M., Munoz, R. F., Youngren, M. A., & Zeiss, A. M. (1986). *Control your depression.* New York: Prentice-Hall.

Lovett, S., & Gallagher, D. (1988). Psychoeducational interventions for family caregivers: Preliminary efficacy data. *Behavior Therapy, 19,* 321–330.

Nezu, A. M. (1986). Efficacy of a social problem-solving therapy approach for unipolar depression. *Journal of Consulting and Clinical Psychology, 54,* 196–202.

Nezu, A. M., Nezu, C. M., Felgoise, S. H., & Zwick, M. L. (2003). Psychosocial oncology In A. M. Nezu, C. M. Nezu, & P. A. Geller (Eds.), *Health psychology* (pp. 267–292). New York: Wiley.

Nezu, A. M., Nezu, C. M., Friedman, S. H., Faddis, S., & Houts, P. S. (1998). *A problem-solving approach: Helping cancer patients cope.* Washington, DC: American Psychological Association.

Nezu, C. M., Nezu, A. M., & Gill-Weiss, M. J. (1992). *Psychopathology in persons with mental retardation: Clinical guidelines for assessment and treatment.* Champaign, IL: Research Press.

Orr, R. R., Cameron, S. J., & Day, D. M. (1991). Coping with stress in families with children who have mental retardation: An evaluation of the double ABCX Model. *American Journal of Mental Retardation, 4,* 444–450.

Roberts, J., Browne, G., Milne, C., Spooner, L., Gafni, A., Drummond-Young, M., et al. (1999). Problem-solving counseling for caregivers of the cognitively impaired: Effective for whom? *Nursing Research, 48,* 162–172.

Sahler, O. J., Varni, J. W., Fairclough, D. L., Butler, R. W., Noll, R. B., Dolgin, M. J., et al. (2002). Problem-solving skills training for mothers of children with newly diagnosed cancer: A randomized trial. *Developmental and Behavioral Pediatrics, 23,* 77–86.

Schmidt, G. L., Bonjean, M. J., Widem, A. C., Schefft, B. K., & Steele, D. J. (1988). Brief psychotherapy for caregivers of demented relatives: Comparison of two therapeutic strategies. *Clinical Gerontologist, 7,* 109–125.

Seltzer, M. M., Greenberg, J. S., & Krauss (1995). A comparison of coping strategies of aging mothers of adults with mental illness and mental retardation. *Psychology and Aging, 10,* 64–75.

Shewchuk, R., Richards, J. S., & Elliott, T. (1998). Dynamic processes in health outcomes among caregivers of patients with spinal cord injuries. *Health Psychology, 17,* 125–129.

Teri, L., Logsdon, R. G., Uomoto, J., & McCurry, S. M. (1997). Behavioral treatment of depression in dementia patients: A controlled clinical trial. *Journal of Gerontology, 52*, 159–166.

Toseland, R. W., Blanchard, C. G. & McCallion, P. (1995). A problem solving intervention for caregivers of cancer patients. *Social Science and Medicine, 40*, 517–528.

Vitaliano, P. P. (1997). Physiological and physical concomitants of caregiving: Introduction to special issue. *Annals of Behavioral Medicine, 19*, 75–77.

Whitlatch, C. J., Zarit, S. H., & von Eye, A. (1991). Efficacy of interventions with caregivers: A reanalysis. *Gerontologist, 31*, 9–14.

Zarit, S. H., Anthony, C. R., & Boutselis, M. (1987). Interventions with caregivers of dementia patients: Comparison of two approaches. *Psychology and Aging, 2*, 225–232.

IV

CONCLUSION

14

SOCIAL PROBLEM SOLVING: CURRENT STATUS AND FUTURE DIRECTIONS

THOMAS J. D'ZURILLA, EDWARD C. CHANG,
AND LAWRENCE J. SANNA

Social problem solving is a construct that refers to problem solving as it occurs in the real world. It is assumed to be a useful and effective general coping strategy for all types of problems in living, including impersonal problems (e.g., property, finances), intrapersonal problems (e.g., behavior, emotions, health), interpersonal problems (e.g., conflicts, disagreements, disputes), as well as broader community and societal problems (e.g., crime, energy resources). Social problem solving is applied routinely to these everyday problems by individuals, couples, and groups (e.g., families, committees) in an attempt to maximize effective functioning and the quality of life.

As several chapters in this volume have shown, social problem solving is associated with many different forms of maladjustment and psychopathology, including depression, anxiety, suicidal ideation, health-related problems, and schizophrenia. In addition, the review in chapter 6 (this volume) indicates that social problem solving is also related to measures of *positive* adjustment, such as positive affectivity, life satisfaction, self-esteem, autonomy, and a sense of environmental mastery. Other chapters in this volume have shown that problem-solving training is a useful and effective treatment and prevention method for a variety of different clinical problems in children, adolescents, and adults.

Despite the many positive research findings and promising clinical applications reported in this volume, there are a number of important directions for future research and clinical practice in the fields of social problem solving and problem-solving training/therapy that would improve on the limitations of previous research as well as add new important research findings. In each chapter in this volume, the authors have presented recommendations for future research for their particular topic. In addition, we present some additional recommendations that follow.

RELATIONS BETWEEN SOCIAL PROBLEM SOLVING AND BEHAVIOR DISORDERS

Most of the research on social problem solving and maladjustment has focused on negative *psychological* conditions (e.g., depression, anxiety). In contrast, much less research has been done on *behavioral* problems and deviations. Most of the studies in this area have focused on the problem of aggression. Social problem-solving deficits have been found to be associated with aggression in children (Lochman & Dodge, 1994; Lochman & Lampron, 1986), adolescents (Deluty, 1981; Jaffee & D'Zurilla, 2003; Lochman, Wayland, & White, 1993), and young adults (D'Zurilla, Chang, & Sanna, 2003; McMurran, Blair, & Egan, 2002). In addition, social problem-solving deficits have been found to be associated with sexual aggression and deviance in male sex offenders (Nezu, Nezu, Dudek, Peacock, & Stoll, 2002).

In addition to the research on aggression, other studies have found that social problem-solving abilities are associated with delinquency in adolescents (Freedman, Rosenthal, Donahue, Schlundt, & McFall, 1978; Jaffee & D'Zurilla, 2003) and with health-compromising behaviors (e.g., substance use, high-risk automobile driving) in both adolescents (Jaffee & D'Zurilla, 2003) and college students (chap. 7, this volume). In other studies, social problem-solving deficits have been found to be related to pathological gambling (Sylvain, Ladouceur, & Boisvert, 1997) and the use of avoidant coping strategies (D'Zurilla & Chang, 1995). In view of these findings, more research is recommended that examines the role of social problem-solving ability in the development and maintenance of behavioral disorders and deviations.

Relations Between Social Problem Solving and Behavioral Competence

Most of the research on social problem solving and adjustment has focused on *maladaptive* functioning and psychopathology. Considering the growing interest in positive psychology (Seligman, 1999; Seligman & Csikszentmihalyi, 2000), more research is needed on the role of social problem solving in predicting and enhancing positive functioning and well-being. Chang et al. (chap. 6, this volume) have reviewed the limited research that has been done on the relations between social problem solving and positive *psychological* functioning and have called for more research in this area. In addition, however, more research is also needed that focuses on positive *behavioral* functioning or behavioral and social competence. Thus far, studies in this area have found that social problem-solving abilities are related to social skills (Sadowski, Moore, & Kelley, 1994); academic performance (D'Zurilla, Nezu, & Maydeu-Olivares, 2002; D'Zurilla & Sheedy, 1992; Rodriguez-Fornells & Maydeu-Olivares, 2000); accident-prevention behaviors (Elliott, Johnson, & Jackson, 1997); and the use of adaptive, problem-focused coping strategies (D'Zurilla & Chang, 1995). In view of these findings, more research is recommended that focuses on other measures of effective functioning or competence in different areas of living, including work, marriage, family, health, public service, sports, and other endeavors that contribute to the quality of life for oneself and society.

Relations Between Social Problem Solving and Optimal Functioning

Continuing with the positive psychology theme, one important hypothesis that has not yet been researched is that *superior* or *creative* problem-solving ability may not only result in effective functioning or competence in dealing with the demands of everyday living but it may also contribute significantly to *optimal* behavioral and psychological functioning, including peak levels of creativity, invention, success, achievement, and positive emotionality that have rarely or never before been attained. Hence, for the betterment of individuals and society, research is needed to develop and evaluate problem-solving training programs that are specifically designed to help individuals and groups realize their potential for higher level functioning and achievement.

THE RECIPROCAL CAUSATION HYPOTHESIS

An important assumption of social problem-solving theory is that the relationship between social problem solving and adjustment is reciprocal (D'Zurilla & Nezu, 1999). That is, ineffective problem solving leads to maladaptive functioning (e.g., depression, anxiety), which in turn inhibits or disrupts subsequent problem solving, resulting in a negative cycle over time of decreasing problem-solving effectiveness and increasing maladjustment or psychological disturbance. Moreover, a reciprocal causal relationship is also assumed to exist between social problem solving and positive adjustment, where effective problem solving enhances positive functioning (e.g., positive affectivity, self-esteem, a sense of mastery), which in turn facilitates subsequent problem solving. Over time, the resulting positive cycle of increasing problem-solving effectiveness and positive functioning not only helps to achieve an optimal level of functioning but also acts as a prophylactic against the negative impact of adverse life conditions on psychological functioning and well-being.

The reciprocal causation hypothesis has important implication for theories of psychopathology as well as for treatment. It also has implications for theories of positive psychology and for interventions that are designed to achieve optimal psychological and behavioral functioning. However, it is a hypothesis that has not yet been adequately researched. To do so, longitudinal studies are needed that use multiple assessments of social problem solving and adjustment variables over time.

The Basic Cognitive Abilities Underlying Social Problem Solving

According to D'Zurilla and Nezu (1999), social problem solving consists of a set of abilities that can be grouped into three levels: (a) the metacognitive level, (b) the performance level, and (c) the basic cognitive level. The metacognitive level consists of a person's general awareness and appraisals of problems in living and his or her own problem-solving ability. The positive and negative problem-orientation components of D'Zurilla and colleagues' social problem solving model are at this level (chap. 1, this volume). The performance level consists of a person's characteristic problem-solving style, or the manner in which he or she typically attempts to solve problems. The three problem-solving styles in the D'Zurilla and colleagues model are at this level (rational problem solving, impulsivity–carelessness style, and avoidance style). Rational problem solving is the constructive style that contains the four major problem-solving skills in the model: (a) problem definition and formulation, (b) generation of alternative solutions, (c) decision making, and (d) solution implementation and verification. At the basic cognitive level are the intellectual and information-processing abilities that underlie and influence the learning and performance of the abilities and skills at the first two levels. It has not yet been determined what basic cognitive abilities are most important for social problem solving, but they are likely to include such abilities as vocabulary and verbal fluency, attention, memory, concentration, comprehension, social perception, social judgment, divergent production (i.e., ability to generate a number of alternative and original ideas), and the ability to distinguish task-relevant from task-irrelevant information.

The D'Zurilla and colleagues model does not address the abilities at the basic cognitive level. It is assumed that most populations, including clinical as well as normal populations, already possess adequate abilities at the basic level to allow them to benefit from learning experiences that result in the acquisition of constructive problem-solving abilities and skills at the metacognitive and performance levels. Hence, most current problem-solving training programs focus only on these two levels. However, there are some populations, including mentally retarded individuals, brain-injured individuals, schizophrenic individuals, and young children, that have significant deficits or underdeveloped abilities at the basic cognitive level. For these populations, research is needed to identify the basic cognitive abilities that are most important for effective social problem solving. In addition, new measuring instruments and methods are needed to assess these abilities and new training methods are needed to improve them, if possible (for an additional discussion of this issue as it pertains to schizophrenic individuals, see chap. 5, this volume; for a discussion pertaining to young children, see chap. 9, this volume).

Age, Gender, and Cultural–Racial Differences

Little research has been done on age, gender, and ethnic–racial differences in social problem-solving ability and its relationship to adjustment. The available data on age and gender differences are based on cross-sectional studies using samples that are made up predominantly of White Americans (see D'Zurilla, Maydeu-Olivares, & Kant, 1998; D'Zurilla et al., 2002). The data on age differences suggest that social problem-solving abilities tend to increase with age from adolescence to young adulthood to middle-age and then decline somewhat in elderly individuals, with the greatest decrease being in problem orientation. Specifically, elderly individuals have been found to score higher on negative orientation than middle-aged individuals and young adults. This result may be related to the fact that elderly individuals report more health problems than young adults, which they may perceive as uncontrollable (D'Zurilla et al., 1998).

The increase in social problem-solving ability from adolescence to middle-age is consistent with the view that social problem solving consists of a set of attitudes and skills that are learned early in life and improve over time with experience or practice in solving problems. Longitudinal research is needed to determine how social problem-solving abilities are learned and what conditions facilitate or inhibit this learning (e.g., parenting styles, modeling, trial-and-error learning). Who are the primary agents or facilitators in this process (e.g., mothers, fathers, teachers)? Are the five problem-solving dimensions learned through a common pathway or are there different pathways to the different dimensions? What methods can be used to facilitate the learning of constructive problem-solving attitudes and skills at an early age? These are some of the questions that need to be addressed in future research.

With regard to gender differences, studies across different age samples suggest that men tend to score higher on positive problem orientation and lower on negative problem orientation than women. In addition, one study focusing on young adults found that men scored higher than women on impulsivity–carelessness style (D'Zurilla et al., 1998). More research is needed on gender differences at different age groups.

Only a few studies have looked at cultural and racial differences in social problem-solving ability. Studies involving Asian Americans have shown that this group, compared to White Americans, scores higher on negative problem orientation (Chang, 1998) and impulsivity–carelessness style (Chang, 1998, 2001). In addition, some preliminary data also suggest that Black Americans, compared with White Americans, may score higher on positive problem orientation, and that Hispanic Americans, compared to White Americans, may score lower on avoidance style (Chang & Banks, in press).

Yet it is interesting to note that despite elevations on maladaptive social problem-solving dimensions for Asian Americans, greater negative problem orientation and impulsivity–carelessness style have *not* been found for this group to be strongly associated with less positive psychological conditions (e.g., life satisfaction; Chang, 2001) and with greater negative psychological conditions (e.g., depressive symptoms, suicidal ideation; Chang, 1998, 2001). Thus, the function of social problem solving in relation to adjustment can vary across different cultural or racial groups. Obviously, we have only begun to scratch the surface in understanding similarities and differences in the form and function of social problem solving across diverse populations.

PROBLEM-SOLVING THERAPY
FOR GENERALIZED ANXIETY DISORDER

According to the *DSM–IV* (American Psychiatric Association, 1994), excessive and uncontrollable worry is the central feature in generalized anxiety disorder (GAD). A number of recent studies have found that problem-solving deficits are significantly associated with worrying (Belzer, D'Zurilla, & Mayeu-Olivares, 2002; Davey, Jubb, & Cameron, 1996; Dugas, Freeston, & Ladouceur, 1997; Dugas, Letart, Rhéaume, Freeston, & Ladouceur, 1995). The findings of these studies have shown that negative problem orientation is the problem-solving dimension that is most strongly and consistently associated with different measures of worrying. However, one study found that when negative problem orientation was controlled, the dimension of impulsivity–carelessness accounted for a significant additional amount of variance in catastrophic worrying (Belzer et al., 2002). Although problem-solving training is often included as one of several treatment components in cognitive–behavioral therapy for GAD (Brown, O'Leary, & Barlow, 1993), its contribution to treatment outcome has not yet been empirically evaluated. Hence, we recommend future research on this issue.

Problem-Solving Training and Therapy for Medical Patients

In recent years, problem-solving therapy has been evaluated as a treatment method for enhancing the quality of life of patients with serious medical conditions and their families, with most of this research focusing on cancer patients (chap. 10, this volume). Because of the positive findings with cancer patients (e.g., Nezu, Nezu, Felgoise, McClure, & Houts, 2003) and patients with obesity (e.g., Black & Scherba, 1983; Perri et al., 2001), we recommend more research in this area that focuses on other serious and chronic medical conditions. In particular, we recommend studies on patients with coronary heart disease. According to Ewart (1990), cardiovascular diseases and cancer have replaced infectious diseases as the leading causes of death in developed nations. Like cancer, cardiovascular disease requires many difficult and often problematic lifestyle changes, such as stopping smoking, starting daily exercising, diet changes, and taking daily medications. Problem-solving training might be particularly useful and effective for dealing with the problems associated with these life changes and, thus, improving one's physical and psychological well-being (see Ewart, 1990).

Problem-Solving Training for Adolescents and Their Parents

Studies have found a link between problem-solving deficits and serious psychological and behavioral problems in adolescents, including depression, suicidal ideation (Sadowski & Kelley, 1993; Sadowski et al., 1994), aggression, delinquency (Freedman et al., 1978; Jaffee & D'Zurilla, 2003; Lochman et al., 1993), substance use (tobacco, alcohol, marijuana) and high-risk automobile driving (Jaffee & D'Zurilla, 2003). Moreover, Jaffee and D'Zurilla (2003) found that adolescents' problem-solving abilities are (a) significantly lower than their parents' problem-solving abilities; (b) significantly, albeit modestly, correlated with their mothers' abilities but not their fathers' abilities; and (c) uniquely related to problem behaviors even after controlling for their parents' problem-solving abilities.

Based on this research, we recommend studies on the evaluation of problem-solving interventions for adolescents and parents (fathers as well as mothers) that are designed to prevent and treat psychological and behavioral problems. The programs for parents should not only focus on problem solving for dealing more effectively with their adolescents' problem behaviors but they should also teach parents how to be more effective in teaching constructive problem-solving attitudes and skills to their pre- and early adolescent children.

Problem-Solving Training for Stress Reduction and Prevention in the Workplace

Except for senior citizens, most American adults spend at least half of their waking hours in the workplace. Hence, daily conflicts and problems at work are a major source of stress for most adults, resulting in such adverse outcomes as absenteeism, low productivity, occupational burnout, lost work days because of illness, high turnover rates, psychological disturbance, and health problems. Social problem solving is likely to be an effective strategy for reducing and preventing stress and its negative effects in the workplace (see D'Zurilla, 1990). However, there is a lack of research on the evaluation of problem-solving training workshops for managers, supervisors, and other employees. If they are proven to be effective, such workshops could have important psychological, health, and economic benefits for individual employees, business owners and executives, and society in general.

Generalization and Maintenance of Training Effects

A number of studies on the evaluation of problem-solving training and therapy programs for children, and some studies focusing on adults, have found that participants learn effective problem-solving skills during the training program, but they do not apply these skills adequately or consistently in the real-life setting, resulting in the failure to obtain significant or durable improvements in adaptive functioning. Because of these findings, research is badly needed to identify training methods that facilitate the generalization and maintenance of effective problem solving in the real-life setting. Based on our assessment of the outcome studies in this area, we believe that two training components are critical for promoting the generalization and maintenance of training effects: (a) training in problem orientation and (b) supervised practice.

In the D'Zurilla and colleagues social problem-solving model (see chap. 1, this volume), a positive problem orientation contains problem-solving self-efficacy beliefs as well as positive problem-solving outcome expectancies. In other words, the person believes (a) that he or she is capable of solving problems effectively and (b) that most problems in life can be solved satisfactorily if one persists in his or her problem-solving efforts and does not give up too easily. Based on self-efficacy theory and research (Bandura, 1997), our hypothesis is that people with a positive rather than negative problem orientation are more likely to apply their problem-solving skills in real life, instead of avoiding problems, and are more likely to show effort and persistence when obstacles occur. Most problem-solving interventions for adults are based on the D'Zurilla and colleagues social problem-solving model, but some of them omit the problem-orientation component and focus only on problem-solving skills. Most programs for children are based on the model described by Spivack, Platt, and Shure (1976), which does not include a problem-orientation component.

Although reports of outcome studies do not always provide a clear and specific description of the treatment program, it appears that the most favorable and durable outcomes are produced by programs that include the problem-orientation component. Some empirical support for this view comes from a study by Nezu and Perri (1989) on problem-solving therapy for major depression. These investigators compared problem-solving therapy with and without the problem-orientation component to a waiting-list control group. Although both treatments were found to be effective in reducing depression, participants who received the training in problem orientation were significantly less depressed at posttreatment and at six months follow-up than participants who only received the problem-solving skills component.

The second critical component, supervised practice, refers to the repeated practice of newly acquired problem-solving skills by applying them to problems in the real-life setting between sessions. The person then reports the results in the next session and receives corrective feedback and additional training, as necessary. In the problem-solving training and therapy program for adults described by D'Zurilla, Nezu, and their colleagues (D'Zurilla & Nezu, 1999; chap. 10, this volume), didactic instruction in the social problem-solving model is only the first phase of the program. Supervised practice in applying the model to actual problems constitutes the second phase. This phase of the program continues until (a) an adequate level of problem-solving competence is achieved in the real-life setting, and (b) the goal level of adaptive functioning is achieved in the targeted problem area (e.g., depression, social competence deficits). Supervised practice is included in most adult training programs but is lacking in most programs for children. What is needed in the latter programs is the training and participation of significant others, such as parents and teachers, to facilitate the generalization and maintenance of effective problem solving in the home, neighborhood, and school. This can be done by using proven behavioral skill-training methods such as prompting, modeling, corrective feedback, and positive reinforcement in the natural environment.

Identification of Mediators and Moderators of Training and Therapy Outcomes

According to social problem-solving theory (D'Zurilla & Nezu, 1999), the major mediator of positive clinical outcomes in problem-solving therapy is social problem-solving ability. In support of this assumption, several outcome studies have found a significant relationship between improvements in social problem-solving ability and positive changes in negative psychological conditions, including psychological stress (D'Zurilla & Maschka, 1988), depression (Nezu & Perri, 1989), and cancer-related distress (Nezu et al., 2003). However, more research is needed to identify *what* specific problem-solving dimensions are the most important mediators for *what* particular problem-solving training and therapy programs. Based on the body of research on social problem solving and adjustment, it appears that positive and negative problem orientation and avoidance style might be the more important mediators in therapy programs for negative psychological conditions, whereas rational problem solving (i.e., problem-solving skills) and impulsivity–carelessness style might be more important in programs focusing on behavioral outcomes.

In addition to social problem-solving ability, other variables might also mediate the effectiveness of problem-solving training and therapy programs. Some potential mediators are positive affectivity, optimism, hope, self-efficacy, self-esteem, and a sense of mastery or control. According to Bandura (1997), self-efficacy might be a significant mediator of psychological and behavioral change in most, if not all, forms of psychotherapy. More research is needed that examines the possible mediating effects of these variables in different problem-solving therapy interventions for different clinical conditions.

Whereas mediators are variables that are influenced by problem-solving training and then influence or account for the psychological and behavioral outcomes of treatment, moderators are variables that interact with treatment to influence the magnitude of outcomes, for better or worse. Such variables might include age, gender, ethnicity, intelligence, educational level, and various personality traits. Research designed to identify moderator variables is important for determining what individuals might benefit most or least from problem-solving therapy.

CONCLUSION

The chapters in this volume show that research on social problem solving and problem-solving training and therapy has been increasing at a rapid pace in recent years. In general, the results thus far have provided strong support for the two major assumptions of social problem-solving theory: (a) that social problem solving is an important general coping strategy that can have a significant effect on a person's ability to cope with stressful problems in living, which in turn can significantly influence that person's adjustment, and (b) that problem-solving training can be a useful and effective treatment or prevention method for a variety of different adjustment problems. However, although the previous findings have generally been supportive and promising, the many future research recommendations in this chapter and other chapters in this volume indicate that much more work needs to be done before the true potential of social problem-solving theory, research, and training can adequately be assessed, not only with respect to the reduction of negative or maladaptive functioning but also for the enhancement of competence and positive psychological well-being.

REFERENCES

American Psychiatric Association. (1994). *Diagnostic and statistical manual of mental disorders* (4th ed.). Washington, DC: Author.

Bandura, A. (1997). *Self-efficacy: The exercise of control*. New York: W.H. Freeman.

Belzer, K. D., D'Zurilla, T. J., & Maydeu-Olivares, A. (2002). Social problem solving and trait anxiety as predictors of worry in a college student population. *Personality and Individual Differences, 33*, 573–585.

Black, D. R., & Scherba, D. S. (1983). Contracting to problem solve versus contracting to practice behavioral weight loss skills. *Behavior Therapy, 14*, 100–109.

Brown, T. A., O'Leary, T. A., & Barlow, D. H. (1993). Generalized anxiety disorder. In D. H. Barlow (Ed.), *Clinical handbook of psychological disorders: A step-by-step treatment manual* (2nd ed., pp. 137–188). New York: Guilford Press.

Chang, E. C. (1998). Cultural differences, perfectionism, and suicidal risk: Does social problem solving still matter? *Cognitive Therapy and Research, 22*, 237–254.

Chang, E. C. (2001). A look at the coping strategies and styles of Asian Americans: Similar and different? In C. R. Snyder (Ed.), *Coping with stress: Effective people and processes* (pp. 222–239). New York: Oxford University Press.

Chang, E. C., & Banks, K. H. (in press). The color and texture of hope: Some preliminary findings and implications for hope theory and counseling among diverse racial/ethnic groups. *Cultural Diversity and Ethnic Minority Psychology*.

Davey, G. C. L., Jubb, M., & Cameron, C. (1996). Catastrophic worrying as a function of changes in problem-solving confidence. *Cognitive Therapy and Research, 20*, 333–344.

Deluty, R. H. (1981). Alternative thinking ability of aggressive, assertive, and submissive children. *Cognitive Therapy and Research, 5*, 309–312.

Dugas, M. J., Freeston, M. H., & Ladouceur, R. (1997). Intolerance of uncertainty and problem orientation in worry. *Cognitive Therapy and Research, 21*, 593–606.

Dugas, M. J., Letarte, H., Rhéaume, J., Freeston, M. H., & Ladouceur, R. (1995). Worry and problem solving: Evidence of a specific relationship. *Cognitive Therapy and Research, 19*, 109–120.

D'Zurilla, T. J. (1990). Problem-solving training for effective stress management and prevention. *Journal of Cognitive Psychotherapy: An International Journal, 4*, 327–354.

D'Zurilla, T. J., & Chang, E. C. (1995). The relations between social problem solving and coping. *Cognitive Therapy and Research, 19*, 547–562.

D'Zurilla, T. J., Chang, E. C., & Sanna, L. J. (2003). Self-esteem and social problem solving as predictors of aggression. *Journal of Social and Clinical Psychology, 22*, 424–440.

D'Zurilla, T. J., & Maschka, G. (1988, November). *Outcome of a problem-solving approach to stress management: I. Comparison with social support.* Paper presented to the Association for Advancement of Behavior Therapy, New York.

D'Zurilla, T. J., Maydeu-Olivares, A., & Kant, G. L. (1998). Age and gender differences in social problem-solving ability. *Personality and Individual Differences, 25*, 241–252.

D'Zurilla, T. J., & Nezu, A. M. (1999). *Problem-solving therapy: A social competence approach to clinical intervention* (2nd ed.). New York: Springer.

D'Zurilla, T. J., Nezu, A. M., & Maydeu-Olivares, A. (2002). *Social Problem-Solving Revised—Inventory (SPSI–R): Technical manual.* North Tonawanda, NY: Multi-Health Systems.

D'Zurilla, T. J., & Sheedy, C. F. (1992). The relation between social problem-solving ability and subsequent level of academic competence in college students. *Cognitive Therapy and Research, 16*, 589–599.

Elliott, T. R., Johnson, M. O., & Jackson, R. (1997). Social problem solving and health behaviors of undergraduate students. *Journal of College Student Development, 38*, 24–31.

Ewart, C. K. (1990). A social problem-solving approach to behavior change in coronary heart disease. In S. Schumaker, E. Schron, & J. Ockene (Eds.), *Handbook of health behavior change* (pp. 153–190). New York: Springer.

Freedman, B. J., Rosenthal, L., Donahue, L. P., Schlundt, D. G., & McFall, R. M. (1978). A social–behavioral analysis of skills deficits in delinquent and non-delinquent boys. *Journal of Consulting and Clinical Psychology, 46*, 1448–1462.

Jaffee, W. B., & D'Zurilla, T. J. (2003). Adolescent problem solving, parent problem solving, and externalizing behavior in adolescents. *Behavior Therapy, 34*, 295–311.

Lochman, J. E., & Dodge, K. A. (1994). Social–cognitive processes of severely violent, moderately aggressive, and nonaggressive boys. *Journal of Consulting and Clinical Psychology, 62*, 366–374.

Lochman, J. E., & Lampron, L. G. (1986). Situational social problem-solving skills and self-esteem of aggressive and nonaggressive boys. *Journal of Abnormal Child Psychology, 14,* 605–617.

Lochman, J. E., Wayland, K. K., & White, K. J. (1993). Social goals: Relationship to adolescent adjustment and to social problem solving. *Journal of Abnormal Child Psychology, 21,* 135–151.

McMurran, M., Blair, M., & Egan, V. (2002). An investigation of the correlations between aggressiveness, impulsiveness, social problem solving, and alcohol use. *Aggressive Behavior, 28,* 439–445.

Nezu, A. M., Nezu, C. M., Felgoise, S. H., McClure, K. S., & Houts, P. S. (2003). Project Genesis: Assessing the efficacy of problem-solving therapy for distressed adult cancer patients. *Journal of Consulting and Clinical Psychology, 71,* 1036–1048.

Nezu, A. M., & Perri, M. G. (1989). Social problem-solving therapy for unipolar depression: An initial dismantling investigation. *Journal of Consulting and Clinical Psychology, 57,* 408–413.

Nezu, C. M., Nezu, A. M., Dudek, J. A., Peacock, M., & Stoll, J. (2002). *Social problem-solving correlates of sexual deviancy and aggression among adult child molesters.* Manuscript submitted for publication.

Perri, M. G., Nezu, A. M., McKelvey, W. F., Schein, R. L., Renjilian, D. A., & Viegener, B. J. (2001). Relapse prevention training and problem-solving therapy in the long-term management of obesity. *Journal and Consulting and Clinical Psychology, 69,* 722–726.

Rodriguez-Fornells, A., & Maydeu-Olivares, A. (2000). Impulsive–careless problem-solving style as a predictor of subsequent academic competence. *Personality and Individual Differences, 28,* 639–645.

Sadowski, C., & Kelley, M. L. (1993). Social problem-solving in suicidal adolescents. *Journal of Consulting and Clinical Psychology, 61,* 121–127.

Sadowski, C., Moore, L. A., & Kelley, M. L. (1994). Psychometric properties of the Social Problem-Solving Inventory (SPSI) with normal and emotionally-disturbed adolescents. *Journal of Abnormal Child Psychology, 22,* 487–500.

Seligman, M. E. P. (1999). The President's address. *American Psychologist, 54,* 559–562.

Seligman, M. E. P., & Csikszentmihalyi, M. (2000). Positive psychology: An introduction. *American Psychology, 55,* 5–14.

Spivack, G., Platt, J. J., & Shure, M. B. (1976). *The problem-solving approach to adjustment.* San Francisco: Jossey-Bass.

Sylvain, C., Ladouceur, R., & Boisvert, J. M. (1997). Cognitive and behavioral treatment of pathological gambling: A controlled study. *Journal of Consulting and Clinical Psychology, 65,* 727–732.

AUTHOR INDEX

Numbers in italics refer to listings in the references.

SUBJECT INDEX

Conduct disorder, 214, 218–219
Conflict management, 213–214
Conscientiousness, 33
Context, mental, 86–87
Coping, 29, 32. *See also* Social problem
    solving; Stress
    and affectivity, 34
    avoidant, 120
    defined, 172
    emotion-focused, 172
    and optimism–pessimism, 34–35
    and perfectionism, 36
    problem-focused, 172
    and problem-solving, 58, 59, 69,
        173–174, 243
    social–contextual model of, 40
Coping Power Program, 161–162
Couples, and problem-solving training, 6,
    193–206
    assessment of problems, 199–200
    and backsliding, 203
    Behavioral Marital Therapy, 195–198
    Integrative Couples Therapy,
        198–203
    interventions in, 201
    Marriage Checkup, 204–205
    and motivational interviewing,
        203–206
    and relationship distress, 193–194
    social problem-solving model,
        194–195
    and tolerance, 202–203
Culture
    and social problem solving, 38–39,
        112, 246

Delinquency, 161–162, 242
Dementia, people with
    and problem-solving training for
        caregivers, 230–231
Depression, 4, 127–128, 215–216
    in caregivers, 224
    future research on, 79
    and medication, 176
    minor, treatment for, 176–177
    and problem orientation, 72
    and problem-solving therapy, 176–
        177, 182–183
    and social problem solving, 49–52,
        57–58, 59, 60, 118

and stroke victims, 233
Developmental disabilities, people with
    and problem-solving training for
        caregivers, 231–232
Diabetes, 127
    and depression, 127–128
    and social problem solving, 127, 128
Dialoguing, 158
Distancing, 158
Divorce, 57, 194
Dopamine, 86, 95
Dysthymia, treatment for, 176–177

Elderly individuals
    and social problem solving, 37–38,
        245
Emotional problems
    and problem-solving therapy,
        177–178
Endurance, 135
Environmental mastery, 104
Ethnicity
    and social problem solving, 38–39,
        112, 246
Everyday Problem Solving Inventory, 22
Everyday Problems Test, 23

Families, and problem-solving training, 6,
    124, 209–220. *See also* Children
    and adolescents, and problem-
    solving training
    and cancer, 179
    collaborative relationships, 218
    conflict management, 213–214
    and depression, 2215–216
    dynamics of, 123
    education, 211–212
    empirical evidence of effects,
        218–219
    engagement of members, 216–218
    facilitation, 212–213
    family system change, 214–216
    future research on, 219–220
    logistics of, 210–211
    motivational tactics for, 217
    and schizophrenia, 218
    screening, 217
    written statement of expectations,
        217–218

Gender. *See also* Women
    and social problem solving, 38, 246
    and suicide risk, 67
Generalized anxiety disorder
    and problem-solving therapy,
        246–250
Genetics
    and social problem solving, 30
Growth, personal, 104

Head Start, 219
Health. *See also* Behavioral health;
    Psychology, positive
    defined, 100
Hope, 35–36, 250
    future research on, 111

"I Can Problem Solve." *See* Interpersonal
    Cognitive Problem Solving
    curricula
Imagination, goals, and affect model and
    timing of events (figure), 139
Improving Social-Awareness/Social
    Problem-Solving Project,
    159–161
    applying, 160
    program assessment, 160–161
    readiness for decision-making,
        159–160
    teaching, 160
Impulsivity–carelessness style, 16, 51,
    110
    in caregivers, 225–226
    men vs. women differences, 246
    and schizophrenia, 85–86
Indulging, 141–142
Integrated Psychological Therapy, 94
Integrative Couples Therapy, 198–203
    assessment of problems, 199–200
Intelligence quotient
    and social problem solving, 88
Internet bulletin boards, 128
Interpersonal Cognitive Problem Solving
    curricula, 156–159
    alternative-solution thinking, 157
    consequential thinking, 157–158
    dialoguing, 158
    distancing, 158
    means–ends thinking, 158

prerequisite skills, 156–157
program assessment, 159
training techniques, 158
Interpersonal Problem-solving Assessment
    Technique, 22
Interviewing, motivational, 204
Inventory of Decisions, Evaluations, and
    Actions, 22

Life satisfaction, 101–103, 105. *See also*
    Psychology, positive
Linking the Interest of Families and
    Teachers program, 162

Marriage. *See* Couples, and problem-
    solving training
Marriage Checkup, 204–205
Means–Ends Problem-Solving Procedure,
    19, 89
    and anxiety, 54
    and depression, 50
    described, 21–22, 91
    and suicide risk, 53, 68, 71
Means–ends thinking, 158
Mediators, of social problem solving, 29–
    41, 250. *See also* Moderators, of
    social problem solving; Social
    problem solving
    affectivity, 33–34
    childhood, 30–31
    and contextual variables, 36–40
    defined, 29–30
    ethnicity, 38–39
    gender, 38
    genetic, 30
    hope, 35–36
    identification of, 250
    life span development and, 37–38
    neuroticism, 31–33
    optimism–pessimism, 34–35
    perfectionism, 36
    social context, 40
Memory
    and schizophrenia, 86
    verbal, and social problem solving,
        88
Mental patient populations
    and problem-solving therapy, 179–
        180, 184–185

ABOUT THE EDITORS

Edward C. Chang, PhD, is an assistant professor of clinical psychology in the Department of Psychology and a faculty associate in Asian/Pacific Islander American Studies at the University of Michigan, Ann Arbor. He received his BA in psychology and philosophy from the State University of New York at Buffalo and his MA and PhD degrees from the State University of New York at Stony Brook. He completed his American Psychological Association accredited clinical internship at Bellevue Hospital Center–New York University Medical Center. He is on the editorial boards of several journals, including the *Journal of Personality and Social Psychology, Cognitive Therapy and Research, Journal of Social and Clinical Psychology,* and the *Asian Journal of Social Psychology.* He has published numerous articles and chapters on optimism and pessimism, perfectionism, social problem solving, and cultural influences on behavior. He is the editor of *Optimism and Pessimism: Implications for Theory, Research, and Practice* (APA, 2001) and *Self-Criticism and Self-Enhancement: Theory, Research, and Clinical Implications* (forthcoming), and he is a coeditor of *Virtue, Vice, and Personality: The Complexity of Behavior* (APA, 2003).

Thomas J. D'Zurilla, PhD, is a professor in the Department of Psychology at Stony Brook University. He received his BA in psychology from Lafayette College and his MA and PhD degrees in clinical psychology from the University of Illinois at Urbana–Champaign. Several decades ago, he spearheaded a new area of study on the role of social problem solving in adjustment and the efficacy of problem-solving training and therapy as a treatment and prevention method. He has published numerous theoretical and research articles, and he is also coauthor with Arthur M. Nezu of the second edition of *Problem-Solving Therapy: A Social Competence Approach to Clinical Intervention*

(1999) and is coauthor with Arthur M. Nezu and Albert Maydeu-Olivares of the *Social Problem-Solving Inventory—Revised (SPSI–R): Technical Manual* (2002). His writings have been translated into Spanish, Japanese, Chinese, and French. He is a member of the American Psychological Association, the Society for a Science of Clinical Psychology, and the Association for the Advancement of Behavior Therapy.

Lawrence J. Sanna, PhD, is an associate professor in the Social Psychology Program at the University of North Carolina at Chapel Hill. He received his BA from the University of Connecticut and his MS and PhD degrees from Pennsylvania State University. Dr. Sanna has previously held positions at Bucknell University and Washington State University and was a visiting scholar at the University of Michigan. He has taught a variety of courses related to social and personality psychology, and he has published numerous articles in the areas of social cognition, personality processes, social judgment, and group influences. He is coauthor of *Group Performance and Interaction* (1999) and coeditor of *Virtue, Vice, and Personality: The Complexity of Behavior* (APA, 2003). He currently serves on the editorial boards of the journals *Personality and Social Psychology Bulletin, European Journal of Social Psychology,* and *Basic and Applied Social Psychology.*